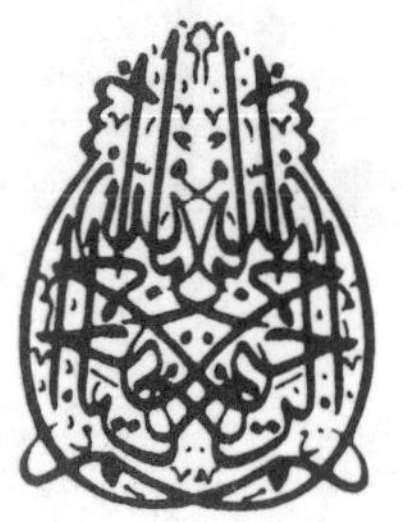

IN THE NAME OF ALLAH
THE MERCIFUL THE COMPASSIONATE

مختصر

الكلم الطيب

لشيخ الإسلام تقي الدين أحمد ابن تيمية
المتوفى سنة ٧٢٨ هـ

اختارها
وترجم معانيها الى الانجليزية

الدكتور عز الدين ابراهيم

دينيس جونسون ديفيز
(عبد الودود)

THE GOODLY WORD

IBN TAYMIYYA

Abridged and translated by
EZZEDDIN IBRAHIM AND
DENYS JOHNSON-DAVIES

THE ISLAMIC TEXTS SOCIETY
CAMBRIDGE

First published by Dar al-Koran al-Kareem in 1992,
second edition 2000.

This edition published in 2003 by
THE ISLAMIC TEXTS SOCIETY
MILLER'S HOUSE
KINGS MILL LANE
GREAT SHELFORD
CAMBRIDGE CB22 5EN, U. K.

Reprint 2010, 2012

British Library Cataloguing-in-Publication Data.
A catalogue record for this book is
available from the British Library.

ISBN 978 1903682 15 9 paper

CONTENTS

Preface

By Dr. Sheikh Yūsuf al-Qaraḍāwī,

Head of the Centre for the illustrious Sunnah and the Sīrah of the Prophet at the University of Qatar and a member of Fiqh academies in the Islamic world and Europe

Praise be to God and peace be upon His Chosen Messenger and his family and Companions, the Leaders of Guidance.

To continue. It was more than half a century ago that I first came to know my dear friend Dr. Ezzeddin Ibrahim: through various Islamic activities and seminars and meetings for research on topics of Islamic thought, also through being colleagues in teaching and administrative educational work. I was always struck by his affable nature, orderly mind and wide range of culture; also his ability to work constructively in initiating various cultural projects in an unassuming manner. It is just such qualities as have fitted him for so many positions of distinction and the accomplishment of such work as the setting up of programmes of study and the compiling of text books for the Ministry of Education in Qatar, the establishment of the Cultural Foundation in Abu Dhabi, holding the post of Professor of Arabic Literature at Riyadh University, being for some years the Rector of the University of the United Arab Emirates, organising and administering the Islamic Solidarity Fund at the Organisation of the Islamic Conference, and participating in organising and running the Sheikh Zayed bin Sultan Organisation for Humanitarian and Charitable Works, and his assistance to African Americans in their religious activities and for his lectures in Arabic and English in various venues and innumerable other activities. I knew Ezzeddin first of all and through him made the acquaintance of Abdul Wadoud Denys Johnson Davies.

Abdul Wadoud Denys Johnson-Davies was well known as a man of letters, especially in the fields of translation and literary criticism. He had lectured on English literature and Arabic translation at Cairo University and later became the pioneer translator of modern Arabic literature, providing translations of books by such figures as Tewfik al-Hakim, Naguib Mahfouz and Tayeb Salih; he has also translated religious works by such writers as al-Imām al-Ghazālī.

When Ezzeddin Ibrahim and Denys Johnson-Davies met they agreed to work closely together on making accurate and acceptable translations into English of various religious texts. It is recognised that Islam's message is a universal one, as is expressed in the words of the Almighty: "We have not sent you, (O Muhammad), except as a mercy to the worlds". (The Prophets: 107); also, "Say: O people, I am the Messenger of God to you all." (The Heights: 157)

And if Islam is universal and the Book of Islam and the words of its Prophet are in the Arabic tongue, how in such circumstances can universality be achieved?

The answer quite simply is that it must be done through translation. However, not any translation will do, for only too many renderings of the Holy Qur'an have distorted its meanings and marred its beauty. In some cases this has been done deliberately, while in others it has been due to the fact that those undertaking such translations lacked the necessary linguistic skills for a proper understanding of the holy Book.

Thus Ezzeddin and his colleague were determined that the translations they had in mind should combine two essential qualities: accuracy on the one hand and an elegantly readable rendering that would come as close as possible to the original. They felt that by cooperating together this could be achieved. Alongside Ezzeddin, whose native language is Arabic and who has a mastery of English, there would be an Englishman whose native tongue was English and who at the same time had a mastery of Arabic. Thus each translator would complement the other and the end result would be arrived at through discussion and consultation.

The two of them decided that initially their efforts should be directed towards making translations into English - the most universal of languages and the one known to the majority of Muslims -of some of the Prophetic Hadith, Hadith having attracted less attention from translators than the Holy Qur'an, of which translations did exist in forms which were at least acceptable.

But the sunnah is a veritable ocean. Where should they start?

Of old it was said that making a choice was part of a man's intelligence. Thus, while praising Abū Tammām for his outstanding poetry, critics have also praised him for his choice of the poetry contained in his well-known anthology entitled al-Ḥamāsah.

They thus chose for their first book the famous short anthology of al-Imām al-Nawawī entitled' al-Nawawī's Forty Hadith', it being a collection that has been universally accepted throughout the Islamic world. When the translation was completed, the book was made available to the public and was immediately well received and has since been reprinted more than twenty times.. The publication of al-Nawawī's Forty Hadith in an English translation encouraged others to pursue the same method of translation and to produce renderings of the work in more than ten languages.

For their second book they made a short anthology of that particular type of Hadith known as 'Qudsī'. Hadith Qudsī are known for their special spiritual quality and are words of the Almighty though spoken by His Prophet (may the blessings and peace of God be upon him). They have the characteristics of Prophetic Hadith rather than those of the Holy Qur'an and contain concepts of divine significance, leading man to a love of God and His glorification, and to an expectation of His mercy and a fear of His torment, thus prompting him to do good and to avoid evil; seldom do such Hadith comprise directly practical rules. This book, entitled 'Forty Hadith Qudsī', was also well received and is often reprinted.

These two books have been followed by a third volume to which it is my pleasure to write this preface. The present volume is a condensed form of the famous 'The Goodly Word', a collection of Hadith made by the renowned scholar and jurist Sheikh al-Islām Ibn Taymiyyah, to which a brief commentary has been added.

This book has been chosen because of the obvious need for a book of prayers and supplications which the ordinary Muslim who depends on English would require for the demands of his daily comings and goings, for those various situations in which a man finds himself: a gust of wind, sudden rainfall, facing up to illness, and the advent of death, all of which are occasions where a man is in need of particular supplications to the Almighty, for supplications are the very core of worship; in fact they are worship itself as the Messenger of God (may the blessings and peace of God be upon him)has taught us.

Many are the volumes, both long and condensed, that contain such prayers and supplications, some of which have explanations and commentaries that extend to no less than seven volumes, as for instance Ibn 'Allān's commentary on al-Nawawī's book ' al-Adhkār'. The choice of Ibn Taymiyyah's 'The Goodly Word' was made because of its reasonable length and the compiler's discerning choice of material, also because Sheikh al-Albānī had already traced the sources of the Hadith quoted in it, specifying those that were either 'authentic' or 'good' - which were the majority – and those that were 'weak'.

However, only those Hadith that were 'authentic' or 'good' were chosen for the present compilation and all others were deleted. The book has been provided with explanations to those words and phrases in the Arabic text that require them. The tracing of the Hadith to their sources was omitted from the first edition but I understand that it has been retained in the second - which I am glad about.

Additionally, the book contains an introduction outlining the importance of prayers and supplications, mentioning what has been written on this subject in all manner of books, also explaining why 'The Goodly Word' was chosen and what work has been done on it. The introduction also demonstrates that prayers need not necessarily be limited to ma'thūr material i.e. those recognised supplications that have been handed down. The justification for such a practice has been derived from the teachings of Hadith itself and is supported by the rulings of renowned scholars in the field of fiqh. Furthermore, the introduction confirmed the need for producing translations of prayers and supplications so that people might worship in their own languages.

It is further pointed out in the conclusion to the introduction that the important thing is for worship to be by prayer and supplication, with an understanding of the meaning, and with the participation of the heart in due humility, and that God Almighty should be turned to with urgent solicitation and with confidence about his good response, while care should be exercised not to articulate unacceptable expressions that may contain - without the person knowing - words that are incompatible with the glorification of God Almighty.

The Muslim should strive to make an effort to maintain such conditions in his prayers and supplications and should have recourse as far as possible to the Arabic tongue. On the other hand, he who is unable to acquire a knowledge of Arabic, should know for certain, when talking to the

Almighty in whatsoever language, that he is addressing a God who is all-Hearing and all-Knowing. The Almighty has said: "And if My servants have asked you about Me, verily I am close by and hear the prayer of him who prays when he prays, so let them pay attention to Me and let them believe in Me so that they may be rightly guided." (The Cow:286)

The two scholars have other projects in mind that aim to provide an understanding of Prophetic Hadith to readers who do not know Arabic or whose knowledge of the language is insufficient for understanding such texts. The most important of these are the following two books:

1.)That most well-known work by al-Nawawī entitled 'Riyāḍ al-Ṣāliḥīn'. It is a long book and they have already started work on it.

2.) A new abridgement of Shu'ab al-Imān along the lines of al-Qazwīnī's abridgement of the large book 'al-Jāmi' li-Shu'ab al-Imān by al-Hāfiz al-Bayhaqī which deals with the authentic Hadith: "Faith is some sixty or seventy branches, the highest of which is 'There is no god but God' and the lowest of which is 'The removal of something harmful from the road' - and bashfulness is a branch of faith.'

The substance of this is that faith is given expression not only in doctrine, nor yet only in worship, but comprises doctrine and behaviour, also worship and conduct, be it one's conduct towards God, towards oneself and one's family, towards society, the Ummah, or the whole of mankind, or towards the whole of the universe around one.

However the most important work on which they are presently engaged, and which they would hope to finish, is a book they have entitled 'Readings from the Holy Qur'an' classified according to subject matter. They have so named it because they felt it would not be appropriate to call it 'Selections from the Holy Qur'an'. The term 'selections' gives the impression that what has not been chosen is in some way inadequate, whereas the Holy Qur'an is wholly beautiful, complete and sublime.

In conclusion, nothing remains for me to say other than to thank the two scholars for the work they are doing for the benefit of their fellow Muslims and to ask God to guide them in their good work. Praise be to God, first and last, and may the blessings of God be upon His Prophet Muḥammad and his family and companions.

He who prays for God's forgiveness.

Yūsuf al-Qaraḍāwī

تقديم

بقلم فضيلة الأستاذ الدكتور يوسف القرضاوي

رئيس مركز السيرة النبوية والسنة المشرفة في جامعة قطر وعضو مجامع الفقه الإسلامي في البلاد العربية والإسلامية وأوروبا

الحمد لله وكفى، وسلام على رسوله المصطفى، وعلى آله وصحبه أئمة الهدى، وبعد،

فقد عرفت أخي الدكتور عز الدين ابراهيم منذ أكثر من نصف قرن، ومن خلاله تعرفت على زميله الأخ الأستاذ عبد الودود دنيس جونسون ديفيز. فأما عز الدين، فقد كانت معرفتي به في مجالات الدعوة الاسلامية، ولقاءات البحث في أمور الفكر الإسلامي المتنوعة، والزمالة في التدريس والإدارة والعمل التربوي. وأعجبني فيه أبداً: شخصيته المحببة، وخلقه السمح، ووجهه المبتسم، وعقله المنظم، وثقافته الرحبة، وحسن تأتيه للأمور، وقدرته على البناء والعمل في صمت وتجرد بعيدا عن الغرور والادعاء والانتفاخ بالباطل، مما أهله لمناصب وأعمال كثيرة مشهودة: في وضع المناهج الدراسية

وتأليف الكتب لوزارة المعارف في قطر، وفي تأسيسه للمجمع الثقافي في أبو ظبي، وتوليه أستاذية الأدب العربي في جامعة الرياض، وإدارته لجامعة الامارات لعدة سنوات، وفي إدارته لصندوق التضامن الإسلامي في منظمة المؤتمر الاسلامي، وفي مساعدة المسلمين الأفارقة في أمريكا، وفي مساهمته بتنظيم وإدارة مؤسسة الشيخ زايد بن سلطان آل نهيان للأعمال الخيرية والإنسانية، وفي محاضراته بالعربية والإنجليزية في أماكن عديدة، وفي عدد من الأعمال التي يشارك فيها بفكره وجهده، ولا أملك أن أحصرها.

وأما الأستاذ عبد الودود دنيس جونسون ديفيز فهو أديب إنجليزي معروف، وخاصة في مجال الترجمة والنقد الأدبي، وقد درس الأدب الإنجليزي وفن الترجمة في كلية الآداب بجامعة القاهرة، وأصدر عدة مجلدات لترجمات من اللغة العربية إلى الإنجليزية تشتمل على أعمال للأدباء توفيق الحكيم، ونجيب محفوظ، والطيب صالح، وغيرهم، كما ترجم للإمام الغزالي، ولكتابات إسلامية أخرى ويعتبر رائدا في مجال الترجمة للأدب العربي الحديث.

وبالتقاء الدكتور عز الدين ابراهيم مع الأستاذ عبد الودود، تم الاتفاق على التعاون الوثيق لإصدار ترجمات دقيقة لبعض الكتب الإسلامية. فمن المؤكد أن رسالة الإسلام رسالة عالمية، كما قال تعالى ﴿ وما أرسلناك إلا رحمة للعالمين ﴾ – الأنبياء ١٠٧ –، وقال ﴿ قل يأيها الناس إني رسول الله إليكم جميعا﴾ – الأعراف ١٥٨ –. وإذا كان الإسلام عالميا، فإن كتاب الإسلام ورسوله عربيا اللسان، فكيف نحقق العالمية في هذه الحالة؟

والجواب أنا نحققها من خلال الترجمة، ولكن ليست أي ترجمة، فكم من ترجمات للقرآن الكريم حرفت معانيه وشوهت جماله، بعضها عن عمد وقصد إلى التحريف والتشويه، وبعضها عن جهل لفقدان أصحابها القدرة على فهم اللغة العربية، ودلالات ألفاظها وتراكيبها، وتذوق جمالياتها.

لهذا كان عز الدين وعبد الودود، حريصين على أن تجمع الترجمة المنشودة بين أمرين أساسيين: الدقة والأمانة من ناحية، والبلاغة والسلاسة - التي تقترب من الأصل ما أمكن ذلك - من ناحية أخرى. ورأى الرجلان أن تعاونهما معا يعين على تحقيق المقصود، فيكون بجوار عز الدين العربي

الأصل، والمتمكن من اللغة الإنجليزية، رجل إنجليزي الأصل والإنجليزية هى لغته الأصلية، وأن تكون له من الأصالة والتمييز في معرفته الإنجليزية ما لعز الدين من الأصالة والتمييز في معرفته العربية، وأن يكون متمكننا من العربية تمكن عز الدين من الإنجليزية، وبهذا يكمل أحدهما الآخر، ويتشاوران ويتحاوران معا حتى يخرج العمل المترجم على أفضل وجه ممكن.

وتوجه الرجلان نحو السنة النبوية، لأن القرآن الكريم له ترجمات عدة من قديم، بعضها مقبول، أو قريب من المقبول. أما السنة، فهى التي لم تجد من يقدمها إلى قراء الإنجليزية - اللغة الأكثر انتشاراً في العالم، وانتشاراً أيضا بين المسلمين - بلغة العصر المفهومة لعموم الناس. والسنة أيضا هى التي يشوبها الكثير من الغموض والالتباس، وتروج حولها الأكاذيب من كثير من الكاتبين.

ولكن السنة بحر واسع وزاخر، فماذا يختار منها ليترجم؟

قديما قالوا: اختيار الرجل جزء من عقله. ولهذا أثنوا على أبي تمام في شعره المتميز، كما أثنوا عليه في اختياراته التي تمثلت في (ديوان الحماسة) المعروف.

ووقـــع الاخـــتيار أن يكـــون أول كـــتاب يترجم هو (الأربعـــون النوويـــة) المعـــروفة، وهى مجموعة أحاديث اخـــتارها الإمام النووي، ولقيت قبولا عاما من المســـلمين في المشـــارق والمغـــارب، طـــوال القرون الماضية وإلى اليوم. وتعـــاون عز الدين مع صاحبه دنيس، حتى أتما الكتاب، ونُشر بيـــن الـــناس، واستقبلوه في كل مكان بقبول حسن، وطُبع منه أكـــثر من عشرين طبعة بالإنجليزية، وترجم إلى بضع عشرة لغـــة، بـــنفس الاشتراط، وهو تعاون اثنين في الترجمة في كل لغة، بحيث يكمل كلاهما صاحبه.

وبعـــد الأربعيـــــن النووية، أُختيرت مجموعـــة أخرى سُـــميت (الأربعـــون القدســـية) وإنما اختيـــرت من هذا الـــنوع مـــن الأحاديث لما تشتمل عليه من روحانية خاصة، فهـــي مـــن كلام الله تعـــالى، ولكن على لســـان رسوله عليه الصـــلاة والسلام، فلها خصائص الحديث النبوي وأحكامه، لا خصـــائص القـــرآن وأحكامـــه، وهـــي تتضمن معاني ربانية وإيمانيـــة، تقـــود الانسان إلى حب الله وتعظيمه، والرجاء في رحمـــته والخشية من عذابه، مما يحفزه إلى عمل الصالحات، واجتـــناب السيئات، وقلما تتضمن هذه الأحاديث أحكاما عملية

مباشرة. وقد حظـــي هذا الكتاب أيضا بالقبول وأعيدت طباعته مرات.

ثم كان هذا الكتاب الثالث الذي شُرفت بأن أكتب له هذه المقدمـــة، وهـــو مختصـــر (الكلم الطيب) لشيخ الاسلام ابن تيمية، مع شرح موجز له.

وإنمـــا اختير هذا الكتاب لحاجة الإنســـان الغربي المسلم إلى معـــرفة مجموعة من الأذكار والدعوات التي يحتاج إليها الإنســـان في يومه وليلته، وفي المواقف المختلفة التي تعرض للإنســـان فـــي الحيـــاة، مثل هبوب الرياح، ونزول الأمطار، وحـــدوث الأمـــراض، ووقوع مصيبة الموت، ليذكر بها ربه، ويدعـــوه منيبا إليه، فالدعاء مخ العبادة، بل الدعاء هو العبادة، كما علمنا رسول الله صلى الله عليه وسلم.

وقـــد ورد في الشرع الكثير من الأذكار والأدعية، ألفت فيهـــا الكـــتب المطولة والمختصرة، ومنها ما شرح في سبعة مجلدات[1] ، ولهذا كان على الكاتب أن يتخير منها ما يراه أليق بالمقام، وأوفى بالمقصد المطلوب. فكان اختيار (الكلم الطيب) لابـــن تيمية لأنه أخصر من غيره، ولحسن انتقاء مؤلفه، ولأن

---

[1] شرح ابن علان للأذكار النووية.

الشيخ الألباني قد خرج أحاديثه، فعرف منها الصحيح والحسن - وهو الأكثر - كما عرف الضعيف.

ولهذا كان اختيار مؤلفنا من الصحاح والحسان، وحذف ما لا حاجة إليه. كما شرح ما لابد منه من المفردات والتراكيب شرحا موجزا بين المراد بالعربية وقد حذف التخريج في الطبعة الأولى، ولكنني فهمت أنه قد أثبت في الطبعة الثانية. وهو خير.

وللكتاب مقدمة حول أهمية الذكر والدعاء، وما أُلف في ذلك من كتب ما بين مطول ومختصر ومتوسط، ولماذا اختير (الكلم الطيب) ، وماذا كان العمل فيه، كما بينت المقدمة حكم الدعاء بغير المأثور، اعتمادا على الحديث الشريف، ومؤيدا بقول العلماء المعتبرين. وكذلك الحاجة إلى ترجمة الأدعية والأذكار، ليتعبد الناس بها بلغاتهم، وأقيم الدليل على ذلك بما يشير إلى حسن الفقه والفهم.

ومما نُبه عليه في ختام المقدمة: أن المهم هو التعبد بالذكر والدعاء بفهم المعنى، وحضور القلب، وخشوع الجوارح. وحسن التوجه إلى الله تعالى بالإلحاح عليه،

والتيقن من حسن إجابته، والحذر من التلفظ بعبارات أعجمية، قد تحتوى على ما ينافي تعظيم الله تعالى دون أن يعلم. وليجتهد المسلم في تحصيل هذه الشروط في دعائه وذكره، وليستعن على ذلك بالاقتراب من اللسان العربي ما وسعه ذلك، وليتيقن العاجز الذي يناجي ربه - بأى لغة مع الصحة والفهم - أنه يناجي ربا سميعا عليما قال تعالى: ﴿ وإذا سألكَ عبادِي عني فإنِّي قريبٌ أُجيبُ دعوةَ الدَّاعِ إذا دعانِ، فليستجيبُوا لِي وليُؤمنُوا بِي لعلَّهم يرشدُونَ ﴾ - البقرة ١٨٦.

وفي جعبة الدكتور عز الدين ابراهيم والأستاذ عبد الودود مشروعات أخرى مهمة في هذه السلسلة الذهبية، التي تهدف إلى تقريب فهم الأحاديث النبوية إلى القراء الذين لا يعرفون اللغة العربية، وأهمها كتابان نافعان، يحتاج إلى كليهما الناس، وهما:

١- **رياض الصالحين** للنووي، وهو أشهر من أن يعرف، وهو قيد الإعداد أو الاستكمال إن شاء الله، وهو عمل كبير، نرجو لهما فيه التوفيق والسداد.

٢- **مختصر جديد لشعب الإيمان** على غرار مختصر القزويني، للكتاب الكبير (الجامع لشعب الإيمان)

لـــلحافظ الـــبيهقي ويدور حول الحديث الصحيح: "الايمان بضـــع وستون أو بضع وسبعون شعبة، أعلاها: لا إله إلا الله، وأدناهـــا: إماطة الأذى من الطريق، والحياء شعبة من الإيمان".

وخلاصـــته: أن الإيمان لا يتمثل في العقيدة وحدها، ولا فـــي العـــبادة وحدهـــا، ولكنه يشمل العقيدة والسلوك، والعبادة والمعامـــلة، ســـواء كانت المعاملة مع الله أم مع النفس أم مع الأسرة أم مع المجتمع، أم مع الأمة، أم البشر كافة أم مع الكون كله من حوله.

ولكن أهم عمل يشتغلان به الآن ويســـألان الله تعالى أن يوفـــق إلى إتمامـــه، ما ســـمياه (قراءات من القرآن الكريم) مبوبـــة وفقاً للموضوعات ولم تستحسن تسميتها (مختارات) لعـــدم مناســـبتها لجلال القرآن، لأن المختار من شيء يوحى بأن ما ترك كأن فيه شيئا جعله لا يصلح للاختيار. والقرآن كله كمال وجمال وجلال. وهذا من دقة النظر ورهافة الحس وبالغ الإجلال للقرآن العظيم.

لايســـعنا في ختـــام هذا التقديم إلا أن نشـــكر للدكتـــور عـــز الدين جهده مع زميله الأخ المسلم عبد الودود، وأسأل الله

تعـــالى أن يسدد خطاهما، وينير طريقهما، وينفع بهما المسلمين فـــيما أصدراه، وما ينويان إصداره، وأن يجعل عملهما خالصا لوجهه، ويثيبهما بذلك في الدنيا والآخرة اللهم آمين. والحمد لله أولا وآخـــرا. وصلى الله على نبيـــه محمد وعلى آله وصحبه وســـلم تسليما كثيرا.

الفقير إلى عفو مولاه

يوسف القرضاوي

In the Name of Allah
the Merciful the Compassionate

INTRODUCTION

Praise be to Allah and blessings and peace on our master the Messenger of Allah and on his family and Companions and on those who summon people to his message.

We have found that the Islamic library is still in need of a book combining a number of *du^{c}ā'* and *dhikr* that are *ma'thūr* (authentically transmitted), together with the translation of their meanings into English. Such *du^{c}ā'* and *dhikr*, being given in the original Arabic form, will be comprehensible to readers of Arabic, both Arabs and others, and are provided with the necessary explanatory aids; at the same time they will in translation be easily understood by readers of English.

For this purpose our choice has fallen on the book *The Goodly Word* by Sheikh al-Islām Taqī ad-Dīn Aḥmad ibn Taymiyyah, who died in A.H. 728, because of its concise nature and because it is confined to those of the Goodly Word that are *ma'thūr*, and owing to its general acceptance among people. This book has been well received and given due attention by scholars in the past. We have nevertheless shortened it slightly in order to make it suitable for publication together with its translation, as explained hereinafter.

We thought it would be useful to provide the book with a short introduction making clear the significance of *duʿā'* and *dhikr* and their place among Islamic religious observances; enumerating the authorised sources for *duʿā'* and *dhikr* that are *ma'thūr*; mentioning the most well-known books composed on this subject; explaining our contribution to the compilation of this book, a shortened version of *The Goodly Word*; and dealing with the well-founded attitude that *duʿā'* and *dhikr* should be restricted to those that are *ma'thūr*, while giving the ruling on using *duʿā'* and *dhikr* that are not *ma'thūr*, and the legal reservations in employing translations of their meanings into other languages.

The status of *duʿā'* and *dhikr* in Islamic religious observances

A *duʿā'* is a calling upon Allah the Almighty in seeking His help, His benevolence, and His mercy in all affairs of religion and daily life. The Prophet (may the blessings and peace of Allah be upon him) has described it by saying "*Duʿā'* is worship,"[1] meaning that it is its essence and innermost core. It is the response to Allah the Almighty's words in the Holy Qur'ān, "And your Lord hath said: Pray unto Me and I will hear your prayer,"[2] and His saying, "And when My servants question thee concerning Me, then surely I am nigh. I answer the prayer of the suppliant when he crieth unto Me,"[3] being an affirmation of the belief in the Oneness of Allah and of sincere

1. It was related by at-Tirmidhī, who said that it was a good and sound Hadith, also by Abū Dāwūd and Ibn Mājah.
2. Qur'ān 40.60.
3. Qur'ān 2.186.

devotion to Him (may He be praised) by describing Him as being He to whom alone prayer is directed, as in the words of the Almighty, "Allah, the eternally besought of all"[1] and in His words, "All unto whom ye cry (for succour) fail save Him alone."[2]

Dhikr is that a man is with his Lord with his mind, thoughts, and feelings, and that he mentions Him constantly with his tongue, repeating the appropriate words of devotion for glorifying Him and exalting Him, praising Him, confirming His Oneness and Uniqueness, and asking His forgiveness, also exalting His sublimeness and His Most Beautiful Names, in pursuance of His words (may He be exalted), "O ye who believe! Remember Allah with much remembrance. And glorify Him early and late,"[3] and His words in describing those who believe, "And men who remember Allah much and women who remember—Allah hath prepared for them forgiveness and a vast reward."[4] And Allah the Almighty has stressed the value of *dhikr* and has made it of more importance than anything else by His words, "And verily the *dhikr* of Allah is greatest."[5] The Messenger of Allah (may the blessings and peace of Allah be upon him) made *dhikr* an indication of the heart being alive, as referred to in his Hadith, "The likeness of him who makes *dhikr* to his Lord to him who does not do so is as the likeness of

---

1. Qur'ān 112.2.
2. Qur'ān 17.67.
3. Qur'ān 33.41–42.
4. Qur'ān 33.35.
5. Qur'ān 29.45.

the living to the dead."[1]

*Du*ᶜ*ā'* and *Dhikr* are largely interlocked and closely associated, so that the phraseology of each of them is complementary to the other, or follows it in the context, as in the words of the Almighty, "Such as remember Allah, standing, sitting, and reclining, and consider the creation of the heavens and the earth, (and say): Our Lord! Thou createst not this in vain. Glory be to Thee! Preserve us from the doom of Fire."[2] They are both to be found throughout the totality of Islamic religious observances such as prayer, fasting, and the Pilgrimage, all of which are so replete with *du*ᶜ*ā'* and *dhikr* that such observances cannot be complete without them. It is the same in respect of other religious practices such as night-prayer, *i*ᶜ*tikāf*, that is, withdrawing to a mosque for a certain time for purposes of worship and meditation, paying *zakāt*, and so on. In fact, the Muslim in his ordinary life should mention Allah in all his circumstances and should call upon Him when he gets up in the morning and enters upon the evening, and on all occasions he faces. Thus books of *du*ᶜ*ā'* and *dhikr* are arranged in accordance with the daily routines: waking up and going to sleep; proceeding to one's work; meeting with people and participating in their social gatherings and their food and drink; undertaking journeys; visiting the sick; changes of weather; encountering the enemy; becoming ill; being struck by misfortune; attaining success; realising happiness in marriage or the birth of offspring; or being favoured with some plentiful boon, and like matters that are part of daily

1. It was related by al-Bukhārī.

2. Qur'ān 3.191. Thus "Glory be to Thee" is *dhikr* while "Preserve us from the doom of Fire" is *du*ᶜ*ā'*.

life. It is for this reason that some books of *du^cā'* and *dhikr* are called 'Devotions for Day and Night,' thus referring to the *du^cā'* and *dhikr* that are on a Muslim's lips during his day and night and which bring him close to his Lord, supplicating Him and asking for His assistance in all circumstances.

One of the benefits of uttering *duᶜā'* and *dhikr* in all the circumstances of the day and night is that customary habits are turned into religious observances, for every ordinary act performed by a Muslim which is accompanied by *duᶜā'* and *dhikr* becomes an act of devotion through the intention of him who practises it, and by the attitude in which it is made, in such a way that it is changed into an act of worship by which the favour of Allah is gained. For instance, travelling is a normal practice which, if begun by someone who recites the *duᶜā'*, "O Allah, we ask You in this journey of ours righteousness and piety and such deeds as You would approve of...,"[1] becomes charged with a collection of refinements and religious and ethical values which will make of it a beneficent journey in which the traveller can be confident of overcoming its hardships, at the same time remembering the family and children he has left behind him, and he can look forward to his return safe and sound and of giving thanks to Allah for the happy outcome. It is in this way that the practice becomes an act of worship.

Sources of *duᶜā'* and *dhikr*

The first source for *duᶜā'* and *dhikr* that are *ma'thūr* is the Holy Qur'ān. It possesses a copious number of them,

---

1. Hadith no. 132 in this book.

which are to be found in four forms.

The first form consists of verses of *du*ʿ*ā'* and *dhikr* that commence with the imperative "Say," as in the two chapters that pronounce incantations, "Say: I seek refuge in the Lord of the Daybreak from the evil of that which He created..."[1] and "Say: I seek refuge in the Lord of mankind..."[2] and in His words "And say: My Lord! Increase me in knowledge,"[3] and His words "And say: 'My Lord! Forgive and have mercy, for Thou art the Best of all who show mercy,'"[4] and the like.

The second form consists of verses that are related on the tongues of angels or prophets. Among those told by angels is "Our Lord! Thou comprehendest all things in mercy and knowledge, therefore forgive those who repent and follow Thy way. Ward off from them the punishment of hell."[5] Among those told by prophets is Dhū 'n-Nūn's *dhikr*, "But he cried out in the darkness, saying: There is no God save Thee. Be Thou Glorified! Lo! I have been a wrong-doer,"[6] and the prayer of Job when seeking restoration of health, "And Job, when he cried unto his Lord, (saying): Lo! Adversity afflicteth me, and Thou art Most Merciful of all who show mercy."[7]

---

1. Qur'ān 113.
2. Qur'ān 114.
3. Qur'ān 20.114.
4. Qur'ān 23.118.
5. Qur'ān 40.7.
6. Qur'ān 21.87.
7. Qur'ān 21.83. And see the supplication of Zakariyyā (on whom be peace) in the same chapter (21.89), when he asks that he may be given offspring; in other chapters that could be quoted there are *du*ʿ*ā'* by other prophets.

The third form consists of *duᶜā'* and *dhikr* that are related on the tongue of the Prophet Muḥammad (may the blessings and peace of Allah be upon him) and the believers who were with him, as in the closing words of the Chapter of al-Baqarah (The Cow), "And they say: We hear, and we obey. (Grant us) Thy forgiveness, our Lord. Unto Thee is the journeying... Our Lord! Condemn us not if we forget, or miss the mark!"[1]

The fourth form consists of *duᶜā'* and *dhikr* that do not fall into any of the previous categories but are recognised by their content. All of Sūrat al-Fātiḥah (The Opening Chapter) is of this category, its first half being *dhikr* of praise, glorification, and exaltation of Allah, while the second half is a *duᶜā'* for guidance.[2]

The *duᶜā'* and *dhikr* in the Holy Qur'ān are distinguished by their being from the Preserved Book, which knows no falsehood of any kind and the recitation of which brings two rewards, the reward of reciting the Holy Qur'ān and the reward of the *dhikr* and *duᶜā'*.[3]

The second source for extracting transmitted texts of *duᶜā'* and *dhikr* are the books of Prophetic Hadith, for they all contain portions allocated to them, in addition to

---

1. Qur'ān 2.286.
2. In the explanation of this Chapter is the Hadith Qudsī (Sacred Hadith) which was given by al-Bukhārī: "Allah the Almighty says 'I have divided prayer between Myself and My servant into two halves, and half of it is for Me [because it is *dhikr* and glorification] and half of it is for My servant [because it is *duᶜā'*] and My servant shall have what he has asked for.'"
3. Refer to Dr. ᶜAbd al-Ḥalīm Maḥmūd, *Fadhkurūnī adhkurkum* (So mention Me and I shall remember you), Dār al-Maᶜārif, Cairo 1981, pp. 67–97.

giving other Hadith that are *ma'thūr* distributed under various chapters in accordance with their subject matter. Thus in the *Saḥīḥ of al-Bukhārī* is a book of *duᶜā'* and *dhikr* under the title *The Book of Prayers*. But it also contains *duᶜā'* and *dhikr* in the chapter on Prayer and others in the chapter on Fasting, the chapter on the Pilgrimage, and so on. *The Book of Prayers (Kitāb ad-daᶜawāt)*[1] consists of sixty-nine chapters and comprises 106 Hadith. In the *Saḥīḥ of Muslim* we find a book under the title *The Book of Duᶜā' and Dhikr, Repentance and Asking for Forgiveness*,[2] which consists of twenty-seven chapters and includes 101 Hadith, apart from the miscellaneous items in the rest of the books. In the *Sunan* of at-Tirmidhī there is *The Book of Prayers*,[3] which comprises 132 chapters and includes 234 Hadith. In the *Sunan* of Ibn Mājah there is the *Book of Duᶜā'*,[4] which comprises twenty-two chapters and includes sixty-five Hadith. The *duᶜā'* and *dhikr* in the *Sunan* of Abū Dāwūd are to be found in *The Book of Good Manners*,[5] which comprises twelve chapters containing sixty-seven Hadith. In the *Musnad* of Imām Aḥmad, *duᶜā'* and *dhikr* are scattered throughout the *musnads* in accordance with the

---

1. *The Saḥīḥ of al-Bukhārī*, Istanbul edition of 1992, offset from the edition of Cairo, volume 7, pp. 145–169.
2. *The Saḥīḥ of Muslim*, the edition of Muḥammad Fu'ād ᶜAbd al-Bāqī, Cairo 1956, volume 3, pp. 2061–2101.
3. *Sunan at-Tirmidhī*, the edition of Ibrahīm ᶜAṭwa ᶜAwaḍ, Cairo 1965, volume 5, pp. 455–582.
4. *Sunan Ibn Mājah*, the edition of Muḥammad Fuād ᶜAbd al-Bāqī, Cairo 1954, volume 2, pp. 1258–1281.
5. *Sunan Abū Dāwūd*, the edition of ᶜIzzat ᶜUbayd ad-Daᶜās, Homs, Syria, 1969, volume 5, pp. 298–337.

particular classification of that book. However, in the edition of the late Sheikh Aḥmad ᶜAbd ar-Raḥmān al-Bannā, which was entitled *al-Fatḥ ar-rabbāni, tartīb musnad al-Imām Aḥmad ibn Ḥanbal ash-Shaybānī,*[1] the book *Duᶜā' and Dhikr* is devoted to them; it comprises forty-two chapters and contains 295 Hadith.

The third source for *duᶜā'* and *dhikr* are those books solely devoted to this subject and whose compilers have a direct chain of authorities to the Messenger of Allah (may the blessings and peace of Allah be upon him) and which are thus one and the same as books of Hadith in that they are regarded as sources for original Hadith on this particular topic. There is a limited number of such books and only two books have come down to us in printed form. These are *Devotions for Day and Night* by Imām Aḥmad ibn Shuᶜayb an-Nasā'ī who died in A.H. 303 and who is also the author of the *Sunan an-Nasā'ī*, and *Devotions for Day and Night* by Abū Bakr ibn as-Sunnī, who died in A.H. 364 and who is the reciter of the *Sunan* of an-Nasā'ī.

As for the book of an-Nasā'ī, its author either composed it in order to include it in his large work, the *Sunan an-Nasā'ī*, and did not do so, which explains why his *Sunan* are alone among the six authorised books of Hadith in being devoid of a section given exclusively to *duᶜā'* and *dhikr*, or the author intentionally made of it a separate and distinct book. It comprises 1121 Hadith, counting the repetitions and variant readings. Thus an-Nasā'ī gathered together more Hadith of *duᶜā'* and *dhikr*

---

1. *Al-Fatḥ ar-rabbāni, tartīb musnad al-Imām Aḥmad*, third edition, Jeddah A.H. 1404, volume 14, pp. 196–312. In this edition the contents have been rearranged according to subject matter.

than any of the other five compilers of collections of Hadith.

As for the book of Ibn as-Sunnī, it is similar to that of an-Nasā'ī; while containing material from an-Nasā'ī, it also provides other material. Additionally, the book includes chapters which are not to be found in an-Nasā'ī. The number of Hadith in Ibn as-Sunnī is 770.

Other books of this sort that are regarded as sources have been compiled; some of these exist in manuscript form, either in their entirety or partly only, whereas in yet other cases only extracts have survived and are to be found in existing publications.[1]

The major books of *du^cā'* and *dhikr*

Owing to the fact that the sources of those *du^cā'* and *dhikr* that are *ma'thūr* are known and authenticated, and the places therein devoted to *du^cā'* and *dhikr* clearly defined, a number of books have been compiled that strive to make the subject more accessible to readers through bringing them together, rearranging them into chapters, making selections, and giving commentaries, and by abridging them and adding to them such studies about *du^cā'* and *dhikr* and their meanings and the manner in which they should be read, and so forth, as the compilers felt would be useful. The door for such books remains open, and we do not think that it will be closed, owing to the eager

---

1. Aḥmad ibn Shu^cayb an-Nasā'ī, *Devotions for Day and Night*, edited by Dr. Fārūq Ḥammādah, second edition, Beirut 1985. See the study of Dr. Ḥammādah on source books of *du^cā'* and *dhikr* in his book, pp. 103–111. And see Muḥammad ibn ^cAllān aṣ-Ṣiddīqī, *al-Futūḥāt ar-rabbāniyyah ^cala 'l-adhkār an-nawāwiyyah*, Dār Iḥyā' at-Turāth al-^cArabī, Beirut, volume 1, p. 18.

desire of Muslims to be informed about their religious devotions. We shall thus refer only to the most important of such books, both old and new, indicating the position enjoyed by the book *The Goodly Word*, which we present here.

1. The oldest books of this kind that must be mentioned are the two books of Imām an-Nasā'ī and Ibn as-Sunnī, which have been previously referred to. Although they are listed among the sources we have enumerated, the fact that they were compiled as separate works and that they are in print has placed them among those books that are readily available to the reader. An-Nasā'ī's book has been edited and twice published, the first edition being that of Dr. Fārūq Ḥammādah in Beirut in A.H. 1405/1985, while the second was also published in Beirut in A.H. 1408/1988.[1] The compiler's aim was to include in his book *du^c^ā'* and *dhikr* of daily life, and he thus gave his book a title which expresses this intention. He begins it with the chapter "Mentioning that which the Prophet used to say when he came into the morning," then he follows it with man's circumstances during his day until what he says during the evening and before going to sleep, and so on. Also in the book is a mention of *du^c^ā'* and *dhikr* relating to certain Islamic religious devotions such as prayer and fasting.

As for the book of Ibn as-Sunnī, it has been published in India and Egypt, after which there appeared an edition edited by ^c^Abd al-Qādir Aḥmad Ṭaha in Cairo in A.H. 1389/ 1969.[2] In its method and contents the book

---

1. Aḥmad ibn Shu^c^ayb an-Nasā'ī: *^c^Amal al-yawm wa 'l-laylah*, edited by Dār al-Kutub al-^c^Ilmiyyah. Beirut, A.H. 1408/1988.

2. Abū Bakr ibn as-Sunnī, *^c^Amal al-yawm wa 'l-laylah, the conduct of the Prophet (may the blessings and peace of Allah be upon him)*

resembles an-Nasā'ī's, though retaining certain of its own characteristics. Scholars are divided as to which of the two books is to be preferred.

2. An-Nawawī's book *al-Adhkār:* The author is Imām Muḥyī 'd-Dīn Yaḥyā ibn Sharaf an-Nawawī ad-Dimishqī, who died in A.H. 676. This work is considered to be midway between the source books predominantly employed by specialists and those used by the general reader for the purposes of practical application in his devotions. We therefore find it has received particular attention from scholars, who lavish praise on it and who have composed commentaries on it, also abridgements, while at the same time gaining widespread acceptance among people generally, to such an extent that there was a saying, "Sell your house and buy *al-Adhkār,*" suggesting that having the book was more worthwhile than owning real estate.[1]

The compiler begins by seeking to shorten his book by deleting the chain of authorities of the Hadith and contenting himself with indicating their sources and showing their degrees of authenticity. However, he soon expands it by including a copious number of Hadith in every category. He likewise includes, as he mentions, "Extracts from the gems of the science of Hadith, the niceties of jurisprudence, the most important fundamental religious rules, spiritual exercises, and good manners, whose knowledge is imperative for those who are

---

with his Lord, edited by ᶜAbd al-Qādir Aḥmad Ṭaha, Cairo A.H. 1389/1969.

1. Muḥammad ᶜAlī ibn ᶜAllān aṣ-Ṣiddīqī, *al-Futūḥāt ar-rabbāniyyah ᶜala 'l-adhkār an-nawāwiyyah,* Beirut edition, volume 1, pp. 1–4.

following the spiritual path";[1] this, though, he does in simple language. The compiler (may Allah have mercy upon him) has thus succeeded in making his book a recognised source which no researcher or scholar of the subject can be without. There was no compiler in this discipline who came after him who did not refer to him.

3. *Al-Kalim aṭ-ṭayyib*[2] by Sheikh al-Islām Taqī ad-Dīn Aḥmad ibn Taymiyyah, who was born at Ḥarrān in A.H. 661 and died in Damascus in A.H. 728. He was well known for his attitude towards the doctrine of the Oneness of Allah, and his writings clarify this doctrine; he was also famed for combatting unacceptable innovations. He took this beautiful and incomparable title for his book from the words of the Almighty, "Unto Him goodly words ascend, and the pious deeds doth He exalt."[3] The book was printed several times in Cairo by the Munīriyyah Press, after which a scholarly edition appeared in A.H. 1385, the work of Sheikh Muḥammad Nāṣir ad-Dīn al-Albānī, presently of Damascus, and of Sheikh Zuhayr ash-Shāwīsh al-Maydānī ad-Dimishqī. This edition contains a full verification of the Hadith so that their degrees of authenticity are determined.

The book contains sixty-one chapters and 253 Hadith. It is clear that the compiler (may Allah have mercy on him) had as an aim that his book should be an easy reference to *duʿā'* and *dhikr* for devotional worship on appropriate

---

1. Muḥyī 'd-Dīn Yaḥyā ibn Sharaf an-Nawawī, *al-Adhkār al-muntakhaba min sayyid al-abrār*, 14th edition, Beirut 1984, pp. 4–5.
2. Taqī ad-Dīn Aḥmad ibn Taymiyyah, *al-Kalim aṭ-ṭayyib*, edited by Sheikh Muḥammad Nāṣir ad-Dīn al-Albānī, 2nd edition, al-Maktab al-Islāmī, Beirut A.H. 1392. See the editor's introduction, p. 13.
3. Qur'ān 35.10.

occasions, without digressing to other related studies. He thus concentrated on simply providing it with a good classification and giving the texts without unnecessary comments, which might otherwise have taken the book outside its intended scope. Because of this, *al-Kalim aṭ-ṭayyib* is regarded as one of the best medium-sized mediaeval books for providing direct access to *du^cā'* and *dhikr* that are *ma'thūr* for the purpose of devotional worship. Most of the books which appeared after that followed his example, and in particular contemporary collections.

4. *al-Wābil aṣ-ṣayyib*[1] *min al-kalim aṭ-ṭayyib* by al-Ḥāfiẓ Abū ᶜAbdullah Muḥammad ibn Abī Bakr, known as Ibn Qayyim al-Jawziyyah, who was born in A.H. 691 and died at Damascus in A.H. 752. He followed his master Ibn Taymiyyah in the naming of his book and in being brief when quoting Hadith of *duᶜā'* and *dhikr* by giving the source alone without mentioning the chain of authorities. The book includes seventy-five chapters, beginning with *dhikr* of morning and evening and comprising *duᶜā'* for occasions to be found in daily life, likewise *dhikr* and *duᶜā'* for most devotional practices. He provided the book with a long introduction of the same size as the book itself, in which he deals with matters relating to spiritual and behavioural practices and those relating to people practising *dhikr* and their gatherings, also about the etiquette of *dhikr*. The book exists in printed form.[2]

---

1. The words mean 'abundant rain,' i.e., that which is of great benefit.

2. Muḥammad ibn Abī Bakr ibn Qayyim al-Jawziyyah, *al-Wābil aṣ-ṣayyib min al-kalim aṭ-ṭayyib*, edited by Sheikh Ibrāhīm al-ᶜAjūz, Dār al-Kutub al-ᶜIlmiyyah, Beirut.

5. *ᶜUddat al-ḥiṣn al-ḥaṣīn min kalām sayyid al-mursalīn* by Ibn al-Jazarī. This book comes at the end of the list of ancient and mediaeval books. The author is the leading Qur'ān reciter Muḥammad ibn Muḥammad ibn al-Jazarī, who died in A.H. 833. The book incorporates 626 Hadith, while being brief in the manner in which they are presented, merely indicating the method whereby the sources are given. It has numerous commentaries, most of which are in print and generally available.[1]

6. *Nuzul al-abrār bi 'l-ᶜilm al-ma'thūr min al-adᶜiyyah wa 'l-adhkār*. This is a recent work by the Indian scholar as-Sayyid Muḥammad Ṣiddīq Ḥasan Khān, who died in A.H. 1307. The author was well informed about the books in this field—and in particular *al-Adhkār* by Imām an-Nawawī—so that his book became a comprehensive work on *dhikr* and *duᶜā'* and included the devotions for day and night and for different occasions in daily life, also *dhikr* for religious observances. The work is in print.[2]

Our work in abbreviating *al-Kalim aṭ-ṭayyib* and translating its meanings

It is evident from the above that the book *al-Kalim aṭ-ṭayyib* by Ibn Taymiyyah is the most suitable to our purpose, which is to present a book of reliable authorship and content which is confined to texts of *duᶜā'* and *dhikr*

---

1. *ᶜUddat al-ḥiṣn al-ḥaṣīn min kalām sayyid al-mursalīn*, with commentary by Sheikh Ḥasanayn Muḥammad Makhlūf, first edition, Cairo A.H. 1381/1961. Muḥammad ᶜAlī ash-Shawkānī, *Tuḥfat adh-dhākirīn bi ᶜuddat al-ḥiṣn al-ḥaṣīn*, first edition, Dār al-Qalam, Beirut 1984.
2. As-Sayyid Muḥammad Ṣiddīq Ḥasan Khān, *Nuzul al-abrār bi 'l-ᶜilm al-ma'thūr min al-adᶜiyya wa 'l-adhkār*, Dār al-Maᶜrifa, Beirut.

that are *ma'thūr* and which is characterised by its brevity. All these distinguishing features make of it a convenient manual for a practising Muslim; one in which he can have confidence, which will be easy for him to understand, and which will stimulate him to commit it to heart for the purpose of reciting from it. Additionally—and for the same reasons—it is suitable for having its meanings translated into other languages.

In order to realise this twin purpose—of being accessible to readers of Arabic and being within easy reach of readers of English—we have followed a well-established practice in making a shortened version of the original book compiled by Sheikh al-Islām ibn Taymiyyah, which we have called *The Goodly Word: A Concise Version*, observing in our shortening of it the following considerations:

1. Restricting ourselves to authentic Hadith, of which there is a rich choice, in preference to Hadith of a lower category. Having confined ourselves solely to *ma'thūr* Hadith, it is natural for us to choose those that are most reliable. We found our task of verifying the Hadith made smooth by the fact that this had already been dealt with in masterly fashion by our venerable traditionist Sheikh Muḥammad Nāṣir ad-Dīn al-Albānī with surpassing expertise in that he had already edited the book, giving the sources of the Hadith and distinguishing those that were authentic from those that were not, with clarity and thoroughness, in his edition of *The Goodly Word* in A.H. 1385 and in compiling his book *Ṣaḥīḥ al-kalim aṭ-ṭayyib*, which appeared in A.H. 1390. We have therefore followed what Sheikh al-Albānī has undertaken. To him and to the publisher of the two books, our respected friend and

scholar Sheikh Muḥammad Zuhayr ash-Shāwīsh, we extend our heartfelt gratitude.

2. For the sake of brevity we have avoided such repetitions as may be found and have omitted Hadith with long preludes if suitable alternatives are to hand, the object being to achieve texts of *duᶜā'* and *dhikr* in abbreviated form,[1] likewise omitting those Hadith for an understanding of which lengthy background information would be required.

Even with such abridgement, the book still remains of a fair size, in that the Hadith included in this shortened version number 180—which is nevertheless a sufficient number for those whom Allah has rightly guided. We have provided in the margin shortened explanations that are not to be found in the original book and have also vocalised Arabic words where necessary.

As for the translation of the meanings into English, we have observed the same considerations as in our translation of the two books *An-Nawawī's Forty Hadith* and *Forty Hadith Qudsī*, these being:

1. That two persons—one of whom is an Arab and the other an English Muslim—should collaborate in the translation, thus ensuring an accurate understanding of the Arabic text and its religious background, together with a readable and accurate rendering in English.

2. That we should exercise extreme care in conveying the meanings and yet should adhere as far as possible to the structure of the original Arabic. If we have been obliged to add a word in order to make clear the meaning,

---

1. This has been done by Imām al-Jazarī in *ᶜUddat al-ḥiṣn al-ḥaṣīn*. In doing so he merely supplied the *duᶜā'* and *dhikr* themselves without giving any chains of authorities.

we have placed it between square brackets and have shown in a marginal note why this was necessary.

3. We have retained the Lord's name in its Arabic form without translating it, also such technical terms as *zakāt*, Hadith, *duᶜā'*, and *dhikr* (all of which we have treated as collective nouns), and have kept the principal phrases of invocation such as *al-ḥamd*, *dhikr*, *tasbīḥ*, and *tahlīl* in Arabic, though in transliteration for ease of reading and so as to make it possible for the non-Arab to read and pronounce them.

4. For translations of the meanings of the Holy Qur'ān we have used *The Meaning of the Glorious Koran* by the English Muslim Muḥammad Marmaduke Pickthall.

5. That the printing of the translation should be placed opposite the Arabic text for ease of reference.

Duᶜā' and *Dhikr* that are not *ma'thūr*

Our examination of books of *duᶜā'* and *dhikr*, old, mediaeval, and contemporary, reveals that the trend of reliable scholars in authentication is unanimously towards the *ma'thūr*, for the *ma'thūr* as we have previously mentioned begins with what is mentioned in the Holy Qur'ān, which is the word of the Almighty, "Who is more true in statement than Allah?" [1] "And who can be more truthful than Allah in utterance?"[2] or with the Hadith of the Messenger of Allah (may the blessings and peace of Allah be upon him), for Allah the Almighty says, "And whatsoever the Messenger giveth you, take it. And

1. Qur'ān 4.87.

2. Qur'ān 4.122.

whatsoever he forbiddeth, abstain (from it)."[1] And he (may the blessings and peace of Allah be upon him) said "If I have ordered you about something in your religion, then act upon it."[2]

The Messenger of Allah (may the blessings and peace of Allah be upon him) was endowed with the gift of words so that his *du^cā'* and *dhikr*, in addition to being things that Allah had taught him, are distinguished by comprehensiveness, eloquence, and succintness. Thus to employ some *du^cā'* or *dhikr* that is *ma'thūr* is to implement the guidance of the Almighty and that of the Noble Messenger by being obedient to both Allah and His Messenger, and by employing the best known *du^cā'* and *dhikr* that are available.

There are none the less things that agitate man's heart and occupy his mind—matters of the soul, of religion, and of the world—that his tongue expresses in words that may or may not be *ma'thūr*. It is also possible that he is surrounded by a group of people who may repeat what he says if they find themselves in similar circumstances. Are such words, if not *ma'thūr*, allowable?

Scholars have provided answers to this, in particular when commenting on two authentic Prophetic Hadith concerning the *du^cā'* to be used after uttering the *tashahhud*[3] in one's prayers. One of them is the Hadith to be found in both al-Bukhārī and Muslim and which is on the authority of ^cAbdullah ibn Mas^cūd (may Allah be pleased with him) and contains the wording of the

1. Qur'ān 59.7.

2. It was related by Muslim.

3. The final part of the set prayer.

tashahhud. At the end of it the Prophet (may the blessings and peace of Allah be upon him) says, "Then let him choose from the *duᶜā'* that which appeals to him most." Imām an-Nawawī says in the explanation of this Hadith, "He may use such *duᶜā'* as he pleases from the matters of the afterlife and of the world so long as it is not wrongful, and this is our doctrine and and that of the majority of scholars." However, Abū Ḥanīfah (may Allah have mercy on him) said, "Only those supplications are allowed that appear in the Qur'ān and the sunnah."[1]

The second Hadith, which was given by Abū Dāwūd on the authority of Muᶜādh (may Allah be pleased with him), is that the Prophet (may the blessings and peace of Allah be upon him) said to a man, "What do you say in your prayers?" He said, "I say the *tashahhud* and I say 'O Allah, I ask You for Paradise and I seek protection of You from Hell-fire.' This is because I do not have the ability or knowledge to murmur the *duᶜā'* as you and Muᶜādh do." The Prophet (may the blessings and peace of Allah be upon him) said, "We murmur about them."[2] Aṣ-Ṣanᶜānī said in commenting on the Hadith, "From this it is inferred that one is permitted to utter any wording one wishes, either *ma'thūr* or otherwise."[3]

If this is permissible in the prayer itself, then it is even more permissible outside it. Such permissibility, however,

---

1. *The Ṣaḥīḥ of Muslim with the commentary of an-Nawawī*, ash-Shaᶜb edition, Cairo, volume 2, p. 41. An-Nawawī's school of jurisprudence is that of ash-Shāfiᶜī.

2. I.e., about Paradise and Hell-fire.

3. Muḥammad ibn Ismāᶜīl al-Kaḥlānī aṣ-Ṣanᶜānī, *Subul as-salām sharḥ bulūgh al-marām min adillat al-aḥkām*, Dār Iḥyā' at-Turāth al-ᶜArabī, fourth edition, A.H. 1379/1960, volume 1, pp. 191–195.

must be accorded its due weight and one should not extend it in practice by deviating from the *ma'thūr* to that which is not *ma'thūr*, which, though permissible, is not preferred. Also, if the door is left wide open, commonplace talk could infiltrate into religious observances and become part of such observances, competing with what has been imparted by the Almighty and His Prophet. Sheikh al-Islām Ibn Taymiyyah has drawn attention to this when he says, "And what is legitimate for one is to employ that which is *ma'thūr* in his *duᶜā'*. Since *duᶜā'* is among the best of devotional practices one should employ in it what has been ordained by the Almighty, just as this is incumbent upon one in other devotional practices. For him who deviates from the *duᶜā'* that is ordained to some other, it is best for him that he should not let the most complete and worthiest pass him by, these being the Prophetic *duᶜā'*, for it is they that are the most perfect by common consent of Muslims."[1]

Duᶜā' and _dhikr_ in Arabic and in other languages

Inasmuch as the majority of Imāms and scholars accord preference to *duᶜā'* and *dhikr* that are *ma'thūr* over others, though allowing those that are not *ma'thūr* to be used in certain parts of the prayer, and likewise outside it, with the reservations that have been instanced, it follows that preference be given to the Arabic wording of *duᶜā'* and *dhikr* over translations of their meanings into languages other than Arabic, for the *ma'thūr* have been taken from the Holy Qur'ān and the Noble Hadith, both of which are in a clear Arabic tongue.

---

1. *Majmūᶜ fatāwā Sheikh al-Islām Ibn Taymiyyah*, first edition, Riyadh A.H. 1382, volume 22, p. 525.

However, this inevitably raises an obvious problem owing to the fact that Islam is a religion directed at the whole of mankind, there being no difference between Arab and non-Arab. The Almighty has said, "And We have not sent thee (O Muḥammad) save as a bringer of good tidings and a warner unto all mankind."[1] The multiplicity of tongues among the peoples of the world are among Allah's signs that do not change. The Almighty has said, "And of His signs is the creation of the heavens and the earth, and the difference of your languages and colours."[2] Whatever the effort made by non-Arabs to learn Arabic when it is not their native tongue, there will always remain multitudes of Muslims who have not been able to learn the language to a standard which enables them to deal with Arabic religious texts with adequate ease and understanding.

Imāms and scholars have since the dawn of Islam given this problem particular attention and have made copious studies that are available in the books of all schools of jurisprudence so that whoever so wishes can clarify these questions in detail by referring to them in those places in the books of jurisprudence where they are treated. Owing to the abbreviated form of this book we have regarded it as sufficient to allude to only three matters arising out of these studies in jurisprudence, matters upon which there is unanimity of opinion or which the majority of scholars agree upon.

The first matter is that, in performing one's prayers, the opening *takbīr* and successive *takbīrs*, the reading of the

1. Qur'ān 34.28.

2. Qur'ān 30.22.

Fātiḥah and such Qur'ānic verses as are recited, the *tasbīḥ* (*subḥān Allah* i.e., how remote is Allah from every imperfection), the reciting of the *tashahhud*, also the *taslīm* with which the prayer is terminated, all these must be wholly in Arabic—and all Muslims must make every possible effort to learn them. The question has throughout Islam's history been made easy in Islamic countries with such languages as Farsi, Turkish, Urdu, Swahili, Malay, and the like. In fact, words from these basic texts have entered the dictionaries of these languages and become part of them. Even in the case of other languages, it is apparent from the observations of teachers of Islam that those who speak these languages do not find it impossible or unusually difficult to learn this limited number of phrases.

For those unable to learn this amount, a legitimate shortened version has been laid down, which is to say: *subḥān Allāh*, *al-ḥamdu lillāh*, *lā ilāha illā Allāh*, *Allāhu akbar*, and *lā ḥawla wa lā quwwata illā billāh;*[1] or to recite the still more shortened version which is: *al-ḥamdu lillāh*, *Allāhu akbar*, and *lā ilāha illā Allāh*; until such time as he succeeds in learning the longer phrases in their totality.[2]

It is not permissible in one's prayers to substitute any of these phrases with the translations made of their meanings, and history records no individual or group of Muslims who have performed their prayers with non-Arabic recitations. In the course of fourteen centuries, Muslims throughout the world, despite the multiplicity of

---

1. *The Sunan of Abū Dāwūd*, volume 5, pp. 75–76 (the chapter on what is permissible for the illiterate or non-Arab person to recite).

2. *Jāmi*ᶜ *at-Tirmidhī*, volume I, p. 186 (the chapter on what has been recorded in the description of prayer).

languages and the disparity in opportunities for education, have prayed and are praying with Arabic recitations, and they have striven and are striving to teach them and to make clear their meanings to their fellow Muslims.[1] This is a clear indication of the spiritual unity of the Islamic world as manifested in the same movements, recitations, and language employed in prayers.

The second matter is that, outside prayers, the Muslim should strive to recite the *duᶜā'* and *dhikr*, both *ma'thūr* and others, in their Arabic wording, in particular those which are from the Qur'ān or Prophetic Hadith. If unable to do so, he should at least endeavour to pronounce *subḥān Allāh*, *al-ḥamdu lillāh*, *lā ilāha illā Allāh*, *Allāhu akbar*, and *lā ḥawla wa lā quwwata illā billāh* in their Arabic wording for the great blessing that this brings. If, though, he wishes to call upon his Lord with more than that and he has recourse to translations of meanings into the native language he knows and in which he is able to express himself well, then this comes under the totality of the Almighty's words "Allah tasketh not a soul beyond its scope."[2]

The Muslim who is obliged to do this should nevertheless remember that the reciting of translations is commensurate to reciting commentaries, it being no more than an attempt to arrive at the transmitted meaning though in an idiom that was not transmitted. He must also remember that the translation of the meanings of the Holy

---

1. Professor ᶜAbd al-Laṭīf aṭ-Ṭībāwī, "Aḥkām tarjamat al-Qur'ān al-karīm wa tarīkhuhā," *Majallat majmaᶜ al-lughat al-ᶜarabiyyah* (Damascus), Dār al-Fikr Press A.H. 1399/1979, volume 54, part 3, p. 4.

2. Qur'ān 2.285.

Qur'ān is not the Qur'ān itself, and that the translation of the meanings of the Noble Hadith is not Hadith. But the great majority of scholars have allowed the translation of the meanings of the Holy Qur'ān so as to make it possible for the person without a knowledge of Arabic to experience divine guidance, and that which is permissible with respect to the Holy Qur'ān is of necessity allowable in respect of Noble Hadith, traditions, and lesser recitations.[1]

The consolation for the person who is incapable of supplicating Allah and invoking Him, worshipping him and calling upon him in a good fashion in the Arabic tongue is that Allah the Almighty is All-hearing of that with which He is called upon and All-knowing of what stirs in men's hearts. The Almighty has said, "And Allah is Hearer, Knower."[2] He is in fact All-hearing and All-knowing even of that which we human beings do not comprehend—the glorification of Him by all His creation. The Almighty has said, "The seven heavens and the earth

---

1. Permitting the translation of the meanings of the Holy Qur'ān has existed from of old, especially in mediaeval writings, such as those of Sheikh al-Islām Ibn Taymiyyah in the seventh century A.H. in *Dar' tanāquḍ al-ᶜaql wa 'n-naql*, to be found in *Fatāwā Ibn Taymiyyah*, first edition, A.H. 1381, volume 3, p. 306, also volume 4, pp. 116–117; and Imām ash-Shāṭibī in the eighth century A.H. in his book *al-Muwāfaqāt*, edited by Muḥammad Muḥyī 'd-Dīn ᶜAbd al-Ḥamīd, volume 2, p. 48. And likewise in contemporary writings by the grand sheikhs of al-Azhar University, Muḥammad al-Khiḍr Ḥusayn, Maḥmūd Shaltūt, and Muḥammad Muṣṭafā al-Marāghī, and by Sheikh Muḥammad Rashīd Riḍā. Refer to Professor ᶜAbd al-Laṭīf aṭ-Ṭībāwī's treatise "Aḥkām tarjamat al-Qur'ān al-karīm wa tarīkhuhā" previously mentioned.

2. Qur'ān 2.256 and 3.34.

and all that is therein praise Him, and there is not a thing but hymneth His praise; but ye understand not their praise."[1] And He said, "Hast though not seen that Allah, He it is Whom all who are in the heavens and the earth praise, and the birds in their flight? Of each He knoweth verily the worship and the praise; and Allah is Aware of what they do."[2]

There is, in all Islamic countries, a superabundance of *du^{c}ā'* and *dhikr* to be used outside prayers in the form of translations of the meanings of *du^{c}ā'* both *ma'thūr* and non-*ma'thūr* for those who have been unable to learn Arabic to assist them in their devotions and meditations, and we have not heard of anyone objecting to this. It is commendable that ulema in these countries begin by giving the *du^{c}ā'* in Arabic in confirmation of the importance of their being in that language and in order that this will assist in fixing some of them in people's minds, then follow up with translations of the meanings.

The third matter is: be the *du^{c}ā'* or *dhikr* recited in the Arabic wording or in the translation of its meaning, what is important is to utter *du^{c}ā'* and *dhikr* in a truly devotional manner: with an understanding of the meaning, with presence of heart, and with complete submissiveness in applying oneself to Allah the Almighty and ardently requesting something of Him and being sure of His favourable answer.

What is demanded of the Muslim is to beware of uttering non-Arabic ambiguous phrases that are incompatible with the glorification of the Lord without his

---

1. Qur'ān 17.44.

2. Qur'ān 24.41.

realising it and without it being possible for someone else who does not possess a knowledge of the language to correct him. For this reason such phrases were regarded as unacceptable. Al-Bayhaqī has related that ᶜUmar ibn al-Khaṭṭāb (may Allah be pleased with him) heard a man talking Farsi while circumambulating the Kaᶜbah and he took him by the shoulders and said, "Strive to find a way of learning Arabic."[1] The same thing can be said about uttering *duᶜā'* and *dhikr* in the Arabic language without a proper understanding of their meaning; also, a person should not utter them when he is not fully conscious of their significance owing to the fact that he is, for example, overcome by sleepiness.[2]

The significance of all this is that, when uttering *duᶜā'* and *dhikr*, one should be in possession of the correct meaning, the correct expression, and the correct understanding of what one is saying. Thus the Muslim should make an effort to fulfil these conditions in his *duᶜā'* and *dhikr*, and to acquire as good an acquaintance as possible with the Arabic tongue, and let him who is incapable of doing so and who calls upon his Lord as best he can in any language or tongue, correctly and with understanding, be sure that he is calling upon a Lord who is All-hearing and All-knowing.

In conclusion, we pray to Allah that this book may be a help in making *duᶜā'* and *dhikr* more accessible to Muslims who wish to refer to them. We hope that he who

---

1. Aḥmad ibn Idrīs al-Qarāfī: *al-Furūq*, volume 4, p. 291.
2. This is recorded in a Hadith to be found in both al-Bukhārī and Muslim: "If one of you when praying is sleepy, he does not know that he is perhaps seeking to ask forgiveness yet is actually cursing himself."

knows Arabic, as also he who is striving to learn it, may find in it an easy manual for choosing such *du^cā'* and *dhikr* as are suitable for the devotions of the day and night, and for the situations and religious observances that he encounters, in a clear Arabic tongue, duly edited and explained; likewise that the reader of English will be able to use it as a simplified aide to the meanings of such *du^cā'* and *dhikr* in a diction with which he is familiar.

Praise be to Allah through Whom good deeds are accomplished.

Ezzeddin Ibrahim Mustafa
Denys Johnson-Davies (Abdul Wadoud)

Abu Dhabi on 15 Jumādā al-Ākhirah A.H. 1419
6 October 1998

بِسْمِ ٱللَّهِ ٱلرَّحْمَٰنِ ٱلرَّحِيمِ

مُقَدِّمَة

الحمد لله، والصلاة والسلام على سيدنا رسول الله، وعلى آله وصحبه، ومن دعا بدعوته إلى يوم الدين، وبعد.

فقد وجدنا أن المكتبة الإسلامية، ما زالت في حاجة إلى كتاب، يجمع طائفة من الأدعية والأذكار المأثورة الصحيحة، مع ترجمة معانيها إلى اللغة الإنجليزية، فتكون هذه الأدعية والأذكار مفهومة لقراء اللغة العربية، من عرب وغيرهم، مع إمدادهم بالضروري من الشروح المساعدة، كما تكون في الوقت ذاته ميسرة وواضحة المعنى لقراء اللغة الإنجليزية.

ووقع اختيارنا لذلك على كتاب (الكَلِم الطيّب) لشيخ الإسلام تقي الدّين أحمد ابن تيمية المتوفى سنة ٧٢٨ هـ لإيجازه، واقتصاره على المأثور من الكلم الطيب، وللقبول الذي يحظى به لدى الناس. وقد لقي هذا الكتاب من العلماء حفاوة وعناية من قبل. ومع ذلك فقد أدخلنا عليه بعض الاختصار غير المخل، ليكون ملائماً للغرض من نشره مع الترجمة، مما سنبينه فيما بعد.

ولعله من المفيد، أن نقدم للكتاب بمقـدمة مختصرة تبين: معنى الدعـاء والذكر ومنزلتـهما بين العـبادات الإسلامـية، والمصادر المعتمدة لمعرفـة الأدعية والأذكار المأثورة، وأشهر الكتب الـتي أُلِّفت في هذا المـوضـوع، وصنـيـعنـا في هذا الكتاب (مـختـصر الكلم الطيب)، كـما تبين حكمـة الالتزام بالمأثور من الأدعية والأذكار، وحكم الدعـاء والذكر بغيرها، والاحترازات الشـرعية في الاستفادة من ترجـمات المعاني إلى اللغات الأخرى.

أولاً - منزلة الدعاء والذكر بين العبادات الإسلامية :

الدعـاء هـو مناداة الله تعـالى، بـطلب عَـوْنه، ولُـطفـه، ورحمـته، في شـؤون الدين والدنيا جـميعـاً. وقد وصـفه النبي صلى الله عليـه وسلم بقوله «الدعـاء هو العـبادة»[١]، بمعنى أنه جوهرها ولُبُّها، وهو استجابة لنداء الله تعالى في القـرآن الكريم ﴿وَقَـالَ رَبُّكـمْ ادْعُـوني أسْـتَـجِبْ لَكُمْ﴾[٢]، وقولـه :﴿وإذا سَألَكَ عِـبادي عَني فـإني قريب، أجِـيبُ دَعْوَةَ الدَّاعِ إذا دَعَانِ﴾[٣]، وتأكـيد للتوحيد وإخلاص العـبودية لله سبحـانه بوصفـه المقصود وحـده بالدعـاء، كـما في قوله تعـالى﴿اللهُ الصَّمَـدُ﴾[٤]، وقـوله ﴿ضَلَّ مَـنْ تَدْعُـونَ إلاّ

(١) رواه الترمذي وقال حديث حسن صحيح، وأبو داود، وابن ماجه.
(٢) سورة غافر، ٤٠: ٦٠.
(٣) سورة البقرة، ٢: ١٨٦.
(٤) سورة الإخلاص، ١١٢: ٢.

إيّاه﴾[١].

والذِّكْـرُ، هو أن يكـون المرء مع ربه : بعـقلـه، وفكره، ووجدانه، وأن يذكـره دَوْماً بلسانه، مـردداً ما يليق به من عبارات التسبيح، والتهليل، والحمـد، والاستغفار، والتمجيد لذاته العَليّة وأسمائه الحسنى، عـملاً بقوله تعالى : ﴿يا أيُّها الَّذِينَ آمَنُوا اذْكُـرُوا اللهَ ذِكْراً كـثـيراً، وسَـبِّـحـوهُ بُكْرة وأصيـلا﴾[٢]، وقولِه في وصف المؤمـنين: ﴿والذَّاكِرِينَ اللهَ كَثيراً والذَّاكراتِ، أعَدَّ اللهُ لَهُمْ مَغْفِرَةً وأجْراً عَظِيماً﴾[٣]. وقد أعلى الله تعالى قـدر الذكر فجعله أكبـر من كل شيء بقوله ﴿وَلَذِكْرُ اللهِ أكْـبَرَ﴾[٤]، وجعله رسـول الله صلى الله وسلم دليلاً على حياة القلب بـقوله «مَثَلُ الّذي يَذْكُرُ رَبَّهُ والذي لا يَذْكُره، مَثَلُ الحيِّ والميِّت»[٥].

والدعاء والذكر متداخلان أو مترافقان غالباً، بحيث تكون عبارة كل منهـما شاملة للآخر، أو تالية له في السـياق، كما في قولـه تعالى ﴿الَّذينَ يَذْكـرونَ اللهَ قِيـاماً وقُعُـوداً وعَلَى جُنُوبِهِمْ، ويَتَـفَكَّرونَ في خَلْـقِ السَّمـواتِ والأرضِ، رَبَّنا مـا

---

(١) سورة الإسراء، ١٧: ٦٧.

(٢) سورة الأحزاب، ٣٣: ٤١ – ٤٢.

(٣) سورة الأحزاب، ٣٣: ٣٥.

(٤) سورة العنكبوت، ٢٩: ٤٥.

(٥) رواه البخاري.

خَلَقْتَ هَذا باطِلاً، سُبْحانَكَ، فَقِنا، عَذَاب النَّارِ﴾[1]. وهما مبثوثان في بقية العبادات الإسلامية، كما في الصلاة والصيام والحج، وكلها مليئة بالأدعية والأذكار بحيث يستحيل أن تكون تامة بدونها. وكذلك في كل ممارسة دينية أخرى كما في قيام الليل، والاعتكاف، وعند إخراج الزكاة، وغيرها. بل إن المسلم في حياته العادية يذكر الله في جميع ظروفه، ويدعوه حينما يصبح ويُمسي، وفي جميع ما يعرض له من أحوال، ولذلك جاءت كتب الأدعية والأذكار مبوبة حسب الممارسات اليومية: من يقظة ونوم وسعي إلى العمل، وملاقاة الناس ومشاركتهم مجالسهم ومأكلهم ومشربهم، والسفر، وعيادة المريض، وتقلب الجو، ومواجهة الأعداء، وحصول المرض، ووقوع المصائب، وإحراز النجاح، وتحقق المسرات في زواج أو ميلاد ذرية، أو نوال رزق واسع، وغير ذلك مما يستوعب أمور الحياة اليومية كلها. ولذلك سميت بعض كتب الأدعية والأذكار **«عمل اليوم والليلة»** ويقصد بذلك ما يلهج به لسان المسلم من دعاء وذكر في يومه وليلته مما يجعله قريباً من ربه، ذاكراً له، ومستعيناً به في جميع الأحوال.

---

(١) سورة آل عمران، ٣ : ١٩١، فعبارة (سُبْحانَكَ) هي ذكر، والعبارة التي تليها (فَقِنَا عَذَابُ النَّار) هي دعاء.

ومن ثمرات الدعاء والذكر في جميع الظروف على مدار اليوم والليلة، أن تتحول العادات إلى عبادات. فكل عمل عادي يمارسه المسلم، ويحوطه بالذكر والدعاء تتطور به نية فاعله، وسلوكه في أدائه، بحيث يتحول إلى عبادة يتأهل بها إلى رضاء الله. فالسفر مثلاً هو من أمور العادات، فإذا بدأ المرء سفره، وقرأ الدعاء المأثور «اللَّهُمَّ إنّا نسألكَ في سَفَرِنا هذا البِرّ والتقوى ومن العمل ما تَرْضى.. إلخ»[1] أصبح السفر محكوماً بمجموعة من الآداب والقيم الدينية والخلقية التي تجعله سفراً خيّراً يتفاءل المسافر بنفعه، والتغلب على مشقاته، مع تذكر من خلَّفهم وراءه من الأهل والولد، والتطلع إلى عودته سالماً غانماً شاكراً لله على توفيقه. وبهذا تصبح العادة عبادة.

ثانياً – مصادر الأدعية والأذكار:

أول مصدر للأدعية والأذكار المأثورة، هو القرآن الكريم، فهو حافل بها، وتأتي فيه على أربعة أنماط:

أولها: أن تُصدَّر آيات الأدعية أو الذكر بأمر القَوْل، كما في المعوِّذتين[2]: ﴿قُلْ أعُوذُ بِربِّ الفَلَقِ مِنْ شَرِّ ما خَلَقَ﴾

---

(١) الحديث رقم ١٣٢ في هذا الكتاب

(٢) سورة رقم ١١٣ و١١٤.

و﴿قُلْ أعُوذُ بِرَبِّ النَّاسِ﴾، وقوله ﴿وقُلْ رَبِّ زِدْني عِلْماً﴾[1]، وقوله ﴿وقُلْ ربِّ اغْفِرْ وارْحَمْ وأنْتَ خَيْرُ الرَّاحِمِينَ﴾[2]، وأشباهها.

وثانيها : أن ترد هذه الآيات حكاية على ألسنة الملائكة أو الأنبياء. فمما حُكي على ألسنة الملائكة ﴿ربَّنا وَسِعْتَ كُلَّ شَيْءٍ رَحْمَةً وَعِلْماً، فاغْفِرْ لِلَّذين تابوا واتَّبَعوا سَبِيلَك، وقِهِمْ عَذاب الجَحِيمِ﴾[3] ومما حُكِي على ألسنة الأنبياء ذكْر ذي النون ﴿فَنَادى في الظُّلُماتِ أن لا إله إلاّ أنْتَ، سُبْحانَكَ إنّي كُنْتُ مِنَ الظَّالِمِينَ﴾[4]، ودعاء أيوب بطلب الشفاء ﴿وأيُّوبَ إذْ نادى، رَبَّهُ أنّي مَسَّنِيَ الضُّرُّ وأنْتَ أرْحَمُ الراحمين﴾[5].

وثالثها : أن ترد آيات الدعاء والذكر حكاية على لسان النبي محمد صلى الله عليه وسلم والمؤمنين معه، كما في خواتيم سورة البقرة ﴿وَقَالُوا سَمِعْنا وَأطَعْنا غُفْرَانَكَ رَبَّنَا

---

(١) سورة طه، ٢٠:١١٤ .

(٢) سورة المؤمنون، ٢٣: ١١٨.

(٣) سورة غافر، ٤٠: ٧.

(٤) سورة الأنبياء، ٢١: ٨٧.

(٥) سورة الأنبياء، ٢١: ٨٣. وانظر دعاء زكريا عليه السلام في السورة ذاتها ٢١: ٨٩ بطلب الذرية. ولغيره من الأنبياء أدعية في سور أخرى يمكن استخراجها.

وَإِلَيْكَ الْمَصيرُ﴾ ﴿رَبَّنا لا تُؤاخِذْنا إنْ نَسِينا أوْ أخْطَأْنا﴾[1].

ورابعها : وهو كثـير، أن ترد الآيات مـرسلة وهي أذكار أو أدعيـة، وسورة الفـاتحة كلهـا من هذا النمط، فنصفـها الأول أذكار حمد وتمجيد وتعظيـم لله، ونصفها الثاني دعاء بالهداية[2]. والقـرآن الكريم حافل بهـذه الأدعيـة والأذكار المرسلة والتي تعرف بمضمونها.

وتتمـيز الأدعيـة والأذكار في القرآن الكـريم بكونها من الكتاب المحفوظ، الذي لا يأتيه الباطل من بين يديه ولا من خلفه، وقراءتُها مَجْلبـة لثوابيْن: ثواب التلاوة للقرآن الكريم، وثواب الدعاء والذكر[3].

والمصدر الـثاني : الذي عليـه الاعتـماد في اسـتخـراج النصـوص المأثورة من الأدعيـة والأذكار هو كتـب الحديث الشريف، ففيها جميعاً أجزاء مخصصة لذلك، بالإضافة إلى ورود مأثورات أخـرى موزعة في أبواب شـتى منها وفـقاً لمناسباتها والموضوعات المرتبطة بهـا. ففي صحيح البخاري

(١) سورة البقرة، ٢: ٢٨٦.

(٢) ورد في بيـان هذه السورة الحـديث القدسي الذي أخـرجه البـخاري. يقول الله عز وجل ﴿قسمتُ الصلاة بَيْني وبَيْنَ عَـبْدي نِصْفَيْن، فَنِصْفُها لي [لأنه ذكر وتمجيد]، ونِصْفُها لِعَبْدي [لأنه دعاء]، ولِعَبْدي ما سَأَلَ﴾.

(٣) راجع في الأدعية القرآنية دراسة المرحوم الدكـتور عبد الحليم محمود : «فـاذكـروني أذكـركم» ص ٦٧ – ٩٧. دار المعـارف، القـاهرة ١٩٨١.

كتاب جامع للأدعية والأذكار بعنوان (كتاب الدعوات)، ومع ذلك فإن فيه أيضاً أدعية وأذكاراً في (كتاب الصلاة) وأخرى في (كتاب الصيام) و(كتاب الحج) وهكذا. ويقع (كتاب الدعوات)(١)، في تسعة وستين باباً تشتمل على مائة وستة أحاديث. وفي صحيح مسلم نجد (كتاب الذكر والدعاء والتوبة والاستغفار)(٢)، ويتضمن سبعة وعشرين باباً تضم مائة حديث وواحداً، عدا المتفرقات في بقية الكتب. وفي سنن الترمذي نجد (كتاب الدعوات)(٣) من مائة واثنين وثلاثين باباً تضم مائتين وأربعة وثلاثين حديثاً. وفي سنن ابن ماجه يوجد (كتاب الدعاء)(٤) من اثنين وعشرين باباً تضم خمسة وستين حديثاً. وترد الأدعية والأذكار في سنن أبي داود ضمن (كتاب الأدب)(٥) الذي يشتمل على اثني عشر باباً، وسبعة وستين حديثاً. وفي مُسند الإمام أحمد ترد الأدعية

---

(١) صحيح البخاري: طبعة استنبول ١٩٩٢م، المصورة عن طبعة القاهرة ج٧، ص ١٤٥-١٦٩.

(٢) صحيح مسلم : طبعة محمد فؤاد عبدالباقي، القاهرة سنة ١٩٥٦م، ج٣ ص ٢٠٦١ - ٢١٠١.

(٣) سنن الترمذي : طبعة ابراهيم عطوة عوض. القاهرة سنة ١٩٦٥ م. ج٥ ص ٤٥٥ - ٥٨٢.

(٤) سنن ابن ماجه : طبعة محمد فؤاد عبد الباقي. القاهرة سنة ١٩٥٤ م. ج٢ ص ١٢٥٨ - ١٢٨١.

(٥) سنن أبي داود : طبعة عزت عبيد الدعاس. حمص سوريا سنة ١٩٦٩ م. ج٥ ص ٢٩٨ - ٣٣٧.

والأذكار مبثوثة في المسانيد حسب تبويب الكتاب. أما في طبعة المرحوم الشيخ أحمد عبد الرحمن البنا، المسماة (الفتح الرباني: ترتيب مسند الإمام أحمد بن حنبل الشيباني)[1]، فقد أُفرد لها كتاب (الأذكار والدعوات)، الذي يشتمل على اثنين وأربعين باباً تضم مائتين وخمسة وتسعين حديثاً.

والمصدر الثالث للأدعية والأذكار، هو الكتب التي أُفردت لهذا الموضوع، ويكون لمؤلفيها إسناد إلى رسول الله صلى الله عليه وسلم، فتكون بذلك صنو كتب الحديث من حيث كونها أصولاً لما ورد فيها بغير نقل عن غيرها. وعدد هذه الكتب محدود، ولم يصلنا منها مطبوعاً إلا كتابان، وهما (عمل اليوم والليلة) للإمام أحمد بن شعيب النسائي المتوفى سنة ٣٠٣هـ، صاحب السنن. وكتاب (عمل اليوم والليلة) لأبي بكر ابن السني المتوفى سنة ٣٦٤هـ راوي سنن النسائي.

فأما كتاب النَّسائي، فإما أن يكون مؤلفه قد ألفه ليلحقه بكتابه الكبير (سنن النَّسائي)، ولم يفعل ذلك، وهذا يُفسِّر تفرد (سنن النسائي) بين كتب الحديث الستة المعتمدة بالخلو من كتاب خاص بالأدعية والأذكار، كما فعل مؤلفو

---

(١) الفتح الرباني ترتيب مسند الإمام أحمد: الطبعة الثالثة. جدة سنة ١٤٠٤هـ ج١٤ ص ١٩٦ - ٣١٢. وفي هذه الطبعة أعيد ترتيب الأحاديث الواردة في المسند وفقاً للأبواب الفقهية، مما سَهَّل تمييز أحاديث الأدعية والأذكار.

الكتب الخمسة الآخرون كما بينا. وإما أن يكون قد قصد إفراده وجَعْلَه كتاباً مستقلاً. وهو يشتمل على ألف ومائة وواحد وعشرين حديثاً، بما فيها المكررات والروايات المختلفة. فيكون النسائي بذلك قد زاد في جمع أحاديث الأدعية والأذكار عما جمع كل من الخمسة الآخرين.

وأما كتاب ابن السني فيشبه كتاب النسائي، وقد يورد فيه روايات عن النسائي، ولكنه ينفرد عنه بروايات أخرى أيضاً، كما أن الكتاب يشتمل على أبواب لم ترد عند النسائي. وعدد أحاديث ابن السني سبعمائة وسبعون حديثاً.

وقد ألفت من هذا النوع من الكتب التي تعتبر من المصادر، كتبٌ أخرى، بقي بعضها تاماً أو مجزوءاً بصورة مخطوطة ، ووصلتنا من بعضها الآخر نقول في كتب أخرى(١).

ثالثاً – أهم كتب الأدعية والأذكار:

نظراً لأن مصادر (الأدعية والأذكار) المأثورة معروفة وموثقة، ومواضع الأدعية والأذكار فيها محددة، فقد أُلفت

---

(١) أحمد بن شعيب النسائي : عمل اليوم والليلة. تحقيق الدكتور فاروق حمادة. ط ثانية. بيروت سنة ١٤٠٥هـ/١٩٨٥م. وانظر دراسة الدكتور حمادة عن الكتب الأصول في الأدعية والأذكار في هذا الكتاب ص ١٠٣-١١١.

وانظر محمد بن علاّن الصديقي : الفتوحات الربانية على الأذكار النواوية ط١، ص١٨. دار إحياء التراث العربي، بيروت.

في هذا الفن مجموعة من الكتب التي حرصت على تقريب الموضوع للقراء: بالجمع، وإعادة التبويب والاختيار، والشرح، والاختصار، وإضافة ما قد يراه المؤلفون نافعاً من دراسات حول الأدعية ومدلولاتها وآداب قراءتها، إلى غير ذلك. وما زال الباب مفتوحاً، ولا نظن أنه سيوصد لحرص المسلمين على معرفة ما يلزم في عباداتهم. ولذلك تكفي الإشارة إلى أهم هذه الكتب قديماً وحديثاً، وبيان موقع كتاب (الكلم الطيب) الذي نقدمه منها :

١- أقدم ما يلزم ذكره في هذا الصدد كتابا **الإمام النسائي وابن السني** المذكوران سابقاً، فمع كونهما من المصادر التي عددناها فإن تأليفهما بصورة كتابين مستقلين ثم طباعتهما قد يسّر استخدامهما ضمن كتب هذا الفن. فأما كتاب الإمام النسائي، فقد حقق ونشر مرتين أولاهما من قبل الدكتور فاروق حمادة في بيروت سنة ١٤٠٥عـ/ ١٩٨٥م، والثانية من قبل دار نشر في بيروت أيضاً سنة ١٥٠٨هـ/١٩٨٨م[1]. وقد حرص المؤلف رحمه الله على أن يستوعب في كتابه أدعية

---

(١) أحمد بن شعيب النسائي : عمل اليوم والليلة. تحقيق دار الكتب العلمية. بيروت ١٤٠٨هـ/١٩٨٨م.

الحيــــــاة اليوميـــــــة وأذكـــارها، ولذلك أعطى الكتــاب عنـــــوانه الذي يعبـــــر عن ذلك، وبدأه بباب (ذكــــر ما كـان النــبي صلى الله عليه وسلم يقـوله إذا أصـبح)، ثم تتـبع أحـوال الإنـــسان في يومه حتى يصل إلى ما يقـوله في مسائه وقبل نومه، وهكذا. وفي الكتـاب أيضـاً ذكـر للأدعـيـة والأذكـار المتعلقة ببعض العبادات الإسلامية كالصلاة والصيام.

وأما كـتـــاب ابن السني فـقد نشـــر في الهنـــد ومصـــر، ثم ظهرت له طبـعة بتحـقيق الأسـتاذ عـبد القـــادر أحـــمـــد طه فـي القـــاهرة سـنة ١٣٨٩هـ/١٩٦٩م[1]. والكتـاب يشـبـه في منهـجه ومضـمونه كـتاب النسـائي، ولكنه يحـتفظ بأوصـافه الخاصة به. والعلماء متفاوتون في تفضيل أي الكتابين على الآخر.

٢ - كتاب الأذكار للنووي :

وهو الإمام مُحيي الدين يحـيى بن شرف النووي الدمشقي المتـوفى سنة ٦٧٦هـ. ويـعـتـبـر هذا الكتـاب همـزة

---

(١) أبو بكر ابن السني : عـمل اليـوم والليلة، سلوك النبي صلى الله عليـه وسلم مع ربه. تحقيق عبد القادر أحمد طه. القاهرة ١٣٨٩هـ/١٩٦٩م.

الوصل بين كتب المصادر التي يغلب التعامل معها من قِبَل المتخصصين، والكتب الموجهة إلى عامة المثقفين والقراء بقصد التطبيق في الممارسات التعبدية. ولذلك نجده يلقى عناية خاصة من العلماء الذين قَرَّظُوهُ، وألفوا له شروحاً وأمالي واختصارات، كما يلقى ذيوعاً بين الناس، حتى إنه قيل «بِعِ الدارَ واشْتَرِ الأذكار» باعتبار أن اقتناء الكتاب أَوْلى من اقتناء العقار[1]. ويبدأ المؤلف كتابه بمحاولة الاختصار، بحذف أسانيد الأحاديث، اكتفاء بتخريجها وبيان درجتها من الصحة، ولكنه لا يلبث أن يتوسع فيضم عدداً وفيراً من الأحاديث في كل باب، كما يضم - كما ذكر - «جملاً من النفائس من علم الحديث، ودقائق الفقه، ومهمات القواعد، ورياضيات النفوس، والآداب التي تتأكد معرفتها على السالكين» ولكن بلغة سهلة ميسرة. وبذلك تحقق للمؤلف رحمه الله أن يصبح كتابه «أصلاً معتمداً لا يستغني عنه باحث أو مراجع في موضوعه. وما من مؤلِّف بعده في هذا الفن إلا رجع إليه»[2].

---

(١) محمد علي ابن عَلاّن الصديقي :الفتوحات الربانية على الأذكار النواوية. ج١ ص ١-٤، بيروت.

(٢) محيي الدين يحيى بن شرف النووي : الأذكار المنتخبة من كلام سيد الأبرار. ط ١٤ بيروت. سنة ١٤٠٤هـ/ ١٩٨٤م. ص ٤-٥.

٣ - الكَلِمُ الطَّيِّب لابن تيمية :

وهو شيخ الإسلام أبو العباس أحمد بن عبد الحليم بن تيمية، المولود بحرَّان سنة ٦٦١هـ، والمتوفى في دمشق سنة ٧٢٨هـ، والمعروف بمواقفه ومؤلفاته في إيضاح عقيدة التوحيد، ومحاربة البدع. وقد استمد هذه التسمية الجميلة والفريدة لكتابه من قول الله تعالى ﴿إِلَيْهِ يَصْعَدُ الكَلِمُ الطَّيِّبُ والعَمَلُ الصَّالِحُ يَرْفَعُهُ﴾[١].

وقد طبع الكتاب عدة مرات في القاهرة من قبل المطبعة المنيرية، ثم ظهرت له طبعة محققة عكف على إخراجها بعناية، المحدث الشيخ محمد ناصر الدين الألباني ثم الدمشقي والأخ الشيخ محمد زهير الشاويش الميداني الدمشقي سنة ١٣٨٥هـ[٢].

ويحتوي الكتاب على واحد وستين باباً، ومائتين وثلاثة وخمسين حديثاً. والواضح أن المؤلف رحمه الله، قد قصد بكتابه أن يكون مرجعاً سهلاً لمعرفة الأدعية والأذكار للتعبد بقراءتها في مناسباتها، دون استطراد إلى ما عدا ذلك من الدراسات المتعلقة بها. ولذلك فقد

---

(١) سورة فاطر، ٣٥ : ١.

(٢) تقي الدين أحمد بن تيمية: الكلم الطيب، تحقيق الشيخ محمد ناصر الدين الألباني. ط٢، المكتب الاسلامي، بيروت ١٣٩٢ انظر مقدمة المحقق ص١٣

ركز على حسن التـبويب، وإيراد النصوص دون تدخل كبير منه قد

يخرج الكـتاب عن مقـصوده. والكتـاب بهذه الصـفة، يعتبـر من أحسن الكتب الوسيطة - تاريخاً وحـجماً - في التـوصل المبـاشـر إلى الأدعـيـة والأذكـار المأثورة بقصد التعبد. وقد حَذَتْ حَذْوه معظم الكتب التي ظهرت بعد ذلك، وخاصة المجموعات المعاصرة.

٤ - الوابِلُ الصَّيِّب[١] من الكَلِم الطيب لابن القَيِّم :

هو الحافظ أبو عبدالله محمـد بن أبي بكر الشهير بابن قيِّم الجَوْزية، المولود سنة ٦٩١هـ والمتوفى في دمشق سنة ٧٥٢هـ. وقد تابع أستـاذه ابن تيمية في تسميـة كتابه، وفي الاقتصار عند إيراد أحـاديث الأدعية والأذكار على التخـريج وحده دون ذكـر الأسانيـد. ويشتمـل الكتاب على خمسة وسبـعين باباً، بادئاً بأذكار الصباح والمساء، ومسـتوعبـاً أذكار المناسبـات للحيـاة اليوميـة، وكذلك أذكار معظـم العبادات وأدعيتـها. وقدم للكتـاب بمقدمة طويلة تبلغ مثل حـجم الكتاب نفسـه، عالج فيهـا أموراً من الريـاضـات السـلوكيـة، وشـؤون أهل الذكـر ومجالسهم، وشيئاً من آداب الذكر، والكتاب مطبوع[٢].

---

(١) الوابل الصيِّب : المطر الغزير، والمقصود العظيم النفع والثواب.

(٢) محـمد بن أبي بكر ابن قيم الجوزية : الوابـل الصيِّب من الكَلِم الطيِّب. بإشراف الشيخ ابراهيم العجوز. دار الكتب العلمية، بيروت.

٥ - عدة الحصن الحصين من كلام سيد المرسلين لابن الجزري :

هذا الكتاب هو خاتمة المطاف فيما وصلنا من الكتب القديمة والوسيطة، ومؤلفه هو شيخ القراء محمد بن محمد بن الجَزَري المتوفى سنة ٨٣٣هـ، وهو يضم ستمائة وستة وعشرين حديثاً، ولكنه يراعي الإيجاز في طريقة عَرْضها، والرمز في طريقة تخريجها. وعليه شروح كثيرة ومعظمها مطبوع ومتداول(١).

٦ - كتاب «نُزُل الأبرار بـ العلم المأثور من الأدعية والأذكار»:

وهو من الكتب المعاصرة للعالم الهندي السيد محمد صديق حسن خان المتوفى سنة ١٣٠٧هـ. وقد اطلع المؤلف على المعروف من كتب هذا الفن وخاصة الأذكار للإمام النووي، فجاء كتابه موسوعة للأدعية والأذكار، شاملة عمل اليوم والليلة، وأذكار المناسبات المختلفة في الحياة اليومية، وأذكار العبادات، وهو مطبوع(٢).

---

(١) محمد بن الجزري : عدة الحصن الحصين من كلام سيد المرسلين، بشرح الشيخ حسنين محمد مخلوف، ط١، القاهرة ١٣٨١هـ - ١٩٦١م.
محمد بن علي الشوكاني : تحفة الذاكرين بعدة الحصن الحصين، ط١، دار القلم، بيروت ١٩٨٤م.

(٢) السيد محمد صديق حسن خان: نُزُل الأبرار بالعلم المأثور من الأدعية والأذكار. دار المعرفة. بيروت.

رابعاً – صنيعنا في اختصار (الكَلِم الطيِّب) وترجمة معانيه :

من العرض السابق، يتضح أن كتاب (الكَلِم الطَّيِّب) لابن تيمية، هو أكثرها ملاءمة لتحقيق غرضنا، وهو تقديم كتاب : موثوق التأليف، موثوق المحتوى، مقتصر على نصوص الأدعية والأذكار المأثورة، متصف بالإيجاز – بحيث يصلح أن يكون دليلاً عملياً للمسلم المتعبد؛ يطمئن إليه، ويسهُل عليه فهمه، ويستنهض هِمَّته لحفظه، وترطيب لسانه بترديد نصوصه، كما يصلح – من ناحية أخرى – ولنفس الأسباب، لترجمة معانيه إلى اللغات الأخرى غير العربية.

ولكي نحقق هذا الغرض المزدوج : التقريب إلى قراء العربية، والتيسير على قراء اللغة الانجليزية، أقدمنا على المألوف مع هذه التآليف، وأخرجنا من الأصل الذي وضعه شيخ الإسلام ابن تيمية، النص المختصر الذي نقدمه، والذي أسميناه (مختصر الكلم الطيب)، مراعين في الاختصار ما يأتي :

١ – الاكتفاء بالأحاديث الصحيحة، ففيها مَنْدوحة وغناء، عما دونها من الأحاديث الأقل رتبة. وما دمنا قد تقيدنا بالمأثور وحده، فليكن خيارنا من المأثور بأوثقه. وقد

وجدنا طريقنا إلى تحقيق أحاديث هذا الكتاب معبداً، إذ اضطلع بهذا الأمر قبلنا، عن فحولة وتخصص، أستاذنا الجليل المحدث الشيخ محمد ناصر الدين الألباني، الذي حقق الكتاب على أحسن وجه، وخرّج أحاديثه، مميزاً صحيحها من غيره باستيفاء ووضوح تامين، وبين ذلك في طبعته المتميزة لكتاب (الكلم الطيب) سنة ١٣٨٥هـ، وفي إصداره كتاب (صحيح الكلم الطيب) سنة ١٣٩٠هـ. فتابعنا في ذلك ما قام به الشيخ الألباني، فله ولناشر الكتابين الأخ الجليل المحقق الشيخ محمد زهير الشاويش، شكرنا وامتناننا واعترافنا بالفضل الكبير.

وقد اكتفينا بهذه الإحالة، عن إيراد تخريجات الأحاديث التي يضمها هذا المختصر، فهي كُلها صحيحة، وواردة: إما في صحيحي البخاري ومسلم أو أحدهما، وإما لدى أحمد وأصحاب السُنن وغيرهم بأسانيد محققة الصحة.

٢ - الحرص على الإيجاز، بتحاشي ما قد يوجد من مكررات، وترك الحديث الذي تكون له مقدمة طويلة إذا وُجد غيره بدون ذلك لأن القصد هو الوصول إلى نصوص الأدعية والأذكار باختصار[1]، وكذلك ترك

---

(١) وقد فعل هذا الإمام الجزري في (عدة الحصن الحصين)، بل وبالغ فيه، بالاقتصار على الدعاء أو الذكر وحدهما.

الحديث الذي يحتاج فهمه إلى خلفية علمية يؤدي تقديمها إلى الإطالة.

وبالرغم من هذا الاختصار، فقد بقي في جوهره بحجم جيد، إذ تبلغ الأحاديث التي يتضمّنها هذا المختصر مائة وثمانين حديثاً، وفيها البركة لمن وفقه الله. وقد أدخلنا في هامش الكتاب شروحاً مختصرة ليست موجودة في أصل الكتاب، كما ضبطنا بالشكل ما يحتاج إلى ذلك.

وأما ترجمة المعاني إلى اللغة الانجليزية، فقد راعينا فيها الاعتبارات التي التزمنا بها في ترجمتنا للكتابيْن (الأربعون النووية) و(الأربعون القدسية) وهي :

١ - أن يتشارك في الترجمة اثنان أحدهما عربي، والثاني انجليزي مسلم، فنضمن بذلك سلامة الفهم للنص العربي وما قد تكون له من خلفية دينية، وسلامة التعبير باللغة الانجليزية.

٢ - أن تراعى الأمانة المطلقة في نقل المعاني، مع محاذاة النص العربي، فإذا اضطررنا إلى زيادة كلمة لإيضاح المعنى جعلناها بين معقوفين، وبينا ما قد يلزم لذلك في الهامش.

٣ - الالتزام بإبقاء لفظ الجـلالة على صيغتـه العربية دون ترجـمة، وكـذلك الكلمـات الاصطلاحيـة مثل (الزكـاة، والحديث، والدعـاء، والذكر)، والالتـزام بكتابة عـبارات الذكر الرئيسـية كالحمد، والذكر، والتسـبيح، والتهليل، بالنص العربي مع تـيسير قـراءتها بالحروف الأجنبـية، ليـتمكن غـيـر العربي من حـسن التلفظ بهـا وقراءتهـا بأصلها العربي.

٤ - عند الحـاجة إلى ترجمـة معنى آية من القـرآن الكريم، اعتمدنا على ترجمة الانجليـزي المسلم محمد مارمديوك بكتهول.

٥ - أن تكون الطبـاعـة بمواجـهـة النص العـربي، للنص الانجليزي، لتـسهل المراجعة، ونظراً لأن الكتـاب موجَّه بصـفـة خاصـة الى القـراء الذين يسـتـعملون اللغـة الانجليزية، فقد رتب الكتاب ليقرأ من اليسار الى اليمين وقـد يوفق الله الى إصـدار طبـعة تناسب قـراء اللغـة العربية باعـتبارها الاصل، فيكون ترتيب الكتـاب حينئذ من اليـمين الى اليسـار. وفي جمـيع الأحوال فـإن هذا

الكتاب معني باللغتين، وكذلك قُرّاؤه.

خامساً - الدعاء والذكر بغير المأثور:

إن مراجعتنا لكتب الأدعية والأذكار القديمة والوسيطة والحديثة، تبين أن اتجاه العلماء الأثبات هو بإجماع نحو المأثور. لأن المأثور كما ذكرنا من قبل يبدأ بما ورد في القرآن الكريم، وهو كلام الله تعالى ﴿وَمَنْ أَصْدَقُ مِنَ اللهِ حَدِيثاً﴾[١] ﴿وَمَنْ أَصْدَقُ مِنَ اللهِ قِيلاً﴾[٢]. ثم بحديث رسول الله صلى الله عليه وسلم، والله تعالى يقول ﴿وما آتاكُمُ الرَّسُولُ فَخُذُوه وما نَهاكُمْ عَنْهُ فانْتَهوا﴾[٣]، وقال صلى الله عليه وسلم «إذا أَمَرْتُكُمْ بشيء من دِينِكمْ فَخُذُوا به»[٤].

وقد أوتي رسول الله صلى الله عليه وسلم جوامع الكلم، فأدعيته وأذكاره، فضلاً عن أنها مما علمه الله، تتصف بالبلاغة والإحاطة والإيجاز. فالأخذ بالمأثور إذن يحقق للداعي والذاكر الالتزام بهَدْي الله تعالى وهَدْي رسوله الكريم، والطاعة لله ورسوله، والدعاء والذكر بأفضل ما وَرَد

(١) سورة النساء، ٤: ٨٧.

(٢) سورة النساء، ٤: ١٢٢.

(٣) سورة الحشر، ٥٩: ٧.

(٤) رواه مسلم.

وعُرف.

ومع ذلك، فإن للإنسان مما يجيش في صدره، ويجول في خاطره، من أمور النفس والدين والدنيا، ما قد يجري به لسانه من القول، مما أثر ومما لم يُؤثر. كما أن مجموعة ممن حوله من الناس، قد تردد ما يقول إذا كانت في مثل ظروفه. فهل لهذا القول إذا خرج عن المأثور إجازة؟

لقد أجاب العلماء عن ذلك، وخاصة عند شرح حديثين نبويين صحيحيْن عن الدعاء بعد التشهد في الصلاة. أحدهما الحديث المتفق عليه عن عبدالله بن مسعود (رضي الله عنه) الذي ترد فيه صيغة التشهد. وفي آخرها يقول النبي صلى الله عليه وسلم «ثم لْيتخيَّرْ من الدُّعاء أعجبَه إلَيْه». قال الإمام النووي في شرح هذا الحديث «يجوز الدعاء بما شاء من أمور الآخرة والدنيا، ما لم يكن إثماً، وهذا مذهبنا ومذهب الجمهور. وقال أبو حنيفة رحمه الله تعالى: لا يجوز إلا بالدعوات الواردة في القرآن والسنة»[1].

والحديث الثاني هو ما أخرجه أبو داود عن مُعاذ (رضي الله عنه) أن رسول الله صلى الله عليه وسلم قال لرجل: كيف تقول في الصلاة؟ قال: أتَشَهَّدُ وأقولُ : اللَّهُمَّ إنّي أسألُكَ الجنَّةَ وأعُوذُ بِكَ مِنَ النَّار. أمَا إنِّي لا أحْسِنُ

(١) صحيح مسلم بشرح النووي. ج٢ ص ٤١. طبعة الشعب، القاهرة. ومذهب النووي هو المذهب الشافعي.

دَنْدَنَتَكَ ولا دَنْدَنَة مُعَاذٍ. فقال النبيُّ صلى الله عليه وسلَّم: حَوْلَها نُدَنْدِنُ. قال الصَّنْعانيُّ تعليقاً على الحديث «ففيه أنه يدعو الإنسان
بأي لفظ شاء من مأثور وغيره»(١).

فإذا جاز هذا في الصلاة، فهو خارجها أكثر جوازاً. إلا أن هذه الإجازة ينبغي أن تُقَدَّر بقدرها، وألا يتوسع المرء في تطبيقها، فيعدل عن المأثور إلى غيره، لأن غير المأثور يظل مفضولاً وإن جاز. ثم إن فتح الباب على مصراعيه يسلك كلام الناس مسلك العبادات، ثم يُصبح جزءاً من هذه العبادات مزاحماً ما ورد عن الله ورسوله. وقد نبه شيخ الإسلام ابن تيمية إلى ذلك فقال: «والمشروع للإنسان أن يدعو بالأدعية المأثورة، فإن الدعاء من أفضل العبادات، فينبغي لنا أن نتبع فيه ما شرع الله وسنّ، كما أنه ينبغي ذلك في غيره من العبادات، والذي يعدل عن الدعاء المشروع إلى غيره، فالأحسن له ألا يفوته الأكمل والأفضل، وهي الأدعية النبوية، فإنها أكمل وأفضل باتفاق المسلمين»(٢).

---

(١) محمد بن اسماعيل الكحلاني الصنعاني : سبل السلام شرح بلاغ المرام من أدلة الأحكام، ج١ ص ١٩١، ١٩٥. دار إحياء التراث العربي، ط٤، ١٣٧٩هـ/ ١٩٦٠م.

(٢) مجموع فتاوى شيخ الإسلام ابن تيمية : ج٢٢، ص ٥٢٥ باختصار، الرياض ط١، سنة ١٣٨٢هـ.

سادساً – الدعاء والذكر باللغة العربية وغيرها :

وما دام جمهور الأئمة والعلماء يقدمون المأثور من الدعاء والذكر على غيره، مع إجازة غير المأثور في مواضع معينة من الصلاة، وكذلك في خارجها بالقيود التي بيّنوها، فإنه ينبني على ذلك تقديم النصوص العربية من الأدعية والأذكار على غيرها من ترجمات معانيها إلى اللغات غير العربية، نظراً لأن المأثور مستمد من القرآن الكريم والسنة المشرّفة، وهما بلسان عربي مبين.

لكن هذه النتيجة قد ترتب عليها إشكال لا يخفى، نظراً لأن الإسلام دين موجه إلى البشرية كافة، لا فرق في ذلك بين عربي وغير عربي. قال تعالى ﴿وما أَرْسَلْنَاكَ إلاّ كَافَّةً لِلنَّاسِ بَشِيراً وَنَذيراً﴾ (١). وتعدد الألسنة واللغات بين البشر هو من آيات الله التي لا تتغير. قال تعالى ﴿وَمِنْ آياتِهِ خَلْقُ السَّمواتِ والأرْضِ واختلافُ ألسِنَتِكُمْ وألوانِكُم﴾ (٢).ومهما اجتهد غير العربي في تعلم العربية، وهي ليست لسانه بالأصالة، فإنه سيتبقى دائماً جموع من المسلمين لا يتمكنون من ذلك بالمستوى الذي يُقدرهم على التعامل مع النصوص الدينية العربية بتفهُّم ويُسْر كافيين.

وقد أولى الأئمة والعلماء، منذ فجر الإسلام، هذا

---

(١) سورة سبأ، ٣٤: ٢٨.

(٢) سورة الروم، ٣٠: ٢٢.

الإشكال عناية فائقة، ولهم في ذلك دراسات تحفل بها كتب الفقه في جميع المذاهب، ويمكن لمن شاء أن يحرر هذه المسألة بتفصيل، أن يرجع إليها في مظانها من كتب الفقه. على أننا استكمالاً للفائدة، ونظراً للطبيعة المختصرة لهذا الكتاب، نكتفي بإيراد ثلاث مسائل مستخلصة من هذه الدراسات الفقهية، مما وقع عليه الإجماع، أو ارتضاه الجمهور.

المسألة الأولى : أنه في أداء الصلوات، يكون الافتتاح والتكبيرات، وقراءة الفاتحة وما تيسر من الآيات القرآنية، والتسبيحات، وقراءة التشهد، وتسليم الخروج من الصلاة – كل ذلك باللغة العربية وحدها. وعلى كل مسلم أن يجتهد في تعلُّم ذلك بأقصى جهده. وقد صار الأمر في ذلك، خلال التاريخ الإسلامي، ميسَّراً في لغات البلاد الإسلامية: كالفارسية، والتركية، والأردية، والسواحيلية، والأندونيسية، وأشباهها. بل لعل مفردات هذه النصوص الأساسية قد دخلت معاجم هذه اللغات، وأصبحت جزءاً منها. وحتى في اللغات الأخرى، فقد اتضح من تجارب دعاة الإسلام وملحوظاتهم، أن المتكلمين بهذه اللغات لا

يجدون استحالة، أو مشقة غير محتملة في تعلُّم هذا القدر المحدود من القراءات.

فمن لم يستطع تعلُّم هذا القدر، فقد نُصب له البدل الشرعي المختصر، وهو قوله باللغة العربية : «سُبْحَانَ اللهِ، والحَمْدُ للهِ، ولا إلهَ إلاّ اللهُ، واللهُ أكْبَرُ، ولا حَوْلَ ولا قُوَّةَ إلا باللهِ»[1]. أو أن يقول البدل الآخر الأكثر اختصاراً وهو: «الحَمْدُ للهِ، واللهُ أكبَرُ، ولا إلهَ إلا اللهُ»[2] وذلك الى أن يوفَّق إلى تعلم هذه القراءات بتمامها.

ولا يجوز، في الصلاة، أن تتم أيٌّ من هذه القراءات بالترجمات الموضوعة لمعانيها. ولم يسجل التاريخ أن فرداً أو مجموعة من المسلمين قد أدّوْا صلواتهم بقراءات غير عربية. وعلى مدى أربعة عشر قرناً، فإن المسلمين في مشارق الأرض ومغاربها، ورغم تعدد لغاتهم وتفاوتهم في فرص التعليم - صلَّوْا ويصلون بالقراءات العربية، واجتهدوا ويجتهدون في تعليمها وإيضاح معانيها لقرائها المتعبدين بها[3]. ولذلك دلالته الواضحة على الوحدة

---

(١) سنن أبي داود : ج٥، ص ٧٥ - ٧٦ (باب ما يجزىء الأمي والأعجمي من القراءة).

(٢) جامع الترمذي : ج١، ص ١٨٦ (باب ما جاء في وصف الصلاة).

(٣) الأستاذ عبد اللطيف الطيباوي: أحكام ترجمة القرآن الكريم وتاريخها. مجلة مجمع اللغة العربية بدمشق، مجلد ٥٤، ج ٣ ، ص ٤، مطبعة دار الفكر ١٣٩٩هـ- ١٩٧٩م.

الروحية للعالم الإسلامي متمثلة في وحدة العبادة بحركاتها وقراءاتها واللغة المستخدمة فيها.

المسألة الثانية : أنه في خارج الصلوات، يجتهد المسلم في قراءة الأدعية والأذكار المأثورة وغير المأثورة، بصيغتها العربية، خاصة ما كان منها قرآناً أو حديثاً نبوياً. فإن لم يستطع ففي الحرص على التسبيح، والحمد، والتهليل، والتكبير، والحَوْقلة، بصيغتها العربية، بركةٌ أيُّ بركة. فإذا أراد أن يتوسع وأن يناجي ربه بما يزيد عن ذلك، مستعيناً بترجمات المعاني إلى اللغة التي يعرفها وفُطر عليها ويُحسن التعبير عما في نفسه بها، فإن ذلك داخل تحت عموم قوله تعالى ﴿لا يُكَلِّفُ اللهُ نَفْساً إلاَّ وُسْعَها﴾[١].

وعلى المسلم الذي يُضطر إلى ذلك أن يتذكر أن قراءة الترجمات هي من قبيل قراءة التفاسير، وأنه محاولة لا مناص منها للوصول إلى المعنى المأثور، ولو بعبارة غير مأثورة. كما أن عليه أن يتذكر أن ترجمة معاني القرآن الكريم ليست قرآناً، وأن ترجمة معاني الحديث الشريف ليست حديثاً. ولكن جمهور العلماء قد أجازوا ترجمة معاني القرآن الكريم، ليتمكن غير العارف بالعربية من معرفة الهداية الإلهية. وما جاز في حق القرآن الكريم يتحتّم جوازه

---

(١) سورة البقرة، ٢: ٢٨٥.

في حق الحديث الشريف، وما دونه من آثار وأقوال[1].

وعزاء العاجز عن دعاء الله وذكره، وحسن تعبُّده ومناجاته، باللغة العربية، أن الله تعالى سميع لما يُدعى به وعليم بما يجيش في الصدور. قال تعالى ﴿واللهُ سَمِيعٌ عَلِيمٌ﴾[2]، بل هو سميع وعليم حتى بما لا نفقه، نحن البشر، من تسبيح جميع خلقه. قال تعالى ﴿تُسَبِّحُ لَهُ السَّمَواتُ السَّبْعُ والأرْضُ وَمَنْ فِيهِنَّ، وَإنْ مِنْ شَيْءٍ إلا يُسَبِّحُ بِحَمْدِهِ، وَلَكِنْ لا تَفْقَهُونَ تَسْبِيحَهُمْ﴾[3]، وقال ﴿أَلَمْ تَرَ أن اللهَ يُسَبِّحُ لَهُ مَنْ في السَّمَواتِ والأرْضِ، والطَّيْرُ صَافات، كُلٌّ قَدْ عَلِمَ صَلاتَهُ وتَسْبِيحَهُ، واللهُ عَلِيمٌ بما يَفْعَلونَ﴾[4].

وقد استفاض الدعاء خارج الصلاة بترجمات المعاني

---

(١) إجازة ترجمة معاني القرآن الكريم قديمة، وخاصة في الكتابات الوسيطة: مثل ما كتبه شيخ الاسلام ابن تيمية في القرن السابع الهجري في فتاويه (طبعة اولى سنة ١٣٨١ هـ ج٣، ص ٣٠٦، وج٤، ص ١١٦-١١٧)، والإمام الشاطبي في القرن الثامن الهجري في الموافقات (تحقيق محمد محيي الدين عبد الحميد ج٢، ص ٤٨)، وكذلك في الكتابات المعاصرة لمشايخ الأزهر محمد الخضر حسين، ومحمود شلتوت، ومحمد مصطفى المراغي، ثم الشيخ محمد حسنين مخلوف والشيخ السيد محمد رشيد رضا. وقد استوعب ذلك الاستاذ عبد اللطيف الطيباوي وحرره في بحثه (أحكام ترجمة القرآن الكريم وتاريخها) المشار إليه سابقاً.

(٢) سورة البقرة، ٢: ٢٥٦، وآل عمران، ٣: ٣٤.

(٣) سورة الإسراء، ١٧: ٤٤.

(٤) سورة النور، ٢٤: ٤١.

للأدعية المأثورة وغير المأثورة في جميع البلاد الإسلامية، تيسيراً على مَنْ عجز عن تعلُّم العربية، وعوْناً له على الخشوع والتدبر، دون أن نسمع باعتراض أحد على ذلك. ويُحمد للعلماء في هذه البلاد البدء بالأدعية بالنص العربي تأكيداً لأهميته، وتثبيتاً لما يمكن أن يعلق بذواكر الناس منه، ثم إردافهم ذلك بترجمات المعاني. ولا حرج على المسلمين في استخدام هذه الترجمات لظهور جوازها في حدود ما بيّناه.

المسألة الثالثة : أنه سواء أكان الدعاء والذكر بالنص العربي، أم بترجمة معناه، فإن المهم هو التعبد بالدعاء والذكر: بفهم المعنى، وحضور القلب، وخشوع الجوارح، وحسن التوجه إلى الله تعالى بالإلحاف عليه، والتيقن من حسن إجابته.

والذي أُمر به المسلم هو عدم التلفظ بعبارات أعجمية قد تحتوي على (ما ينافي تعظيم الله)، دون أن يعلم، ودون توفر الفرصة لتصحيحه لعدم المعرفة باللغة التي يستعملها، ولذلك اعتبرت هذه العبارات رطانة غير مقبولة. وقد أخرج البيهقي عن عمر بن الخطاب رضي الله عنه أنه سمع رجلاً يتكلم بالفارسية في الطواف، فأخذ بعضديه وقال «ابتغ إلى

العربية سبيلاً». ومثل هذا يقال عن التلفظ بأدعية أو أذكار عربية اللسان، دون فهم صحيح لمعناها[1]، أو أن يتلفظ بها المرء وهو ناقص الوعي بمدلولها بسبب غلبة النعاس مثلاً[2]. ومدلول ذلك كله أن يتوافر في الدعاء والذكر: صحة المعنى، وصحة التعبير، وصحة الإدراك لما يردده اللسان.

فليجتهد المسلم في تحصيل هذه الشروط في دعائه وذكره، وليستعن على ذلك بالاقتراب من اللسان العربي ما وسعه ذلك. وليتيقن العاجز الذي يناجي ربه بما يقدر عليه، بأي لغة أو لسان، مع الصحة والفهم، أنه يناجي رباً سميعاً عليماً قال تعالى ﴿وإذا سَألَكَ عِبادِي عَنِّي فَإنِّي قَرِيبٌ، أجِيبُ دَعْوَةَ الدَّاعِ إذا دَعَانِ، فَلْيَسْتَجِيبُوا لي وَلْيُؤْمِنُوا بِي، لَعَلَّهُمْ يَرْشُدُونَ﴾[3].

وأخيراً، فإننا ندعو الله مخلصين، أن يكون هذا الكتاب عَوْناً على تقريب الأدعية والأذكار المأثورة، للمسلمين الذين يرجعون إليه، فيجد فيه العارف بالعربية والمجتهد في تعلُّمها دليلاً ميسَّراً لما يناسب حاله من (أعمال اليوم والليلة

---

(١) أحمد بن ادريس القرافي : الفروق. ج٤، ص ٢٩١.

(٢) كما ورد في الحديث الذي أخرجه البخاري ومسلم «فإن أحَدَكم إذا صلى وهو ناعِسٌ، لا يَدْري لعله يذهبُ يستغفر فيسب نفسه».

(٣) سورة البقرة، ٢: ١٨٦.

وأدعـية المناسـبات والعـبادات وأذكـارها) باللسان العـربي المبين مُـحقّـقـاً ومشـروحاً، كـمـا يجد فـيـه قارىء اللغـة الانجليـزية، وسيلة مـبسـطة لمعرفـة معـاني هذه الأدعيـة والأذكار، بـعبارة مـحررة يألفـها لسـانه. والحمـد لله الذي بنعـمتـه تتم الصـالحات. وآخـر دعـوانا أن الحمـد لله ربّ العالمين.

عزالدين ابراهيم مصطفى،ودنيس جونسون ديڤيز(عبد الودود)

أبو ظبي في ١٥ جمادى الآخرة ١٤١٩ هـ

٦ اكتوبر ١٩٩٨ م

مختصر

الكَلِم الطيِّب

Shaykh al-Islam Ibn Taymiyyah's Introduction

O Allah, bless the most noble of Your creation, Muḥammad, and to Allah be praise, and that is all that need be said, and peace be upon His servants whom He has chosen. I bear witness that there is no god but Allah alone, He having no associate, and I bear witness that Muḥammad is His servant and His messenger.

Allah Almighty said: "O you who believe, guard your duty to Allah, and speak words truthful and He will put to rights your works for you and will forgive you your sins."[1]

And the Almighty said: "Unto Him goodly words ascend, and the pious deed does He exalt."[2] And the Almighty said: "Therefore remember Me, and I shall remember you, and give thanks to Me."[3] And the Almighty said: "Remember Allah with much

1. The Chapter of the Clans 33:70–71.
2. The Chapter of the Creator 35:10.
3. The Chapter of the Cow 2:152.

مقدمة شيخ الإسلام ابن تيمية

بِسْمِ ٱللَّهِ ٱلرَّحْمَٰنِ ٱلرَّحِيمِ

اللهم صلِّ على أَشْرَف خَلْقِك مُحمَّد، ولله الحَمْدُ وكفى، وسلامٌ على عِباده الَّذينَ ٱصطفى. وأَشهدُ أَنْ لا إِلٰه إلاَّ اللهُ وحدِه لا شَريكَ له، وأَشهد أَنَّ مُحمَّداً عبْدُه ورسُوله.

قال الله تعالى: ﴿يا أَيُّها الَّذينَ آمنُوا اتَّقُوا اللهَ وَقُولُوا قَوْلاً سَدِيداً[1] يُصْلِحْ لَكُمْ أَعْمالَكُمْ وَيَغْفِرْ لَكُمْ ذُنُوبَكُمْ﴾ [الأحزاب ٣٣: ٧٠ ـ ٧١]. وقالَ تعالى: ﴿إِلَيْهِ يَصْعَدُ[2] ٱلْكَلِمُ الطيِّبُ وَٱلْعَمَلُ الصَّالحُ يَرْفَعُهُ[3]﴾ [فاطر ٣٥: ١٠]. وقال تعالى: ﴿فَاذْكُرُوني أَذْكُرْكُمْ وَٱشْكُرُوا لي﴾ [البقرة ٢: ١٥٢]. وقال تعالى: ﴿اذْكُروا اللهَ

---

(١) سديداً: صادقاً بقصد الوصول إلى الحق.

(٢) يصعد: يرتفع إلى الله فيقبله بالرضا.

(٣) يرفعه: يرفعه الله ويقبله ويرضى عنه.

remembrance."[1] And the Almighty said: "And men and women who remember Allah much."[2]

And the Almighty said: "Those who remember Allah, standing, sitting, and reclining."[3] And the Almighty said: "When you come up against a group (of fighting men), hold firm and remember Allah much."[4]

And the Almighty said: "And when you have completed your devotions, then remember Allah as you remember your fathers or with a more intense remembrance."[5] And the Almighty said: "Let not your wealth nor your children distract you from remembrance of Allah."[6] And the Almighty said: "Men whom neither commerce nor sale beguiles

---

1. The Chapter of the Clans 33:41.
2. The Chapter of the Clans 33:35.
3. The Chapter of the Family of ᶜImrān 3:190.
4. The Chapter of the Spoils of War 8:45.
5. The Chapter of the Cow 2:200.
6. The Chapter of the Hypocrites 63:9.

ذِكْـراً كَثِيـراً﴾ [الأحـزاب ٣٣: ٤١]، وقـال تعالى: ﴿وَالذَّاكِرِينَ اللهَ كَثِيراً وَالذَّاكِراتِ﴾ [الأَحزاب ٣٣: ٣٥]. وقال تعالى: ﴿الَّذِينَ يَذْكُرُونَ اللهَ قِياماً وَقُعُوداً وَعَلَى جُنُوبِهِمْ﴾ [آل عمـران ٣: ١٩٠]. وقـال تعـالـى: ﴿إِذَا لَقِيتُـمْ فِئَـةً[١] فَـاثْبُتُـوا وَاْذْكُـرُوا اللهَ كَثِيـراً﴾ [الأَنفال ٨: ٤٥]. وقالَ تعالى: ﴿فَإِذَا قَضَيْتُمْ مَنَاسِكَكُمْ[٢] فَاذْكُرُوا اللهَ كَذِكْرِكُمْ آباءَكُمْ أَوْ أَشَدَّ ذِكْراً﴾ [البقرة ٢: ٢٠٠]. وقالَ تعالى: ﴿لا تُلْهِكُمْ[٣] أَمْوَالُكُمْ وَلا أَوْلادُكُمْ عَنْ ذِكْرِ اللهِ﴾ [المنـافقـون ٦٣: ٩]. وَقـالَ تعـالـى: ﴿رِجَالٌ لا تُلْهِيهِمْ تِجارَةٌ وَلا بَيْعٌ عَنْ ذِكْرِ اللهِ

(١) فئة: جماعة مقاتلة.
(٢) مناسككم: عبادات الحج.
(٣) لا تلهكم: لا تشغلكم.

from remembrance of Allah and the performance of prayer and paying zakāt[1] to the poor."[2]

And the Almighty said: "Remember your Lord within yourself humbly and with awe, without raising your voice, at morn and evening. And be not you of the neglectful."[3]

***

---

1. Often rendered as 'alms tax' or 'poor due,' it is a tax levied on a man's wealth and distributed among the poor.
2. The Chapter of the Light 24:37.
3. The Chapter of the Heights 7:205.

وإِقَامِ الصَّلاةِ وَإِيتَاءِ الزَّكَاةِ﴾ [النور ٢٤: ٣٧]. وَقالَ تعالى: ﴿وَٱذكُرْ رَبَّكَ في نَفْسِكَ تَضَرُّعاً وَخِيفَةً(١) وَدُونَ الجَهْرِ مِنَ ٱلْقَوْلِ بِالغُدُوِّ(٢) وَالآصَالِ(٣) وَلا تَكُنْ مِنَ الْغَافِلينَ﴾ [الأعراف ٧: ٢٠٥].

***

(١) تَضَرُّعاً وخِيفة: تذلُّلاً لله وخوفاً من مؤاخذته.

(٢) الغُدُوُّ: بين الفجر وطلوع الشمس.

(٣) الآصال: جمع أصيل وهو بين العصر وغروب الشمس.

1. The Merit of Remembrance

1) The Messenger of Allah (may the blessings and peace of Allah be upon him) said:

"Shall I not inform you of the best of your deeds, and the most pure in the eyes of your King, and the loftiest of them in your grades (of merit), (deeds) that are better for you than the spending of gold and silver, and better for you than meeting your enemy and striking their necks and they striking your necks?" They said: Yes indeed, O Messenger of Allah. He said: "The remembrance of Allah."

(Related by at-Tirmidhī and Ibn Mājah)

2) The Prophet (may the blessings and peace of Allah be upon him) said:

"The mufarridūn[1] (devotees) have surpassed (others)." They said: And who are the mufarridūn, O Messenger of Allah? He said: "The men and women who remember Allah much."

(Related by Muslim)

1. Those who isolate themselves and devote themselves to the praise of Allah

١ ـ فضل الذكر

١ ـ قالَ رسُولُ اللهِ ﷺ:

«ألا أُنبِّئُكُمْ بِخَيْرِ أعْمالِكُمْ، وأزْكاها عِنْدَ مَلِيكِكُمْ، وأرْفَعِها في دَرَجاتِكُم، وَخَيْرٌ لَكُمْ مِنْ إنْفاقِ الذَّهَبِ وَالْوَرِقِ[١]، وَخَيْرٌ لكمْ مِنْ أنْ تَلْقَوْا عَدُوَّكُمْ فَتَضْرِبُوا أعْناقَهُمْ وَيَضْرِبُوا أعْناقَكُمْ»؟ قالُوا: بلى يا رسولَ اللهِ. قالَ: «ذِكْرُ اللهِ».

التِّرْمذي وابنُ ماجَه

٢ ـ قالَ النَّبِيُّ ﷺ:

«سَبَقَ المُفَرِّدُونَ». قالوا: وما المُفرِّدون[٢] يا رَسولَ اللهِ؟ قال: «الذَّاكِرونَ اللهَ كَثيراً وَالذَّاكِراتُ».

مسلم

---

(١) الورِق: الفضة.

(٢) فرَّد الرجل: اعتزل الناس واشتغل بطاعة الله وذكره.

3) ᶜAbdullah ibn Busr mentioned that a man said: O Messenger of Allah, the revealed laws of faith have become too many for me, so tell me of one thing to hold fast to. He said: "Let your tongue continue to be moist with the remembrance of Allah the Almighty."

(Related by at-Tirmidhī)

4) On the authority of the Prophet (may the blessings and peace of Allah be upon him) who said:

"The likeness of him who remembers his Lord to him who does not remember his Lord is as the likeness of the living to the dead."

(Related by al-Bukhārī)

٣ ـ وَذَكَرَ عبدُ اللهِ بْنُ بُسْرٍ أَنَّ رجُلاً قالَ: يا رسُولَ اللهِ إِنَّ شَرائِعَ[١] الْإِيمانِ قَدْ كَثُرَتْ عَلَيَّ، فأَخْبِرْني بِشَيْءٍ أَتَشَبَّثُ بِهِ. قالَ: «لا يَزالُ لِسانُكَ رَطْباً[٢] مِنْ ذِكْرِ اللهِ تعالى».

التِّرْمذي

٤ ـ عَنِ النَّبيِّ ﷺ قالَ:

«مَثَلُ الَّذي يَذْكُرُ رَبَّهُ والَّذي لا يَذْكُرُ رَبَّهُ مَثَلُ الحَيِّ والميِّتِ».

البخاري

---

(١) كثرت الشرائع: أي كثرت عليه العبادات المشروعة وصعُب عليه أداؤها جميعاً.

(٢) الرطب ضد اليابس. قال الطيبي: رطوبة اللسان جريانه. وجريان اللسان عبارة عن مداومة الذكر، فكأنه قال: داوم الذكر. وقد يكون المعنى أن الذكر يكسب اللسان الرطوبة والنعومة والعذوبة، كناية عن جريان الخير للذاكرين. انظر ابن علان جـ ٧ ص ٢٦٤.

5) From the Messenger of Allah (may the blessings and peace of Allah be upon him), who said:

"He who sits down without remembering Allah the Almighty has committed an omission which Allah the Almighty will hold against him, and he who lies down without remembering Allah the Almighty has committed an omission which Allah the Almighty will hold against him."

(Related by Abū Dāwūd)

٥ ـ عَنْ رَسولِ اللهِ ﷺ قالَ:

«مَنْ قَعَدَ مَقْعَداً لَمْ يَذْكُرِ اللهَ تَعالى فيهِ، كانَتْ عَلَيه مِنَ اللهِ تَعالى تِرَةٌ، وَمَنِ اضْطَجَعَ مَضْجَعاً لا يَذْكُرُ اللهَ تعالىٰ فيهِ، كانتْ عليهِ مِنَ اللهِ تِرَةٌ» أَي: نَقْصٌ، وَتَبِعَةٌ، وَحَسْرَةٌ.

أبو داود

2. The merit of taḥmīd,[1] tahlīl,[2] and tasbīḥ[3]

6) The Messenger of Allah (may the blessings and peace of Allah be upon him) said:

"He who says: There is no god but Allah alone, He having no associate, He has dominion, and thanks are due to Him and He is able to do all things—a hundred times a day—will have the reward equivalent to manumitting ten slaves. He will have written for him a hundred good deeds and will have erased for him a hundred bad deeds. He will have sanctuary from the devil for that day of his until he enters upon the evening, and no one will have brought anything better than he has, except for a man who has done more than he."

(Related by al-Bukhārī and Muslim)

1. To say "al-ḥamdu lillāh."
2. To say "lā ilāha illa 'llāh."
3. To say "subḥāna 'llāh."

٢ ـ فَضْلُ التَّحْمِيدِ والتَّهْليلِ والتَّسْبيحِ

٦ ـ قالَ رسولُ اللهِ ﷺ:

«مَنْ قالَ: لا إِلٰهَ إلاَّ اللهُ وَحْدَهُ لا شَرِيكَ لَهُ، لهُ المُلْكُ، ولهُ الحَمْدُ، وَهُوَ علىٰ كُلِّ شَيْءٍ قَدِيرٌ، في يَوْمٍ مِائَةَ مَرَّةٍ، كانَتْ لَهُ عِدْلَ عَشْرِ رِقابٍ(١)، وكُتِبَتْ لَهُ مِائَةُ حَسَنَةٍ، ومُحِيَتْ عنه مِائَةُ سَيِّئَةٍ، وكانَتْ لَهُ حِرْزاً(٢) مِنَ الشَّيْطانِ يَوْمَهُ ذٰلِكَ حَتَّىٰ يُمْسِيَ، ولم يَأْتِ أَحَدٌ بِأَفْضَلَ مِمَّا جاءَ بِهِ إِلاَّ رَجُلٌ عَمِلَ أَكْثَرَ مِنْهُ».

البخاري ومسلم

---

(١) أي له مثل ثواب من أعتنق عشرة من الرقيق

(٢) حرْزاً : وقاية .

7) And he said: “Whoever has said subḥāna ’llāh wa bi-ḥamdih (How far is Allah from every imperfection!—and praise is due to Him) a hundred times in a day, his sins will be taken from him even if they are as the foam of the sea.”

(Related by al-Bukhārī and Muslim)

8) The Messenger of Allah (may the blessings and peace of Allah be upon him) said:

“(There are) two phrases that are light upon the tongue, heavy in the Scales, beloved of the Merciful: subḥāna ’llāh wa bi-ḥamdih (How far is Allah from every imperfection!—and praise is due to Him) and subḥāna ’llāh al-ᶜAẓīm (How far is Allah the Great from every imperfection!).”

(Related by al-Bukhārī and Muslim)

٧ ـ وَقـالَ: «مَـنْ قـالَ سُبْحـانَ اللهِ[١] وبِحَمْدِهِ في يَوْمٍ مِائَةَ مَرَّةٍ، حُطَّتْ[٢] عنهُ خَطاياهُ وإِنْ كانَتْ مِثْلَ زَبَدِ البَحْرِ».

البخاري ومسلم

٨ ـ قالَ رَسولُ اللهِ ﷺ:

«كَلِمَتان خَفِيفَتانِ على اللِّسانِ، ثَقِيلَتانِ في الْمِيزانِ، حَبِيبَتانِ إِلى الرَّحْمٰنِ: سُبْحانَ اللهِ وَبِحَمْدِهِ، سُبْحانَ اللهِ الْعَظِيمِ».

البخاري ومسلم

---

(١) نزَّه الله وقدَّسه.

(٢) حُطت الخطايا: غُفرت وأسقطت.

9) The Messenger of Allah (may the blessings and peace of Allah be upon him) said:

"For me to say subḥāna 'llāh (How far is Allah from every imperfection!), al-ḥamdu lillāh (Praise be to Allah), lā ilāha illā 'llāh (There is no god but Allah), and Allāhu akbar (Allah is greatest) is dearer to me than that over which the sun comes out."

(Related by Muslim)

10) The Messenger of Allah (may the blessings and peace of Allah be upon him) said:

"The phrases most dear to Allah the Almighty are four, and it matters not to you which of them you begin with: subḥāna 'llāh (How far is Allah from every imperfection!), al-ḥamdu lillāh (Praise be to Allah), lā ilāha illā 'llāh (There is no god but Allah), and Allāhu akbar (Allah is greatest)."

(Related by Muslim)

٩ ـ قالَ رسولُ الله ﷺ:

«لأَنْ أَقُولَ سُبْحانَ اللهِ، وَالْحَمْدُ للهِ، وَلا إِلٰهَ إِلا اللهُ، وَاللهُ أَكْبَرُ، أَحَبُّ إِلَيَّ مِمَّا طَلَعَتْ عَلَيْهِ الشَّمْسُ».

مسلم

١٠ ـ قالَ رَسولُ اللهِ ﷺ:

«أَحَبُّ الكَلامِ إِلى اللهِ تعالى أَرْبَعٌ، لا يَضُرُّكَ بِأَيِّهِنَّ بَدَأْتَ: سُبْحانَ اللهِ، وَالْحَمْدُ للهِ، وَلا إِلٰهَ إِلا اللهُ، وَاللهُ أَكْبَرُ».

مسلم

11) The Messenger of Allah (may the blessings and peace of Allah be upon him) said:

"Is any one of you incapable of gaining each day a thousand good deeds?" One of those who were sitting with him asked him: How does one us of gain a thousand good deeds? He said: "He says subḥāna 'llāh (How far is Allah from every imperfection!) a hundred times and there is written for him a thousand good deeds, or there are taken from him a thousand sins."

(Related by Muslim)

12) On the authority of Juwayriyah, Mother of the Believers[1] (may Allah be pleased with her), that the Prophet (may the blessings and peace of Allah be upon him) went out from her home early in the morning when he had performed the dawn prayer, while she was in her place of prayer. Then he returned after the morning had come, and she was

1. I.e., the wife of the Prophet.

١١ ـ قالَ رَسولُ اللهِ ﷺ:

«أَيَعْجزُ أَحَدُكُمْ أَنْ يَكسِبَ كُلَّ يَوْمٍ أَلْفَ حَسَنَةٍ؟ فَسأَلَهُ سائِلٌ مِنْ جُلَسائِهِ: كَيْفَ يَكْسِبُ أَحَدُنا أَلْفَ حَسَنَةٍ؟ قال: يُسبِّحُ مِائَةَ تَسْبيحَةٍ، فتُكْتَبُ لَهُ أَلْفُ حَسَنَةٍ، أَو تُحَطُّ عَنْهُ أَلْفُ خَطِيئَةٍ».

مسلم

١٢ ـ عن جُوَيْرِيَةَ أُمِّ المؤْمِنينَ رَضِيَ اللهُ عَنْها، أَنَّ النَّبيَّ ﷺ خَرجَ مِنْ عِنْدِها بُكْرَةً حِينَ صَلَّىٰ الصُّبْحَ وَهِيَ في مَسْجِدِها، ثُمَّ رَجعَ بَعْدَ

sitting down. He said "Are you still in the state in which I left you?" She said: Yes. Then the Prophet (may the blessings and peace of Allah be upon him) said:

"After (leaving) you I said four phrases three times. Were they to be weighed against what you have said today they would outweigh them: I glorify Allah as many times as the number of His creatures, I glorify Allah as much as it pleases Him, I glorify Allah with a weight like that of His throne, I glorify Allah with (a quantity like that of) the ink (required) for His words."

(Related by Muslim)

أَنْ أَضْحَىٰ وَهِيَ جَالِسَةٌ فقَالَ: «ما زِلْتِ على الْحَالِ التي فارَقْتُكِ عَلَيْها؟» قالتْ: نَعَمْ. فقالَ النَّبيُّ ﷺ:

«لَقَدْ قُلْتُ بَعْدَكِ أَرْبَعَ كَلِماتٍ، ثَلاثَ مَرَّاتٍ، لَوْ وُزِنَتْ بِما قُلْتِ مُنْذُ الْيوم لَوَزَنَتْهُنَّ(١): سُبْحانَ اللهِ عَدَدَ خَلْقِهِ، سُبْحَانَ اللهِ رِضَىٰ نَفْسِهِ، سُبْحانَ اللهِ زِنَةَ عَرْشِهِ، سُبْحانَ اللهِ مِدادَ كَلِماتِهِ».

مسلم

---

(١) رجحت عليهنّ.

13) He (may the blessings and peace of Allah be upon him) said to an Arab of the desert: "Say: I glorify Allah, there is no god but Allah alone, He having no associate, Allah is truly the Greatest and much praise be to Allah, Lord of the Worlds, there is no strength nor power except through Allah, the Mighty, the Wise." He said: These are for my Lord, so what is for me? He said: "Say: O Allah, forgive me, and have mercy on me, and guide me, and keep me in health, and provide for me."

(Related by Muslim)

١٣ ـ قالَ ﷺ لِأَعْرابِيٍ: «قُلْ: لا إِلٰهَ إِلا اللهُ وَحْدَهُ لا شَرِيكَ لَهُ، اللهُ أَكْبَرُ كَبِيراً، والحَمْدُ للهِ كَثِيراً، وسُبْحانَ اللهِ رَبِّ العالَمِينَ، ولا حَوْلَ ولا قُوَّةَ إِلا بِاللهِ العَزِيزِ الحَكِيمِ».

قالَ: فَهٰؤُلاءِ لِرَبِّي، فما لي؟ قالَ: «قُلْ: اللَّهُمَّ اغْفِرْ لِي، وَارْحَمْنِي، واهْدِنِي، وعافِنِي[١]، وَارْزُقْنِي».

مسلم

---

(١) عافني: ارزقني الصحة وجنِّبني العلل.

14) On the authority of Abū Mūsā al-Ashᶜarī (may Allah be pleased with him), who said that the Prophet (may the blessings and peace of Allah be upon him) said to him:

"Shall I not direct you to one of the treasures of Paradise?" So I said: Yes indeed, O Messenger of Allah. He said: "Say: 'Lā ḥawla wa lā quwwata illā billāh' (There is no strength or power except through Allah)."

(Related by al-Bukhārī and Muslim)

١٤ ـ قال أبو موسى الأَشْعَرِيُّ، رَضِيَ اللهُ عنه، قالَ لِي النَّبيُّ ﷺ:

«أَلا أَدُلُّكَ على كَنْزٍ مِنْ كُنُوزِ الْجَنَّةِ؟»

فقُلتُ: بَلى يا رَسولَ اللهِ. قالَ: «قُلْ لا حَوْلَ ولا قُوَّةَ إلا بِاللهِ».

البخاري ومسلم

3. Remembrance of Allah the Almighty at the two ends of the day

Allah the Almighty has said: "O you who believe, remember Allah with much remembrance, and glorify Him morning and evening."[1] And the Almighty has said: "And remember your Lord within yourself humbly and with awe, without raising your voice, mornings and evenings. And be not you of the neglectful."[2] And the Almighty has said: "And extol the praise of your Lord at fall of night and in the early hours."[3] And the Almighty has said: "And extol the praise of your Lord before the rising and before the setting of the sun."[4] And the Almighty has said: "Repel not those who call upon their Lord at morn and evening, seeking His Countenance."[5] And the Almighty has said: "And he

1. The Chapter of the Clans 33:41.
2. The Chapter of the Heights 7:205.
3. The Chapter of the Forgiver 40:55.
4. The Chapter of Qāf 50:39.
5. The Chapter of the Cattle 6:52.

٣ ـ ذِكْرُ اللهِ تعالى طَرَفَي النَّهارِ

قالَ اللهُ تعالىٰ: ﴿يَا أَيُّهَا الَّذِينَ آمَنُوا اذْكُرُوا اللهَ ذِكْراً كَثِيراً وَسَبِّحُوهُ بُكْرَةً[١] وَأَصِيلاً﴾ [الأحزاب ٣٣: ٤١]، ـ الأَصيلُ: ما بَيْنَ العَصْرِ إلى المَغْرِبِ ـ وقالَ تعالىٰ: ﴿وَاذْكُرْ رَبَّكَ فِي نَفْسِكَ تَضَرُّعاً وَخِيفَةً وَدُونَ الجَهْرِ مِنَ القَوْلِ بِالغُدُوِّ[٢] وَالآصالِ وَلا تَكُنْ مِنَ الغَافِلِينَ﴾ [الأعراف ٧: ٢٠٥]، ﴿وَسَبِّحْ بِحَمْدِ رَبِّكَ بِالعَشِيِّ والإِبْكارِ﴾ [غافر ٤٠: ٥٥] وقالَ تعالىٰ: ﴿وَسَبِّحْ بِحَمْدِ رَبِّكَ قَبْلَ طُلُوعِ الشَّمْسِ وَقَبْلَ الغُرُوبِ﴾ [قٓ ٥٠: ٣٩] ﴿وَلا تَطْرُدِ الَّذِينَ يَدْعُونَ رَبَّهُمْ بِالغَدَاةِ وَالعَشِيِّ[٣] يُرِيدُونَ وَجْهَهُ﴾

(١) البُكرة: أول النهار إلى طلوع الشمس.
(٢) الغُدُوّ: جمع غُدْوة وهي ما بين الفجر وطلوع الشمس.
(٣) الغداة والغدوّ بمعنى واحد والعشي من زوال الشمس إلى المغرب.

signified to them: Glorify your Lord at break of day and fall of night."[1] And the Almighty has said: "And in the night-time also glorify Him, and at the setting of the stars."[2] And the Almighty has said: "So glory be to Allah when you enter the night and when you enter the morning."[3] And the Almighty has said: "Perform prayers at the two ends of the day and in some watches of the night. Verily good deeds annul bad deeds."[4]

15) The Prophet (may the blessings and peace of Allah be upon him) said:

"He who says when he enters upon the morning and when he enters upon the evening subḥāna 'llāh wa bi-ḥamdih (How far is Allah from every imperfection!—and praise be to Him)—a hundred times—will not have anyone come on the Day of

1. The Chapter of Mary 19:11.
2. The Chapter of the Mountain 52:49.
3. The Chapter of the Romans 30:17.
4. The Chapter of Hūd 11:114.

[الأنعام ٦ : ٥٢] ﴿فَأَوْحَىٰ إِلَيْهِمْ أَنْ سَبِّحُوا بُكْرَةً وَعَشِيّاً﴾ [مريم ١٩ : ١١]. ﴿وَمِنَ اللَّيْلِ فَسَبِّحْهُ وَإِدْبَارَ النُّجُومِ[1]﴾ [الطور ٥٢ : ٤٩] ﴿فَسُبْحَانَ اللهِ حِينَ تُمْسُونَ وَحِينَ تُصْبِحُونَ﴾ [الروم ٣٠ : ١٧] ﴿وَأَقِمِ الصَّلاةَ طَرَفَيِ النَّهَارِ وَزُلَفاً مِنَ اللَّيْلِ[2] إِنَّ الحَسَنَاتِ يُذْهِبْنَ السَّيِّئَاتِ﴾ [هود ١١ : ١١٤].

١٥ ـ قالَ النبيُّ ﷺ:

«مَنْ قالَ حِينَ يُصْبِحُ وَحِينَ يُمْسِي: سُبْحانَ اللهِ وبِحَمْدِهِ، مِائَةَ مَرَّةٍ، لَمْ يَأْتِ أَحَدٌ

(١) إدبار النجوم: وقت غيبتها آخر الليل.
(٢) زُلَف: جمع زُلْفة وهي قَدْر من الليل.

Resurrection with anything better than he has brought, except for someone who has said as he has said or has said more."

(Related by Muslim)

16) The Prophet of Allah (may the blessings and peace of Allah be upon him), when he entered upon the evening, used to say: "We have come upon the evening and dominion has come to Allah, and praise is to Allah. There is no god but Allah alone, He having no associate. To Him is dominion and to Him is praise, and He is able to do all things. O my Lord, I ask you for the good that is in this night and for the good that is after it, and I take refuge in You from the evil that is in this night and from the evil that is after it. O my Lord, I take refuge in You from laziness and baneful old age. O my Lord, I take

يَوْمَ القِيامَةِ بأَفْضَلَ مِمَّا جاءَ بِهِ إلاَّ أَحَدٌ قالَ مِثْلَ ما قالَ، أَوْ زادَ عَلَيْهِ».

مسلم

١٦ ـ «كانَ نَبِيُّ اللهِ ﷺ إذا أَمْسَىٰ قالَ: أَمْسَيْنا وأَمْسَىٰ المُلْكُ لِلَّهِ، والحمْدُ لِلَّهِ، لا إِلٰهَ إلا اللهُ وَحْدَهُ لا شَرِيكَ لَهُ، لَهُ المُلْكُ ولهُ الْحَمْدُ، وَهُوَ على كُلِّ شَيْءٍ قَدِيرٌ، رَبِّ أَسْأَلُكَ خَيْرَ ما في هٰذِهِ اللَّيْلَةِ، وَخَيْرَ ما بَعْدَها، وأَعوذُ بِكَ مِنْ شَرِّ ما في هٰذِهِ اللَّيْلَةِ، وَشَرِّ ما بَعْدَها، رَبِّ أَعوذُ بِكَ مِنَ الكَسَلِ، وسُوءِ الكِبَرِ، رَبِّ

refuge in You from torment in the Fire, and from torment in the grave." And when he entered upon the morning he used also to say: "We have come upon the morning and dominion has come to Allah."[1]

(Related by Muslim)

17) ᶜAbdullah ibn Khubayb said: We went out on a night of rain and great darkness to ask the Prophet (may the blessings and peace of Allah be upon him) to pray for us. We arrived where he was and he said: "Speak." I did not say anything. Then he said: "Speak." I said: O Messenger of Allah, what should I say? He said: "Say: He is Allah the One"[2] and "the two Muᶜawwidhahs—the two cries for refuge and protection"[3] when you enter upon the evening and when you enter upon the morning—three times—and that will suffice you (as protection) from everything."

(Related by Abū Dāwūd, an-Nasā'ī and at-Tirmidhī)

---

1. The rest of the prayer continues as above but with the relevant changes.
2. I.e., the Chapter of the Unity (112).
3. I.e., the Chapter of the Daybreak (113) and the Chapter of Mankind (114).

أَعوذُ بِكَ مِنْ عَذابٍ في النَّارِ، وَعَذابٍ في القَبْـرِ». وإذا أَصْبـحَ قَـالَ ذٰلِـكَ أَيْضـاً[1]: «أَصْبَحْنا وأَصْبَحَ المُلْكُ لِلَّهِ».

مسلم

١٧ ـ وَقَالَ عَبْدُ اللهِ بْنُ خُبَيْبٍ: خَرجْنا في لَيْلَةِ مَطَرٍ، وظُلْمةٍ شَدِيدَةٍ، نَطلُبُ النبيَّ ﷺ لِيُصَلِّيَ لنا، فأَدْرَكْناهُ، فقالَ: «قُلْ»، فَلَمْ أَقُلْ شَيْئاً، ثُمَّ قالَ: «قُلْ»، فَلَمْ أَقُلْ شَيْئاً، قالَ: «قُلْ» قُلْتُ: يا رسولَ اللهِ ما أَقولُ؟ قالَ: «قُلْ هُوَ اللهُ أَحَدٌ»، والمُعَوِّذَتَيْنِ[2]، حينَ تُمْسي وَحِينَ تُصْبِحُ، ثَلاثَ مَرَّاتٍ، يَكْفيكَ مِنْ كُلِّ شَيْءٍ».

أبو داود والنَّسائي والترمذي

---

(١) أي كرر الدعاء المذكور، مع استبدل (أصبح) بـ (أمسى).

(٢) أي اقرأ سورة الإخلاص والسورتيْن المعوذتيّن بتمامها جميعاً.

18) The Prophet (may the blessings and peace of Allah be upon him) used to teach his Companions, saying:

"If one of you comes upon the morning, then let him say: O Allah, by You we have entered upon the morning, and by You we have entered upon the evening, and by You we live, and by You we die, and to You is the Resurrection. And if he comes upon the evening, let him say: O Allah, by You we have entered upon the evening, and by You we have entered upon the morning, and by You we live, and by You we die, and to You is the final destiny."

(Related by at-Tirmidhī)

19) On the authority of the Prophet (may the blessings and peace of Allah be upon him), who said: "The master prayer for forgiveness is: O Allah, You are my Lord, there is no god but You. You have created me and I am Your servant, and I am (keeping) my covenant to You and my promise to You as much as I am able. I take my refuge in You

١٨ ـ كانَ النبيُّ ﷺ يُعَلِّمُ أصحابَهُ، يقولُ:

«إذا أَصْبَحَ أحدُكُم فَلْيَقُلْ: اللَّهُمَّ بِكَ أَصْبَحْنا، وبِكَ أَمْسَيْنا، وبِكَ نَحْيَا، وبِكَ نَموتُ، وإِلَيْكَ النُّشُورُ(١). وإذا أَمْسَىٰ فَلْيَقُلْ: اللَّهُمَّ بِكَ أَمْسَيْنا، وبِكَ أَصْبَحْنا، وبكَ نَحْيا وَبِك نَموتُ، وإِلَيْكَ المَصيرُ(٢)».

التِّرْمذي

١٩ ـ عَنِ النبيِّ ﷺ قالَ: «سَيِّدُ الاسْتِغْفارِ: اللَّهُمَّ أَنْتَ ربِّي، لا إِلٰهَ إلاَّ أَنْتَ، خَلَقْتَني وأَنا عَبْدُكَ، وأَنا على عَهْدِكَ وَوَعْدِكَ

(١) النشور: بعث الموتى يوم القيامة.
(٢) المصير: نهاية الخَلق.

from the evil that I have done, I acknowledge to You Your favour to me. And I acknowledge my wrongdoing, so forgive me, for there is no one who forgives sins other than You. He who says that, when he enters upon the evening and then dies that night, enters heaven; and he who says it when he enters upon the morning and dies that day, enters heaven."

(Related by al-Bukhārī)

20) Abū Bakr aṣ-Ṣiddīq (may Allah be pleased with him) said: The Messenger of Allah (may the blessings and peace of Allah be upon him) said: "Say, if you have entered upon the morning or have entered upon the evening: O Allah, Knower of the invisible and the visible, Creator of the heavens and the earth, Lord of everything and its King, I bear witness that there is no god but You. I take refuge in You from the evil of myself, and from the evil of the

ما ٱسْتَطَعْتُ، أَعوذُ بِكَ مِنْ شَرِّ ما صَنَعْتُ، أَبُوءُ[١] لكَ بِنعْمَتِكَ عَلَيَّ، وأَبوءُ بِذَنْبي، فاغْفِرْ لي، فإِنَّهُ لا يَغْفِرُ الذُّنُوبَ إِلا أَنْتَ». مَنْ قالَها حِينَ يُمْسي فَماتَ مِنْ لَيْلَتِهِ، دَخَلَ الجَنَّةَ، ومَنْ قالَها حِينَ يُصبحُ فماتَ مِنْ يَوْمِه دَخَلَ الْجَنَّةَ».

البخاري

٢٠ ـ قال أَبو بَكْرٍ الصِّدِّيقُ رَضِيَ اللهُ عَنْهُ: قالَ رسولُ الله ﷺ: «قلْ: إِذا أَصْبَحْتَ وإِذا أَمْسَيْتَ، اللَّهُمَّ عالِمَ الغَيْبِ وَالشَّهادةِ، فـاطِـرَ السَّمٰـواتِ والأَرضِ، ربَّ كـلِّ شـيءٍ ومَلِيكَهُ، أَشْهَدُ أَن لاَّ إِلٰهَ إِلا أَنتَ أَعُوذُ بِكَ مِن

(١) أبوء: أُقِرُّ وأعترف.

devil and his idolatry."[1] And in one version (it says): "And I take refuge in You so that I may not commit against myself some evil, or bring it down upon a Muslim. Say it when you enter upon the morning, and when you enter upon the evening, and when you have taken to your place of sleep."

(Related by at-Tirmidhī)

21) The Messenger of Allah (may the blessings and peace of Allah be upon him) said: "There is no servant (of Allah) who says on the morning of each day, and on the evening of each night: In the name of Allah, with whose name nothing in the earth or in the sky brings harm, and He is the all-hearing, the all-knowing—three times—to whom any harm will come."

(Related by at-Tirmidhī)

---

1. I.e., his tempting mankind with idolatry.

شَرِّ نَفْسي، وَشَرِّ الشَّيْطانِ وشِرْكِهِ[1]، وفي رِوايةٍ: [وَأَنْ أَقْتَرِفَ على نَفْسي سُوءًا أو أَجُرَّهُ إلى مُسْلِمٍ] ـ قُلْهُ إذا أَصْبَحْتَ، وإذا أَمْسَيْتَ، وإذا أَخَذْتَ مَضْجَعَكَ».

التّرْمذي

٢١ ـ قال رسولُ اللهِ ﷺ: «مَا مِن عَبْدٍ يقولُ في صَباحِ كُلِّ يَوْمٍ، ومَساءِ كُلِّ لَيْلَةٍ: بِسْمِ اللهِ الَّذي لا يَضُرُّ مع اسْمِهِ شَيْءٌ في الأَرْضِ ولا في السَّماءِ، وهوَ السَّمِيعُ العَلِيمُ، ثلاثَ مَرَّاتٍ، لمْ يَضُرَّهُ شيءٌ».

التّرْمذي

---

(١) أي ما يدعو إليه من الإشراك بالله.

22) The Messenger of Allah (may the blessings and peace of Allah be upon him) said: "He who has said when he enters upon the evening: I am content with Allah as a Lord, with Islam as a religion, and with Muḥammad (may the blessings and peace of Allah be upon him) as a prophet, it is incumbent upon Allah that He should cause him to be content."

(Related by at-Tirmidhī)

23) The Prophet (may the blessings and peace of Allah be upon him) did not fail to say these prayers when entering upon the evening or entering upon the morning:

"O Allah, I ask of You well-being in this world and in the Hereafter. I ask of You forgiveness and well-being in my religion and in my worldly needs,

٢٢ ـ قال رَسُولُ الله ﷺ: «مَنْ قالَ حينَ يُمْسي: رَضِيتُ باللهِ ربّاً، وبالإسْلام ديناً، وبمُحمَّدٍ ﷺ نبِيّاً، كان حقاً على اللهِ أَن يُرْضِيَه».

التّرْمذي

٢٣ ـ لمْ يكُنِ النبيُّ ﷺ يَدَعُ هٰؤلاءِ الدَّعواتِ حينَ يُمْسي وحينَ يُصْبِحُ:

«اللَّهُمَّ إنِّي أَسْأَلُكَ العافِيةَ في الدُّنيا والآخِرةِ، اللَّهُمَّ أَسْأَلُكَ العَفْوَ والعافِيةَ في

and in my family and in my wealth. O Allah, conceal my shortcomings and protect me against frights. O Allah, guard me from in front and guard me from behind, and from my right side and from my left, and from above me, and I take refuge in Your sublimity lest I be taken unawares from below me."

(Related by Abū Dāwūd, an-Nasā'ī and Ibn Mājah)

دِيني ودُنْيايَ، وأَهْلي ومَالي، اللَّهم ٱسْتُرْ عَوْراتي[(١)]، وآمِن رَوْعاتي[(٢)]، اللهمَّ احْفَظْني مِنْ بَيـن يَـدَيَّ ومِـن خَلْفـي، وعَـن يَميـني وعَـنْ شِمالي، ومِن فَوْقي وأَعوذُ بِعَظَمَتِكَ أَنْ أُغْتالَ مِن تَحْتي[(٣)]».

أبو داود والنَّسائي وابن ماجة

---

(١) العَوْرات: جمع عَوْرة وهي الخلل والعيب والمعنى: استر عيوبي.

(٢) الروْعات: جمع رَوْعة وهي الفَزْعة والمعنى: آمني من الفزع والخوف.

(٣) يعني الخَسف.

4. What is to be said on going to sleep

24) The Messenger of Allah (may the blessings and peace of Allah be upon him), when he wanted to sleep, would say: "In Your name, O Allah, I die and I live." And when he awoke from his sleep he would say: "Thanks be to Allah who has brought us to life after having caused us to die, and to Him is the Resurrection."

(Related by al-Bukhārī and Muslim)

25) The Prophet (may the blessings and peace of Allah be upon him), on repairing to his bed each night, used to bring the palms of his hands together and blow on them. Then he would recite into them: "Say: He is Allah the One… and Say: I seek refuge in the Lord of the Daybreak… and Say: I seek refuge in the Lord of Mankind…"[1] He would then wipe as much as he could of his body with them,[2] starting with his head and face and (so down) the front of his body. He would do this three times.

(Related by al-Bukhārī and Muslim)

---

1. I.e., the recitation of the whole of the Chapters of the Unity (112), of the Daybreak (113) and of Mankind (114).
2. I.e., with the palms of his hands.

٤ ـ ما يقال عند المنام

٢٤ ـ كان رسولُ الله ﷺ إذا أراد أَنْ يَنامَ قال: «بِٱسْمِكَ اللَّهمّ أَمُوتُ وَأَحْيا» وإذا استَيقظ مِن مَنامِه، قال: «الحَمْدُ لله الَّذي أَحْيانا بَعْدَ ما أَماتَنا وإِلَيْهِ النُّشُورُ».

البخاري ومسلم

٢٥ ـ «كان النبيُّ ﷺ إذا أوىٰ إلى فِراشِه كلَّ لَيْلَةٍ، جَمَعَ كَفَّيْه ثمَّ نَفَثَ[1] فيهما فقرأَ فيهما (قُلْ هُوَ اللهُ أَحَدٌ)، و (قُلْ أَعُوذُ بربِّ الفَلَق)، و (قُلْ أَعُوذ بِرَبِّ النّاس)[2]، ثم يمسحُ بهما ما استطاعَ من جَسَدِهِ، يَبْدأُ بهما على رَأْسِهِ وَوَجْهِهِ، وما أَقبلَ منْ جَسَدِهِ، يَفْعَلُ ذلك ثلاثَ مَرّاتٍ».

البخاري ومسلم

(١) النَّفث: نَفْخ لطيف.

(٢) أي قرأ سور الإخلاص، والفَلَق، والناس بتمامها.

26) On the authority of the Prophet (may the blessings and peace of Allah be upon him), who said: "When you have repaired to your bed, then recite the Verse of the Throne[1]—Allah, there is no god but He, the Ever-living, the Sustainer, the Self-sustainer... until you complete it, and it will continue to be from Allah a protection for you and no devil will approach you until you enter upon the morning."

(Related by al-Bukhārī)

---

1. The Verse of the Throne 2:255 reads:
   Allah, there is no god but He, the Ever-living, the Sustainer, the Self-sustainer. Neither drowsiness nor sleep comes to Him. To Him belongs all that is in the heavens and all that is on the earth. Who is he who shall intercede with Him save by His permission? He knows what lies before them and what behind them and they comprehend none of His knowledge except that which He wishes. His throne encompasses the heavens and the earth, and He is not wearied by guarding them. He is the all-high, the all-exalted.

٢٦ ـ عن النبي ﷺ قال: إذا أَوَيْتَ إلى فِراشِكَ، فاقرأ آيةَ الكُرْسيِّ: ﴿اللهُ لا إِلَهَ إِلاَّ هُوَ الحَيُّ القَيُّومُ﴾ حتى تَخْتِمَها فإِنَّهُ لنْ يَزالَ عليْكَ مِنَ اللهِ حافظٌ، ولا يَقْرَبُكَ شيطانٌ حتى تُصْبِحَ».

البخاري

وآيَةُ الكُرْسِيْ هي قولُه تَعالىٰ: ﴿ٱللَّهُ لَآ إِلَـٰهَ إِلَّا هُوَ ٱلْحَيُّ ٱلْقَيُّومُ لَا تَأْخُذُهُۥ سِنَةٌ وَلَا نَوْمٌ لَّهُۥ مَا فِي ٱلسَّمَـٰوَٰتِ وَمَا فِي ٱلْأَرْضِ مَن ذَا ٱلَّذِي يَشْفَعُ عِندَهُۥٓ إِلَّا بِإِذْنِهِۦ يَعْلَمُ مَا بَيْنَ أَيْدِيهِمْ وَمَا خَلْفَهُمْ وَلَا يُحِيطُونَ بِشَيْءٍ مِّنْ عِلْمِهِۦٓ إِلَّا بِمَا شَآءَ وَسِعَ كُرْسِيُّهُ ٱلسَّمَـٰوَٰتِ وَٱلْأَرْضَ وَلَا يَـُٔودُهُۥ حِفْظُهُمَا وَهُوَ ٱلْعَلِيُّ ٱلْعَظِيمُ * لَآ إِكْرَاهَ فِي ٱلدِّينِ قَد تَّبَيَّنَ ٱلرُّشْدُ مِنَ ٱلْغَيِّ فَمَن يَكْفُرْ بِٱلطَّـٰغُوتِ وَيُؤْمِن بِٱللَّهِ فَقَدِ ٱسْتَمْسَكَ بِٱلْعُرْوَةِ ٱلْوُثْقَىٰ لَا ٱنفِصَامَ لَهَا وَٱللَّهُ سَمِيعٌ عَلِيمٌ﴾ [البقرة ٢: ٢٥٥].

27) On the authority of the Prophet (may the blessings and peace of Allah be upon him), who said: "He who recites the two verses from the end of the Chapter of the Cow[1] at night will find them sufficient for him."

(Related by al-Bukhārī andMuslim)

---

1. The Chapter of the Cow 2:285–286 reads:

285. The Messenger believes in that which has been revealed to him from his Lord and (so do) the believers. Each one believes in Allah and His angels and His scriptures and His messengers—we make no distinction between any of His messengers—and they say: We hear, and we obey. (Grant us) Your forgiveness, our Lord. Unto You is the journeying.

286. Allah tasks not a soul beyond its scope. For it (is only) that which it has earned, and against it (only) that which it has deserved. Our Lord! condemn us not if we forget or miss the mark! Our Lord! lay not on us such a burden as You laid on those before us! Our Lord! impose not on us that which we have not the strength to bear! Pardon us, absolve us, and have mercy on us, You, our Protector, and give us victory over the disbelieving folk.

٢٧ ـ عن النبيِّ ﷺ قال: «مَن قَرَأَ الآيَتَيْنِ مِن آخرِ سُورةِ (البَقَرةِ) في لَيْلَةٍ كَفَتاهُ».

البخاري ومسلم

والآيتان هما قوله تعالى: ﴿ءَامَنَ ٱلرَّسُولُ بِمَآ أُنزِلَ إِلَيْهِ مِن رَّبِّهِۦ وَٱلْمُؤْمِنُونَ كُلٌّ ءَامَنَ بِٱللَّهِ وَمَلَـٰٓئِكَتِهِۦ وَكُتُبِهِۦ وَرُسُلِهِۦ لَا نُفَرِّقُ بَيْنَ أَحَدٍ مِّن رُّسُلِهِۦ وَقَالُوا سَمِعْنَا وَأَطَعْنَا غُفْرَانَكَ رَبَّنَا وَإِلَيْكَ ٱلْمَصِيرُ * لَا يُكَلِّفُ ٱللَّهُ نَفْساً إِلَّا وُسْعَهَا لَهَا مَا كَسَبَتْ وَعَلَيْهَا مَا ٱكْتَسَبَتْ رَبَّنَا لَا تُؤَاخِذْنَا إِن نَّسِينَا أَوْ أَخْطَأْنَا رَبَّنَا وَلَا تَحْمِلْ عَلَيْنَا إِصْراً كَمَا حَمَلْتَهُ عَلَى ٱلَّذِينَ مِن قَبْلِنَا رَبَّنَا وَلَا تُحَمِّلْنَا مَا لَا طَاقَةَ لَنَا بِهِۦ وَٱعْفُ عَنَّا وَٱغْفِرْ لَنَا وَٱرْحَمْنَا أَنتَ مَوْلَـٰنَا فَٱنصُرْنَا عَلَى ٱلْقَوْمِ ٱلْكَـٰفِرِينَ﴾ [البقرة: ٢٨٥ ـ ٢٨٦].

28) The Messenger of Allah (may the blessings and peace of Allah be upon him) said: “If one of you goes to his place of sleep, let him say: In Your name, O Lord, have I laid myself down on my side and by You shall I raise myself up. If You take hold of my soul, then have mercy on it; and if You let it go, then guard it with that which You guard Your pious servants. And if one of you wakes, then let him say: Thanks be to Allah who has protected me in my body and returned to me my soul and permitted me to remember Him.”

(Related by at-Tirmidhī)

٢٨ ـ قـــال رســـولُ اللهِ ﷺ: «وإذا اضْطَجَعَ أَحدُكُمْ فَلْيَقُلْ: باسْمِكَ ربِّي وَضَعْتُ جَنْبـي وَبِـكَ أَرْفَعُـهُ، فـإِنْ أَمْسَكْـتَ نفسـي فارْحَمْها، وإن أَرسَلْتَها فاحْفَظْها بِمَا تَحْفَظُ به عِبادَكَ الصَّالِحينَ». «فإذا اسْتيقظ أَحَدُكم فلْيَقُلْ: الحَمْدُ لِلَّهِ الَّذي عافاني في جَسَدي وَرَدَّ عَلَيَّ رُوحي، وأَذِنَ لي بِذِكْرِهِ».

الترمذي

29) He (may the blessings and peace of Allah be upon him) said to ᶜAlī and Fāṭimah: "If you have repaired to your bed, then say subḥāna 'llāh (How far is Allah from any imperfection!)—thirty-three times—and al-ḥamdu lillāh (Praise be to Allah)—thirty-three times—and Allāhu akbar (Allah is greatest)—thirty-four times."

(Related by al-Bukhārī and Muslim)

30) The Prophet (may the blessings and peace of Allah be upon him), when wanting to go to sleep, would place his right hand under his cheek and then say: "O Allah, protect me from Your punishment on the day You resurrect Your servants"—three times.

(Related by Abū Dāwūd and at-Tirmidhī)

٢٩ ـ قال ﷺ لعليٍّ وفاطمة: «إذا أَوَيْتُما إلى فِراشِكُما، فسَبِّحا ثَلاثاً وَثَلاثِين، واحْمَدا ثلاثاً وثلاثينَ، وكَبِّرا أَرْبَعاً وثلاثينَ».

البخاري ومسلم

٣٠ ـ كان النبيُّ ﷺ إذا أَرادَ أَن يَرْقُدَ وَضَعَ يَدَهُ اليُمْنى تَحتَ خدِّهِ ثم يقولُ: «اللَّهُمَّ قِني عَذابَكَ يَوْمَ تَبْعثُ عِبادَكَ» ـ ثلاثَ مَرّاتٍ.

أبو داود والترمذي

31) The Prophet (may the blessings and peace of Allah be upon him), on repairing to his bed, used to say: "Thanks be to Allah who has given us to eat and to drink and who has met all our requirements and who has sheltered us. And how many are there who have no one to provide for them and give them shelter!"

(Related by Muslim)

32) He (may the blessings and peace of Allah be upon him) ordered a man on going to his place of sleep to say: "O Allah, You have created my soul, and You will take it to Yourself. You possess its death and its life. If You make it live, then guard it; and if You make it die, then forgive it. O Allah, I ask of You well-being."

(Related by Muslim)

٣١ ـ كان النبيُّ ﷺ إذا أوىٰ إلى فِراشِهِ قال: «الحَمْدُ للهِ الَّذي أَطْعَمَنا وَسَقَانا، وكفانا، وآوانا، فَكَمْ مِمَّن لا كافيَ لَهُ ولا مُؤْوِيَ».

مسلم

٣٢ ـ أَمَرَ ﷺ رجلاً إذا أَخَذَ مَضْجَعَهُ أَنْ يقولَ: «اللَّهُمَّ أَنْتَ خَلَقْتَ نفْسِيَ، وأَنت تَوَفَّاها[١]، لَكَ مَماتُها وَمَحْياها، إِنْ أَحْيَيْتَها فاحْفَظْها، وإِنْ أَمَتَّها فاغْفِرْ لَها، اللهُمَّ إِني أَسأَلُكَ العافِيَةَ».

مسلم

---

(١) تتوفَّاها: تقبضها بالوفاة.

33) He (may the blessings and peace of Allah be upon him) used to say when he had repaired to his bed: "O Allah, Lord of the heavens and Lord of the earth, and Lord of the Great Throne, O our Lord and Lord of everything, the Cleaver of the dry grain and of the date-stone, and He who has sent down the Torah, the Gospel, and the Qur'ān,[1] I take refuge in You from the evil of anyone capable of evil. It is You who are in control of him.[2] O Allah, You are the First, there being nothing before You, and You are the Last, there being nothing after You. And You are the Outward, there being nothing above You, and You are the Inward, there being nothing below You. Discharge debts for us and free us from poverty."

(Related by Muslim)

---

1. The Arabic word here used is "Furqān" which literally means "that which distinguishes right from wrong." It is one of the terms used for the Qur'ān.
2. Lit. have him by the forelock.

٣٣ ـ كان ﷺ يقولُ إذا أوىٰ إلى فِراشِهِ:
«اللَّهُمَّ ربَّ السَّمٰواتِ، وَرَبَّ الأَرضِ، وَرَبَّ العَرْشِ العَظِيمِ، ربَّنا وَرَبَّ كُلِّ شَيْءٍ، فالِقَ الحَبِّ والنَّوىٰ، ومُنَزِّلَ التَّوْرَاةِ والإِنجيلِ والفُرْقانِ، أَعوذُ بِكَ من شَرِّ كُلِّ ذي شَرٍّ أَنْتَ آخِذٌ بناصِيَتِهِ[1]، اللَّهمَّ أَنتَ الأَوَّلُ فلَيْسَ قَبْلَكَ شَيْءٌ، وأَنتَ الآخِرُ فلَيسَ بَعْدَكَ شيءٌ، وأَنتَ الظاهِرُ فليس فوْقَكَ شَيْءٌ، وأَنْتَ الباطِنُ فليسَ دُونكَ شيْءٌ، اقْضِ عَنَّا الدَّيْنَ، وَأَغْنِنا مِنَ الفَقْرِ».

مسلم

(١) الناصية: مقدم الرأس والمعنى مسيطر عليه ومالكٌ أمره.

34) The Messenger of Allah (may the blessings and peace of Allah be upon him) said: "If you have come to your bed, make your ablutions for prayer then lie down on your right side and say: O Allah, I have delivered myself to You, and have directed my face to You, and have entrusted myself to You, and have supported myself against You in both desire and awe of You. There is no refuge and no haven from You except to You. I believe in Your book which You have revealed and in Your Prophet whom You have sent. —If you die that very night, you will have died in professing the natural and true faith—and make them the last words you say."

(Related by al-Bukhārī and Muslim)

٣٤ ـ قال رسولُ الله ﷺ: «إذا أتيْتَ مَضْجَعَكَ فَتَوَضَّأْ وُضُوءَكَ لِلصَّلاةِ، ثمَّ اضْطَجِعْ على شِقِّكَ الأيْمَنِ، وقُلْ: اللهُمَّ أَسْلَمْتُ نفسي إليْكَ، وَوَجَّهتُ وَجهي إلَيْكَ، وفوَّضْتُ أَمْري إليْكَ، وألْجأْتُ ظَهْري إليْكَ، رَغْبةً وَرَهْبَةً إليْك، لا مَلْجَأَ ولا مَنْجَىٰ منك إلا إلَيْك، آمَنْتُ بكتابِكَ الذي أَنْزَلْتَ، وبنبيِّكَ الَّذي أَرْسَلْتَ؛ فإنْ مُتَّ من لَيْلَتِكَ مُتَّ على الفِطْرةِ، واجْعَلْهُنَّ آخِرَ ما تقُولُ».

البخاري ومسلم

5. What is to be said by the person awakening from sleep at night

35) On the authority of the Prophet (may the blessings and peace of Allah be upon him), who said: "He who wakes up at night and says: There is no god but Allah alone, He having no associate, to Him is dominion, and to Him is praise, and He is able to do everything. Praise be to Allah and How far is He from every imperfection! There is no god but Allah and Allah is greatest. There is no strength or power save through Allah the Supreme, the Mighty. If after this he says: Allah, forgive me, or he asks (for something), it will be granted him. And if he has made his ablutions and has performed his prayer, his prayer will be accepted."

(Related by al-Bukhārī)

٥ ـ ما يقولُهُ المُسْتيقِظُ من نَوْمِهِ ليلاً

٣٥ ـ عن النبيِّ ﷺ قال: «مَنْ تَعارَّ[1] من اللَّيل فقال: لا إِلٰهَ إلا اللهُ وحدَهُ لا شَرِيكَ له، لهُ المُلْكُ، ولهُ الحَمْدُ، وهُوَ على كُلِّ شَيءٍ قَديرٌ، الحمْدُ للهِ، وسُبْحانَ اللهِ، ولا إِلٰهَ إلا اللهُ، واللهُ أكبرُ، ولا حَوْلَ ولا قُوَّةَ إلا باللهِ العليِّ العَظيمِ، ثُمَّ قال: اللَّهُمَّ اغْفِرْ لي، أَوْ دَعَا، اسْتُجيبَ لهُ، فإِنْ توضَّأَ وصلَّى قُبِلَتْ صَلاتُهُ».

البخاري

(١) تعارّ: استيقظ.

36) The Messenger of Allah (may the blessings and peace of Allah be upon him) said: “No one betakes himself to his bed clean and pure[1] and remembers Allah Almighty until sleep comes upon him, and he does not wake up for an instant in the night and asks Allah for something of the good of this world and the Hereafter without Allah granting him it.”

(Related by at-Tirmidhī)

37) On the authority of the Prophet (may the blessings and peace of Allah be upon him) who said: “When one of you wakes up, let him say: Thanks be to Allah who has returned to me my soul and has protected me in my body and has permitted me to remember Him.”

(Related by Ibn as-Sunnī)

1. I.e., in a state of ablution.

٣٦ ـ قال رسولُ اللهِ ﷺ: «مَنْ أوىٰ إلى فِراشِهِ طاهِراً، وذكَرَ اللهَ تعالى حتى يُدْرِكَهُ النُّعاسُ، لم يَنْقَلِبْ(١) ساعةً مِنَ اللَّيْلِ يَسْأَلُ اللهَ شيئاً من خَيْرِ الدُّنْيا والآخِرَةِ إلا أَعطاهُ اللهُ إيّاهُ».

الترمذي

٣٧ ـ عَنِ النَّبي ﷺ قال: «إذا اسْتَيْقظَ أَحَدُكُمْ فَلْيَقُلْ: الحَمْدُ للهِ الَّذي رَدَّ عليَّ رُوحي، وعافاني(٢) في جَسَدي، وأَذِنَ لي بِذِكْرِهِ».

ابن السُّنّي

---

(١) ينقلب: تتغير حاله من النوم إلى اليقظة.
(٢) أي جعلني صحيح الجسد سليماً من الأمراض.

38) The Messenger of Allah (may the blessings and peace of Allah be upon him) used to teach them[1] words (to be used) against fright: "I take refuge in the consummate words of Allah from His anger and from the evil of His servants, and from the temptations whispered by devils and from their presence."[2]

(Related by Abū Dāwūd and at-Tirmidhī)

---

1. I.e., his Companions.
2. See the Chapter of the Believers 23:97–98.

٣٨ ـ كـان رسـولُ اللهِ ﷺ يُعَلِّمُهُـمْ مِـنَ الْفَـزَعِ كلمـاتٍ: «أَعُـوذُ[١] بكلمـاتِ اللهِ التَّـامَّـةِ[٢]، مِـنْ غَضَبِـهِ وشَـرِّ عِبـادِهِ، ومِـنْ هَمَزاتِ[٣] الشَّياطينِ وأَنْ يَحْضُرونِ».

أبو داود والترمذي

---

(١) أعوذ بكلمات الله: أعتصم بها.

(٢) التامة: المتصفة بالكمال المنزهة عن النقص.

(٣) هَمَزات الشياطين: وسوستهم للإنسان بارتكاب المعاصي. وحضورهم إيذان بالوسوسة والدعاء تضمين لقوله تعالى: ﴿وقل ربِّ أعوذُ بك من همزات الشياطين وأعـوذ بـك ربِّ أن يَحْضُـرُونِ﴾ [المؤمنون ٢٣: ٩٧ ـ ٩٨].

6. What one should do on seeing something in a dream

39) Abū Salamah ibn ᶜAbdurraḥmān said: I heard Abū Qatādah ibn Ribᶜī say: I heard the Messenger of Allah say: "(Good) dreams are from Allah and (bad) dreams are from the devil. If one of you has seen (in a dream) something he dislikes, let him blow to his left three times when he awakes, and let him seek the protection of Allah from its evil, and it will bring him no harm, Allah willing."

Abū Salamah said: I used to have dreams (and regard them as) heavier upon me than a mountain, but when I heard this Hadith I paid them no attention. And in (another) version he said: I used to have dreams that would disquiet me until I heard Abū Qatādah say: I used to have dreams which

٦ ـ ما يَصْنعُ مَنْ رأىٰ رُؤيا

٣٩ ـ قال أَبو سَلَمَةَ بْنُ عبدِ الرَّحمٰنِ: سمعتُ أَبا قَتادَةَ بْنَ رِبْعِيٍّ يَقولُ: سمعتُ رسولَ اللهِ ﷺ يقولُ: «الرُّؤْيا مِنَ اللهِ والحُلْمُ مِنَ الشَّيْطانِ، فإذا رأىٰ أَحَدُكُمْ شيئاً يكرَهُهُ فلْيَنْفُثْ[١] عَنْ يَسارِهِ ثلاثَ مَرَّات إذا اسْتَيْقَظَ، وَلْيَتَعَوَّذْ باللهِ مِنْ شرِّها، فإنها لن تَضُرَّهُ إنْ شاءَ اللهُ».

قال أَبو سَلَمَةَ: إنْ كُنْتُ لأَرىٰ الرؤْيا هِيَ أَثقَلُ عليَّ من الجَبَلِ، فلمَّا سمعْتُ بهذا الْحَديثِ، فما كنت أُبالِيها، وفي رواية: «قال: إن كنْتُ أَرىٰ الرُّؤْيا تُهِمُّني، حتَّى سمعْتُ أَبا قَتادَةَ يقولُ: وأَنا كنتُ لأَرى الرُّؤْيا فتُمْرِضُني حتى سَمِعْتُ رسولَ اللهِ ﷺ يقولُ: الرُّؤْيا الصَّالِحَةُ مِنَ اللهِ، فإذا رأَىٰ أَحدُكمْ ما

---

(١) النفث: نفخ لطيف.

would make me ill until I heard the Messenger of Allah (may the blessings and peace of Allah be upon him) say: "Good dreams are from Allah, so if one of you sees something (in a dream) that he likes, let him not talk of it other than to those he likes; and if he sees something (in a dream) that he dislikes, let him not talk of it at all."

(Related by al-Bukhārī and Muslim)

40) And in a version on the authority of Jābir, the Messenger of Allah (may the blessings and peace of Allah be upon him) added: "And let him change over from the side on which he was."

(Related by Muslim)

يُحِبُّ، فلا يُحَدِّثْ بِهِ إلا مَنْ يُحِبُّ، وإِنْ رأَى ما يَكْرَهُ، فلا يُحدِّثْ بِهِ ، وليتعوَّذْ باللهِ مِنَ الشَّيْطانِ الرَّجيمِ مِنْ شرِّ ما رأَىٰ فإِنَّها لَنْ تَضُرَّهُ».

البخاري ومسلم

٤٠ ـ وفي رواية جابر عن رسول الله ﷺ، أضاف: «وَلْيَسْتَعِذْ بالله مِنَ الشَّيْطانِ ثلاثاً، وَلْيَتَحَوَّلْ عن جَنْبِهِ الَّذي كانَ عَلَيهِ».

مسلم

7. The merit of acts of devotion at night

Allah the Almighty has said: "O you wrapped in your raiment, keep vigil the night long, save a little—a half thereof, or abate a little thereof or add (a little) thereto—and recite the Qur'ān (in slow measured tones), for we shall charge you with a word of weight. Verily the vigil of the night is (a time) when impression is more keen and speech more certain."[1] And the Almighty has said: "And keep awake some part of the night for additional devotions, so that your Lord may raise you to a glorious state."[2] And the Almighty has said: "And prostrate yourself to Him (a portion of) the night, and glorify Him throughout the lifelong night."[3]

1. The Chapter of the Wrapped-up 73:1–5.
2. The Chapter of the Children of Israel 17:79.
3. The Chapter of Time 76:26.

٧ ـ فضل العبادة بالليل

قال الله تعالى: ﴿يَا أَيُّها المُزَّمِّلُ[(١)] قُم اللَّيْلَ إِلاَّ قَلِيلاً﴾ إلى قوله: ﴿إِنَّ نَاشِئَةَ اللَّيْلِ[(٢)] هِـيَ أَشَـدُّ وَطْـأً[(٣)] وَأَقْـوَمُ قِيـلاً[(٤)]﴾ [المزمل: ٧٣ ١ ـ ٥] وقال تعالى: ﴿وَمِنَ اللَّيْلِ فَتهَجَّدْ[(٥)] بِهِ نَافِلَةً[(٦)] لَكَ عَسىٰ أَنْ يَبْعَثكَ رَبُّكَ مَقاماً مَحْمُوداً﴾ [الإِسراءُ ١٧: ٧٩]، ﴿وَمِنَ اللَّيْلِ فَاسْجُدْ لَهُ وَسَبِّحْهُ لَيْلاً طَوِيلاً﴾ [الدهر ٧٦: ٢٦].

---

(١) المزَّمِّل: المتلفف في ثياب نومه.

(٢) ناشئة الليل: العبادة التي تحدث في الليل.

(٣) اشد وطأ: أي أشد وقعاً على النفس وأرسخ أثراً.

(٤) أقومُ قيلاً: أوضح قولاً لصفاء الفكر واكتمال الهدوء.

(٥) التهجد: صلاة الليل.

(٦) نافلة: أي عبادة زائدة على الفرائض.

41) On the authority of the Prophet (may the blessings and peace of Allah be upon him), who said: "Our Lord descends each night to the lowest sky when there remains the final third of the night, and He says: Who is saying a prayer to Me that I may answer it? Who is asking something of me that I may give it him? Who is asking forgiveness of Me that I may forgive him?"

(Related by al-Bukhārī and Muslim)

42) The Prophet (may the blessings and peace of Allah be upon him) said: "The Lord is at His most near to the servant in the middle of the final part of the night. If you are able to be among those who are remembering Allah at that hour, then be so."

(Related by at-Tirmidhī)

٤١ ـ عن النبي ﷺ قال: «يَنْزِلُ ربُّنا كُلَّ لَيْلَةٍ إلى السَّماءِ الدُّنْيا حينَ يَبْقَىٰ ثُلُثُ اللَّيْلِ الآخِرِ، فيقول: مَنْ يَدْعوني فَأَسْتَجيبَ لهُ، ومَنْ يَسْأَلُني فأُعْطيَهُ، ومَن يَسْتَغْفِرُني فأَغْفِرَ لَهُ».

البخاري ومسلم

٤٢ ـ قال النبيُّ ﷺ: «أَقْرَبُ ما يَكونُ الرَّبُّ مِنَ الْعَبْدِ في جَوْفِ اللَّيلِ الآخِرِ، فإنِ اسْتَطَعْتَ أَن تكونَ ممَّن يَذْكُرُ اللهَ في تلكَ السَّاعَةِ فكُنْ».

الترمذي

43) The Prophet (may the blessings and peace of Allah be upon him) said: "Verily in the night there is a period of time which no Muslim man happens upon and wherein he asks Allah (Exalted be He!) for something good from the things of this world and the Hereafter, without his being given it—and this is so every night."

(Related by Muslim)

44) The Messenger of Allah (may the blessings and peace of Allah be upon him) said: "He who says on leaving his house: Bismillāh (in the name of Allah), I have put my trust in Allah, there is no strength or power save in Allah, it is said to him: All

٤٣ ـ قــال النبــيُّ ﷺ: «إنَّ فــي اللَّيــلِ لَساعةً لا يُوافِقُها رَجُلٌ مُسْلِمٌ يسأَلُ اللهَ عَزَّ وَجَلَّ خيْراً مِن أَمْرِ الدُّنيا والآخِرَةِ إلا أَعْطاهُ إِيَّاهُ، وذٰلك كُلَّ لَيْلَةٍ».

مسلم

٤٤ ـ قال رسولُ الله ﷺ: «مَنْ قالَ ـ إذا خَرَجَ مِنْ بيتِهِ ـ: «بِسْمِ اللهِ، تَوَكَّلْتُ على اللهِ، لا حَوْلَ ولا قُوَّةَ إلّا باللهِ تعالى، يُقالُ لهُ:

requirements have been met for you, you have been protected, and you have been guided; also the devil turns away from him and says to another devil: What can you do with a man who has been guided, whose requirements have been met, and who has been protected?"

(Related by Abū Dāwūd, an-Nasā'ī and at-Tirmidhī)

45) Umm Salamah (may Allah be pleased with her) said: The Messenger of Allah (may the blessings and peace of Allah be upon him) never left my house without glancing up at the sky and saying: "O Allah, I take refuge in You lest I go astray, or I am caused to go astray, or I commit a slip, or I am caused to commit a slip, or I oppress or I am oppressed, or I behave foolishly or am behaved foolishly against."

(Related by Abū Dāwūd, at-Tirmidhī, an-Nasā'ī and Ibn Mājah)

كُفِيتَ، وَوُقِيتَ، وهُدِيتَ، وتنحَّى عنه الشيطانُ، فيقُولُ لِشَيْطانٍ آخر: كيْفَ لكَ برجُلٍ قَد هُدِيَ وكُفِيَ ووُقِيَ؟

أبو داود والنّسائي والترمذي

٤٥ ـ وقالت أُمُّ سَلَمَةَ رَضِيَ اللهُ عنها: ما خَرَجَ رَسُولُ اللهِ ﷺ مِنْ بيتي قَطُّ إلا رَفَعَ طَرْفَهُ إلى السَّماءِ فقال: «اللَّهُمَّ إني أَعُوذُ بك أَن أَضِلَّ أَو أُضَلَّ أَو أَزِلَّ أَوْ أُزَلَّ، أَو أَظْلِمَ أَو أُظْلَمَ، أَوْ أَجْهَلَ أَو يُجْهَلَ[1] عليَّ».

أبو داود والترمذي والنّسائي وابن ماجة

---

(١) جهِل الرجل على غيره: تسافه.

8. On entering one's home

46) The Prophet (may the blessings and peace of Allah be upon him) said: "When a man enters his house and has remembered Allah Almighty on entering, and on partaking of food, the devil says: There is no shelter for the night for you[1] and no supper. And if he has entered without remembering Allah Almighty on entering, he says: You[1] have attained shelter for the night. And if he has not remembered Allah Almighty on partaking of food, he says: You[1] have attained shelter for the night and supper."[2]

(Related by Muslim)

1. He is addressing devils in general.
2. The meaning is that he who remembers Allah on entering his house and on partaking of food protects himself against the devil, but he who does not do so allows the devil access to himself.

٨ ـ في دخول المنزل

٤٦ ـ قال النَّبيُّ ﷺ: «إذا دخلَ الرجلُ بَيْتَهُ، فذَكَرَ اللهَ تعالىٰ عِندَ دُخولِهِ، وعندَ طَعامِه، قال الشَّيطانُ: لا مَبيتَ لَكُمْ ولا عَشاءَ[١]، وإذا دخلَ فلمْ يذْكُرِ اللهَ تَعالى عِندَ دُخولِهِ، قال الشيطانُ: أدركْتُمُ المَبِيتَ. وإذا لم يَذْكُرِ اللهَ تعالىٰ عندَ طَعامِه قال: أَدركْتُمُ المَبيتَ والعَشاءَ».

مسلم

(١) معناه أن الذي يذكر الله محفوظ من الشيطان ووسوسته عند مبيته وعشائه، والذي لا يذكر الله يتيح للشيطان أن ينفذ إليه.

47) The Messenger of Allah (may the blessings and peace of Allah be upon him) said: "When a man enters his house, let him say: O Allah, I ask of You the best entrance and the best exit. In the name of Allah we have entered, and in the name of Allah we have gone out, and on Allah our Lord we have depended. After that he should greet his family."

(Related by Abū Dāwūd)

48) Anas (may Allah be pleased with him) said: The Messenger of Allah (may the blessings and peace of Allah be upon him) said to me: "O my son, when you enter upon your family, give greetings—it shall be a blessing on you and on the family of your house."

(Related by at-Tirmidhī)

٤٧ ـ قال رسولُ الله ﷺ: «إذا وَلَجَ الرَّجلُ بيتهُ فليقُلْ: اللَّهُمَّ إني أَسْأَلُكَ خَيْرَ الْمَوْلَجِ[١]، وخيرَ الْمَخْرَجِ بسمِ الله وَلَجْنا، بسمِ اللهِ خَرَجْنَا، وعلى اللهِ ربِّنا تَوَكَّلْنا. ثم لِيُسَلِّمْ على أَهلِهِ».

أبو داود

٤٨ ـ قال الحسنُ رضِيَ اللهُ عنه: قال لي رسولُ الله ﷺ: «يا بُنيَّ إذا دَخلْتَ على أَهلِكَ فَسَلِّمْ يَكُنْ بَرَكَةً عليْكَ وعلى أَهلِ بيتِكَ».

التِّرْمذي

---

(١) المولَج: المدْخل.

9. On entering and leaving the mosque

49) The Messenger of Allah (may the blessings and peace of Allah be upon him), when entering and leaving the mosque would say: "Bismillāh (in the name of Allah), O Allah, bless Muḥammad, and when he left he used to say: Bismillāh (in the name of Allah), O Allah, bless Muḥammad."

(Related by Ibn as-Sunnī and at-Tirmidhī)

50) The Messenger of Allah (may the blessings and peace of Allah be upon him) said: "When one of you enters the mosque, let him say greetings on the Prophet[1] and let him say: O Allah, open for me the doors of Your mercy, and when he leaves let him say: O Allah, I ask for Your favour." And in one version he added the saying of greetings on the Prophet when leaving.

(Related by Muslim)

---

1. I.e., by saying: "Allāhumma ṣallī wa sallim ᶜala Muḥammad."

٩ ـ في دخولِ المسجدِ والخروجِ منه

٤٩ ـ كان رسول الله ﷺ إذا دخلَ المسجِدَ قال: «بسمِ اللهِ، اللَّهُمَّ صَلِّ على محمدٍ وإذا خرجَ، قال: بسم الله، اللهمَّ صلِّ على محمدٍ».

ابن السُّني والترمذي

٥٠ ـ قال رسول الله ﷺ: «إذا دخلَ أَحَدُكُمْ الْمَسْجِدَ فَلْيُسَلِّمْ على النبيِّ[١] ﷺ، ولْيَقُلْ: اللَّهُمَّ افْتَحْ لي أَبوابَ رَحْمَتِكَ، وإذا خرجَ فليَقُلْ: اللَّهُمَّ إني أَسْأَلُكَ منْ فَضْلِكَ».

وزاد في رواية: التسليمَ عند الخروج.

مسلم

(١) أي بقوله: اللهم صَلِّ وسلِّمْ على محمد.

51) The Prophet (may the blessings and peace of Allah be upon him), when entering the mosque would say: "I take refuge in Allah the Mighty, and in His noble face, and in His ancient authority, from the accursed devil. He said: If he says that, the devil says: He is protected from me for the rest of the day."

(Related by Abū Dāwūd)

٥١ ـ كانَ النبيُّ ﷺ إذا دخلَ المسجدَ قال: «أعوذُ باللهِ العظيمِ، وبِوَجهِهِ الكَريمِ وبِسُلْطانِهِ القَديمِ مِنَ الشَّيطانِ الرَّجيمِ». قال: «فإذا قال ذلك، قال الشَّيطانُ: حُفِظَ منِّي سائرَ اليَوْمِ».

أبو داود

10. The call to prayer and he who hears it

52) The Messenger of Allah (may the blessings and peace of Allah be upon him) said: "Were people to know what (merit) there is in giving the call to prayer and in (being in) the first rank (in communal prayers), and then found no way (to achieve this) other than by drawing lots, they would do so."

(Related by al-Bukhārī and Muslim)

53) The Messenger of Allah (may the blessings and peace of Allah be upon him) said: "Neither djinn nor man hears the reach of the voice of the muezzin without acknowledging him on the Day of Resurrection."

(Related by al-Bukhārī)

54) The Messenger of Allah (may the blessings and peace of Allah be upon him) said: "If you hear the call to prayer, say as the muezzin is saying."

(Related by al-Bukhārī and Muslim)

١٠ ـ الأَذانُ ومَنْ يسمعُه

٥٢ ـ قال رسولُ الله ﷺ: «لَوْ يَعْلَمُ النَّاسُ ما في النِّداءِ والصَّفِّ الأَوَّلِ، ثُم لم يَجِدوا إلا أَن يَسْتَهِمُوا[1] عليهِ لَاسْتَهَمُوا[1]».

البخاري ومسلم

٥٣ ـ قال رسولُ اللهِ ﷺ: «لا يسمعُ مَدىٰ صَوْتِ المؤَذِّنِ جِنٌّ ولا إِنْسٌ إلا شهِدَ له يومَ القيامةِ».

البخاري

٥٤ ـ قال رسولُ اللهِ ﷺ: «إذا سَمِعْتُمُ النِّداءَ فقُولوا مِثْلَ ما يقولُ المؤَذِّنُ».

البخاري ومسلم

---

(١) استهموا: اقترعوا فيما بينهم.

55) The Prophet (may the blessings and peace of Allah be upon him) said: "When you hear the muezzin, say the same as he is saying, then say blessings on me, for he who says a blessing on me, Allah shall say on him ten. Then ask of Allah that I be granted the *wasīlah*, for it is a rank in heaven which is given to one of the servants of Allah (who is truly devout), and I hope that I am he; and he who asks for me the *wasīlah*, intercession (by me for him) will be permitted."

(Related by Muslim)

56) The Messenger of Allah (may the blessings and peace of Allah be upon him) said: "When the muezzin says: Allah is greatest, Allah is greatest, and one of you says: Allah is greatest, Allah is greatest;

٥٥ ـ قال النبيُّ ﷺ: «إذا سَمِعتُمُ المؤَذِّنَ فقُولوا مِثْلَ ما يقولُ: ثمَّ صَلُّوا عَلَيَّ، فإنَّه من صَلَّى عَلَيَّ صلاةً صلَّى الله عليه بها عَشْراً، ثم سَلُوا اللهَ لِيَ الْوَسِيلةَ[١]، فإنَّها مَنْزِلةٌ في الجنَّةِ لا تَنبغي إلا لِعَبْدٍ[٢] مِن عبادِ اللهِ، وأَرْجُو أَن أكونَ أَنا هُوَ، فَمَنْ سأَلَ لِيَ الْوَسيلةَ حَلَّتْ له الشَّفاعَةُ».

مسلم

٥٦ ـ قال رسول الله ﷺ: «إذا قال المؤذِّن: اللهُ أَكبرُ اللهُ أَكبر، فقال أَحدُكُم: اَللهُ

(١) الوسيلة: بينها الحديث بأنها منزلة في الجنة. وأصلها من التوسُّل إلى الله أي التقرب إليه بوسيلة العمل الصالح لنوال هذه المنزلة والدرجة الرفيعة.

(٢) أي لعبد كامل العبودية لله.

then he says: I bear witness that there is no god but Allah, and one of you says: I bear witness that there is no god but Allah; then he says: I bear witness that Muḥammad is the Messenger of Allah, and one of you says: I bear witness that Muḥammad is the Messenger of Allah; then he says: Come to prayers, and one of you says: There is no strength or power save in Allah; then he says: Come to success, and one of you says: There is no strength or power save in Allah; then he says: Allah is greatest, Allah is greatest, and one of you says: Allah is greatest, Allah is greatest; then he says: There is no god but Allah, and one of you says from his heart: There is no god but Allah—then he will enter Heaven."

(Related by Muslim)

أَكبرُ الله أَكبر، ثمَّ قال: أَشهدُ أَن لا إِلٰهَ إِلا اللهُ، قال: أَشهدُ أَن لا إِلٰهَ إِلا اللهُ، ثم قال: أَشهدُ أَنَّ محمداً رسُولُ الله، قال: أَشهدُ أَنَّ محمداً رسُولُ الله، ثم قال: حيَّ على الصَّلاةِ، قال: لا حولَ ولا قُوَّةَ إِلا باللهِ، ثم قال: حيَّ على الْفَلاحِ، قال: لا حَوْلَ ولا قُوَّةَ إِلا باللهِ، ثم قال: اللهُ أَكْبَرُ اللهُ أَكبرُ، قال: اللهُ أَكبرُ اللهُ أَكبرُ، ثم قال: لا إِلٰه إِلا اللهُ، قال: لا إِلٰه إِلا اللهُ، مِنْ قَلْبِهِ، دَخلَ الجنةَ».

مسلم

57) The Messenger of Allah (may the blessings and peace of Allah be upon him) said: "He who, when he hears the call to prayer, says: O Allah, Lord of this consummate call and the present prayers, grant Muḥammad the wasīlah[1] and the faḍīlah,[2] and bring him to the glorious state that You have promised him,[3] intercession (by me for him) will be permitted on the Day of Resurrection."

(Related by al-Bukhārī)

58) And on the authority of ᶜAbdullah the son of ᶜUmar (may Allah be pleased with them both) that a man said: O Messenger of Allah, the muezzins surpass us (in merit). And the Messenger of Allah (may the blessings and peace of Allah be upon him) said: "Then say as they say and, when you have finished, ask (something) and you shall be given it."

(Related by Abū Dāwūd and Ibn Ḥibbān)

---

1. Wasīlah is a rank in heaven granted to the most devout of Allah's servants.
2. Faḍīlah is an enhanced state in heaven.
3. With reference of the Chapter of the Night Journey 17:79, which reads: "And pray in the small watches of the morning an additional prayer for you, so that your Lord may raise you to a glorious state."

٥٧ ـ قالَ رسولُ اللهِ ﷺ: «مَنْ قالَ حينَ يَسْمَعُ النِّداءَ: اللهُمَّ ربَّ هَـٰذِهِ الدَّعْوَةِ التَّامَّةِ، والصَّلاةِ القائمةِ، آتِ مُحمَّداً الوَسيلةَ والفَضِيلةَ[1]، وابْعَثْهُ مَقاماً مَحْمُوداً الَّذي وَعَدْتَهُ[2]، حَلَّتْ لَهُ شَفاعَتي يومَ القِيامةِ».

البخاري

٥٨ ـ وعن عبد الله بن عمر رضي الله عنهما، أَن رجلاً قال: يا رسولَ الله إنَّ الْمُؤَذِّنِينَ يَفْضُلونَنا، فقالَ رسولُ الله ﷺ: «قُلْ كما يَقُولونَ، فإذا انْتهيْتَ فَسَلْ[3] تُعْطَهْ».

أبو داود وابنُ حِبّان

---

(١) الفَضيلة: الدرجة الزائدة.

(٢) لقوله تعالى لنبيه ﷺ: ﴿عسى أن يبعثك ربُّك مقاماً محموداً﴾ [الإسراء ١٧: ٧٩].

(٣) ادع الله بعد الفراغ من ترديد الأذان بما تشاء من الدعاء، فسوف يُستجاب لك.

59) The Messenger of Allah (may the blessings and peace of Allah be upon him) said: "The invocation (which is made) between the call to prayers and the call indicating the start of prayers is not rejected." He said: What shall we say, O Messenger of Allah? He said: "Ask Allah for well-being in this world and in the Hereafter."

(Related by at-Tirmidhī)

60) And on the authority of Sahl ibn Sa[c]d (may Allah be pleased with him), who said: "The Messenger of Allah (may the blessings and peace of Allah be upon him) said: Two things are not rejected—or are seldom rejected: a supplication at (the time of) the call to prayer and at (the time) when people engage in close combat."

(Related by Abū Dāwūd)

٥٩ ـ قـــالَ رســـولُ اللهِ ﷺ: «لا يُــرَدُّ الدُّعاءُ بينَ الأَذانِ والإِقامةِ، قالوا: فماذا نَقولُ يا رسولَ اللهِ؟ قال: سَلوا اللهَ العافِيَةَ في الدُّنيا والآخِرَةِ».

الترْمذي

٦٠ ـ وعن سَهْلِ بنِ سَعْدٍ رضي اللهُ عنه قال: قال رسولُ اللهِ ﷺ «ثِنْتان لا تُرَدَّان ـ أَو قَلَّما تُرَدَّان ـ: الدُّعاءُ عندَ النِّداءِ[1]، وعندَ الْبَأْسِ[2] حين يُلْحِمُ بَعْضُهم بَعْضاً».

أبو داود

(١) النداء: الأذان.

(٢) والبأس لقاء العدو في حرب مشروعة.

11. At the commencement of prayers

61) The Messenger of Allah (may the blessings and peace of Allah be upon him) used to be silent for a short while when commencing the prayers. Abū Hurayrah said: O Messenger of Allah, by my father and my mother,[1] tell me about your silence between saying "Allah is greatest" and the recitation (of the prayers)? What do you say then? He said: I say: "O Allah, make a distance between me and my sins as You have made a distance between the east and the west. O Allah, cleanse me of my sins as the white robe is cleansed of staining. O Allah, wash me of my sins with snow, water and hail."

(Related by al-Bukhārī and Muslim)

1. Lit. "I would ransom my father and mother for you."

١١ - في استفتاح الصلاة

٦١ - كَانَ رسولُ اللهِ ﷺ إذا اسْتفتحَ الصَّلاةَ سَكَتَ هُنَيْهَةً قبلَ أَنْ يَقْرَأَ، فقال أبو هُرَيْرَةَ: يا رسولَ اللهِ بأَبي وأُمِّي أرأَيْتَ سُكوتَكَ بينَ التَّكبيرِ والقِراءَةِ، ما تقولُ؟ قال: أَقُولُ: «اللَّهُمَّ باعِدْ بَيْني وبينَ خَطَايايَ كما باعَدْتَ بينَ المَشْرِقِ والمَغْرِبِ، اللهُمَّ نَقِّني مِن خطايايَ كما يُنَقَّىٰ الثَّوْبُ الأَبيضُ مِنَ الدَّنَس، اللَّهُمَّ اغسِلْني مِن خَطايايَ بالثَّلْجِ والماءِ والبَرَدِ».

البخاري ومسلم

62) And on the authority of Jubayr ibn Muṭᶜim that he saw the Messenger of Allah (may the blessings and peace of Allah be upon him) performing a prayer. He said: "Allah is truly the greatest, and much praise be to Allah, and Allah is glorified at early morning and late afternoon"—three times. "I take my refuge in Allah from the accursed devil, from his pride, his exhalations of noxious poetry, and his ability to derange."

(Related by Abū Dāwūd)

63) And on the authority of ᶜĀ'ishah (may Allah be pleased with her) and of Abū Saᶜīd and others: That the Prophet, when starting the prayers, would say: "How far are You from every imperfection! and praise be to You, and may Your name be blessed and may Your sublimity be exalted, and there is no god but You."

(Related by Abū Dāwūd, at-Tirmidhī, an-Nasā'ī and Ibn Mājah)

٦٢ ـ وعن جُبَيْرِ بْنِ مُطْعِمٍ أَنَّهُ رأىٰ رسولَ اللهِ ﷺ يُصلِّي صلاةً قال: «اللهُ أَكْبَرُ كَبيراً، والحَمْدُ للهِ كثيراً، وسُبْحانَ اللهِ بُكْرَةً وأَصِيلاً، ثلاثاً، أعوذُ باللهِ مِنَ الشَّيطانِ الرَّجيمِ، مِنْ نَفْخِهِ وَنَفْثِهِ وَهَمْزِهِ»، نفخُهُ: الكِبْرُ. وَنَفْثُهُ: الشِّعْرُ(١)، وهَمْزُهُ: المُوتَةُ(٢).

أبو داود

٦٣ ـ وعن عائشةَ رضي الله عنها، وأَبي سَعِيدٍ وغيرِهِما: أَنَّ النبيَّ كان إذا افْتَتَحَ الصَّلاةَ قالَ: «سُبحانَكَ اللهُمَّ وبحَمْدِكَ، وتَبارَكَ اسْمُكَ، وتَعالى جَدُّكَ(٣)، ولا إِلٰهَ غَيْرُكَ».

أبو داود والترمذي والنَّسائي وابنُ ماجَه

---

(١) المقصود الشعر المذموم الذي لا تحكمه الضوابط الدينية.

(٢) المُوتَة: ما يصيب العقل ويُغَيِّبه كالجنون والصرع والغَشْية إلى أن يفيق ومثله السُّكر والنوم الثقيل.

(٣) الجَدُّ: المقام والمنزلة.

64) On the authority of ᶜUmar (may Allah be pleased with him) that he[1] said "Allāhu Akbar," then opened the prayers with it.[2]

(Related by Muslim)

65) The Messenger of Allah (may the blessings and peace of Allah be upon him), when he began his prayer would say: "I have directed my face, as a true believer and not one of the polytheists, to Him who has created the heavens and the earth. My prayers and my devotions, my life and my death, belong to Allah, Lord of the worlds; He has no associate, and thus have I been instructed, and I am one of the Muslims. O Allah, You are the Supreme Sovereign,

---

1. I.e., the Prophet.
2. I.e., with the invocation given in 63.

٦٤ ـ عن عُمَرَ رَضِيَ اللهُ عنه، أَنَّه كبَّرَ ثُمَّ اسْتَفْتَحَ به[(١)].

مسلم

٦٥ ـ كان رسولُ اللهِ ﷺ إذا قام إلى الصَّلاةِ قال: «وَجَّهْتُ وَجْهِيَ لِلَّذي فَطَرَ السَّمٰواتِ والأَرْضَ حَنِيفاً وَمَا أَنَا مِنَ المُشْرِكِينَ، إِنَّ صَلاتي ونُسُكي ومَحْيَايَ وَمَماتي للهِ رَبِّ العَالَمِينَ، لا شَرِيكَ لَهُ وَبِذٰلِكَ أُمِرْتُ وأَنَا مِنَ المُسْلِمِينَ، اللَّهُمَّ أَنْتَ المَلِكُ،

(١) أي بدعاء الاستفتاح الوارد في الحديث السابق.

there is no god but You. You are my Lord and I am Your servant. I have done wrong to myself, and I acknowledge my guilt, so forgive me all my sins; there is no one who forgives sins but You. Guide me to the best of morals, and no one guides to the best of them but You; and avert from me the worst of them, and no one averts the worst of them but You. Here I present myself to You and seek Your approval. All good is in Your hands. Evil is not Yours, and I am of You and to You. May You be blessed and glorified. I ask forgiveness of You and I turn to You in repentance."

(Related by Muslim)

لا إِلٰهَ إِلاَّ أَنْتَ، أَنْتَ رَبِّي وأَنا عَبْدُكَ، ظَلَمْتُ نَفْسي، واعْترفتُ بذنْبي، فاغفرْ لي ذُنوبي جَميعاً، إنَّه لا يَغْفِرُ الذُّنوبَ إلا أَنتَ، واهدِني لأَحْسَنِ الأَخلاقِ لا يَهْدي لأَحسَنِها إلا أَنْتَ، واصْرِفْ عَنِّي سيِّئَها لا يَصْرِفُ عنِّي سَيِّئَها إلا أَنْتَ، لبَّيْكَ وَسَعْدَيْك[1]، والخَيْرُ كُلُّهُ في يَدَيْك، والشرُّ ليس إليْك، أَنا بكَ وإليكَ، تَباركْتَ وتَعالَيْتَ، أَسْتَغْفِرُكَ وأَتوبُ إِلَيْك».

مسلم

---

(١) تلبيةً بعد تلبية وإسعاداً بعد إسعاد. والمعنى أنني أستجيب لك وأقدم من الطاعات ما يرضيك عني.

66) The Messenger of Allah (may the blessings and peace of Allah be upon him) would commence his prayers when he performed them at night (with the words): "O Allah, Lord of Gabriel and of Mikā'īl and of Isrāfīl, Creator of the heavens and the earth, Knower of the invisible and the visible. You judge between Your servants in that about which they differ. Guide me by Your permission to the truth about which people hold divergent views. Verily You guide whom You will to a straight path."

(Related by Muslim)

67) The Messenger of Allah (may the blessings and peace of Allah be upon him) would say when he rose to prayer in the middle of the night: "O Allah, praise be to You, You are the light of the heavens and of the earth and of those therein; and praise be to You; You are the Upholder of the heavens and the earth

٦٦ ـ كان رسولُ اللهِ ﷺ يفْتَتِحُ صلاتَهُ إذا قام من اللَّيلِ: «اللَّهُمَّ رَبَّ جِبْريلَ، وَمِيكائِيلَ، وإسْرافيلَ، فاطِرَ السَّمٰواتِ والأَرضِ، عالِمَ الغَيْبِ والشَّهادَةِ، أَنْتَ تحكُمُ بينَ عِبادِكَ فيما كانوا فيه يَختَلِفونَ، اهْدِني لما اخْتُلِفَ فيهِ مِنَ الحقِّ بإِذْنِكَ، إِنَّكَ تَهدي مَن تَشاءُ إِلى صِراطٍ مُستقيمٍ».

مسلم

٦٧ ـ كان رسولُ اللهِ ﷺ يقولُ: إِذا قامَ إِلى الصَّلاةِ من جَوْفِ اللَّيلِ: «اللَّهُمَّ لكَ الحَمْدُ، أَنتَ نُورُ السَّمٰواتِ والأَرضِ ومَنْ فيهِنَّ، ولَكَ الحَمْدُ، أَنتَ قَيَّامُ السَّمٰواتِ[١]

(١) قَيَّام السموات وقَيُّومها: الحافظ لها.

and of those therein; and praise be to You, You are the Lord of the heavens and of the earth and of those therein; and praise be to You, You are real, and Your promise is real, and Your words are real, and the meeting with You is real, and Heaven is real, and Hell-fire is real, and the prophets are real, and Muḥammad is real, and the Day of Judgement is real. O Allah, to You have I submitted, and in You have I believed, and upon You have I relied, and to You I have returned in repentance, and for You have I contended in dispute, and to You have I submitted judgement, so forgive my early sins and my late sins, those I have kept secret and those I have done openly. You are my God, there is no god save You."

(Related by al-Bukhārī and Muslim)

والأَرضِ ومَن فيهِنَّ، ولَكَ الحَمْدُ، أَنْتَ ربُّ السَّمٰواتِ والأَرْضِ ومن فيهنَّ، ولكَ الْحَمْدُ أَنتَ الحقُّ، وَوَعْدُكَ الحقُّ، وقَوْلُكَ الحقُّ، ولِقاؤُكَ حَقٌّ، والجَنَّةُ حَقٌّ، والنارُ حَقٌّ، والنَّبِيُّونَ حَقٌّ، ومحمَّدٌ حقٌّ، والساعَةُ حقٌّ، اللَّهُمَّ لَكَ أَسْلَمْتُ، وبِكَ آمَنْتُ، وعَلَيْكَ تَوَكَّلْتُ، وإِلَيْكَ أَنَبْتُ، وبكَ خاصَمْتُ، وإِلَيْكَ حاكَمْتُ، فاغْفِرْ لي ما قَدَّمْتُ وما أَخَّرْتُ، وما أَسْرَرْتُ وما أَعْلَنْتُ، أَنْتَ إِلٰهي، لا إِلٰهَ إِلا أَنتَ».

البخاري ومسلم

12. On the invocations to be said when bowing and rising therefrom, and when prostrating oneself, and when sitting between the two prostrations

68) On the authority of Ḥudhayfah (may Allah be pleased with him) that he heard the Prophet (may the blessings and peace of Allah be upon him) say when he bowed down: subḥāna rabbiya 'l-ᶜAẓīm (Glorified is my Great Lord!)—three times. And when he prostrated himself he said: subḥāna rabbiya 'l-'Aᶜlā (Glorified is my most Sublime Lord!)—three times.

(Related by Abū Dāwūd, at-Tirmidhī, an-Nasā'ī and Ibn Mājah)

69) And in the Hadith of ᶜAli (may Allah be pleased with him) concerning the prayers of the Messenger of Allah (may the blessings and peace of Allah be upon him), (it is said) that when he had bowed down he would say: "O Allah, to You have I bowed down, and in You have I believed and to You have I

١٢ ـ في دعاءِ الرُّكوعِ والقيامِ منهُ والسجودِ والجلوسِ بينَ السَّجْدتَيْنِ

٦٨ ـ عن حُذَيْفَةَ رَضِيَ اللهُ عنهُ، أَنهُ سَمِعَ النبيَّ ﷺ يقولُ إِذا رَكَعَ: «سُبْحانَ ربِّيَ العظيمِ» ثلاثَ مَرَّاتٍ، وإِذا سَجَدَ قالَ: «سُبحانَ ربِّيَ الأَعلىٰ» ثَلاثَ مرَّاتٍ.

أبو داود والتِّرْمذي والنَّسائي وابنُ ماجَه

٦٩ ـ وفي حديثِ عليٍّ رضيَ اللهُ عَنْهُ، عَنْ صلاةِ رسولِ اللهِ ﷺ وإِذا رَكَعَ يقولُ في رُكُوعِهِ: «اللَّهُمَّ لَكَ رَكَعْتُ، وبكَ آمَنْتُ،

submitted. My hearing and my sight, my brain, my bones and my nerves have humbled themselves to You." And when he had raised his head from the bowing position he would say: "Allah hears him who has praised Him, O our Lord, and to You be praise filling the heavens and filling the earth and filling that which is between them, and filling anything further that You want." And when he prostrated himself he would say in his prostrate position: "O Allah, to You have I prostrated myself, and in You have I believed, and to You have I submitted. My face has prostrated itself to Him who created and fashioned it and who opened out its hearing and its sight. May Allah, the best of creators, be blessed."

(Related by Muslim)

ولكَ أَسلَمْتُ، خَشَعَ لك سَمْعِي، وَبَصَرِي، ومُخِّي، وَعَظْمِي، وَعَصَبِي». وإذا رَفَعَ رأْسَهُ مِنَ الرُّكوع يقولُ: «سَمِعَ اللهُ لِمَنْ حَمِدَهُ، ربَّنا وَلكَ الحَمْدُ، مِلْءَ السَّمٰواتِ وَمِلْءَ الأَرْضِ وَمِلْءَ ما بَيْنَهُما، وَمِلْءَ ما شِئْتَ مِنْ شَيْءٍ بَعْدُ»

وإذا سجدَ يقولُ في سجوده:

«اللَّهُمَّ لَكَ سَجَدْتُ، وَبِكَ آمَنْتُ، وَلَكَ أَسْلَمْتُ، سَجَدَ وَجْهِي للَّذي خَلَقَهُ وصوَّرَهُ، وشقَّ سَمْعَهُ وَبَصَرَهُ، تَبارَكَ اللهُ أَحْسَنُ الخالِقِينَ».

مسلم

70) And ᶜĀ'ishah (may Allah be pleased with her) said: The Messenger of Allah (may the blessings and peace of Allah be upon him) would often say in his position of bowing down and prostration: "Glory be to You, O Allah, our Lord, and praise be to You. O Allah forgive me"—following the injunction of the Qur'ān. She refers to His (Exalted is He) words: "Glorify your Lord, giving praise to Him, and ask His forgiveness, He is ever-accepting of repentance."[1]

(Related by al-Bukhārī and Muslim)

71) The Messenger of Allah (may the blessings and peace of Allah be upon him) would say when in the position of bowing down and of prostration: "Most perfect, most holy, the Lord of the angels and of the soul."[2]

(Related by Muslim)

---

1. The Chapter of Succour 110:3.
2. I.e., Gabriel.

٧٠ ـ وقالتْ عائِشَةُ رضيَ اللهُ عَنْها: كانَ رسولُ اللهِ ﷺ يُكْثِرُ أَنْ يقولَ في رُكُوعهِ وسُجودِهِ: «سُبحانَكَ اللَّهُمَّ ربَّنا وبِحمْدِك، اللَّهُمَّ اغفِرْ لي» يتأوَّلُ القرآنَ. تُريدُ قولَهُ تعالى: ﴿فَسَبِّحْ بِحَمْدِ رَبِّكَ وَٱسْتَغْفِرْهُ إِنَّهُ كَانَ تَوَّابَاً﴾ [النصر ١١٠ ٣].

البخاري ومسلم

٧١ ـ كان رسولُ اللهِ ﷺ يقولُ في رُكوعِه وسُجودِه: «سُبُّوحٌ قُدُّوسٌ[1] رَبُّ الملائِكَةِ والرُّوحِ»[2].

مسلم

(١) السُّبُّوح: المتنزه عن كل سوء. القُدُّوس: المنزه عن النقائص.
(٢) الروح: أي جبريل.

72) The Messenger of Allah (may the blessings and peace of Allah be upon him) said: "Take note that I was forbidden to recite the Qur'ān when bowing down and in prostration. As for bowing down, extol therein the Lord; and as for prostration, exert yourself in making supplication, for it is sure to be answered to you."

(Related by Muslim)

73) ᶜAwf ibn Mālik said: I stayed up one night with the Messenger of Allah (may the blessings and peace of Allah be upon him) and he rose and recited the Chapter of the Cow. He did not pass by a verse of mercy without stopping and asking for mercy, and he did not pass by a verse of punishment without stopping and saying "I take refuge in Allah." He said: Then he bowed down for as long as he had

٧٢ ـ قال رسول الله ﷺ: «ألا وإني نُهيتُ أَنْ أَقْرَأَ القُرآنَ راكِعاً أو ساجِداً، فَأَمَّا الرُّكُوعُ، فَعَظِّموا فيهِ الرَّبَّ، وأَمَّا السُّجودُ، فاجْتَهِدُوا في الدُّعاء، فَقَمِنٌ[1] أن يُسْتجابَ لَكُمْ». مسلم

٧٣ ـ وقال عَوْفُ بْنُ مالِكٍ: قُمتُ مَعَ رَسولِ الله ﷺ لَيْلةً، فَقامَ فقَرأَ سُورةَ (البقَرَةِ)، لا يمُرُّ بآيَةِ رَحْمَةٍ إلا وَقَفَ وسَأَلَ، ولا يمُرُّ بآيَةِ عَذابٍ إلا وَقَفَ وتَعَوَّذَ، قالَ: ثم ركَعَ

---

(١) قَمِن: جدير.

been standing in prayer, saying in his bowed position: "Glory be to Him who possesses omnipotence and sovereignty, pride and greatness." Then he said likewise in his prostration.

(Related by Abū Dāwūd and an-Nasā'ī)

74) The Messenger of Allah (may the blessings and peace of Allah be upon him) would say:

"Sami[c]a 'llāhu liman ḥamidah" (Allah hears him who has praised Him) when he was straightening up from the position of being bowed down; then, standing, he would say:

"Rabbana wa laka 'l-ḥamd" (O our Lord, and praise be to You). And in another version: "Rabbana laka 'l-ḥamd" (O our Lord, praise be to You).

(Related by al-Bukhārī and Muslim)

بِقَدْرِ قِيامِهِ، يقولُ في رُكُوعِهِ: «سُبْحانَ ذي الجَبَرُوتِ والمَلَكوتِ، والكِبْرِياءِ والعَظَمَةِ».
ثم قالَ في سُجُودِهِ مِثلَ ذلكَ.

أبو داود والنّسائي

٧٤ ـ كانَ رسولُ اللهِ ﷺ يقولُ:
«سَمِعَ اللهُ لِمَنْ حَمِدَهُ» حينَ يرفعُ صُلْبَهُ مِنَ الرُّكوعِ، ثم يقولُ وهُوَ قائِمٌ:
«ربَّنَا وَلَكَ الحَمْدُ»، وفي لَفْظٍ: «ربَّنا لَكَ الحَمْدُ».

البخاري ومسلم

75) The Messenger of Allah (may the blessings and peace of Allah be upon him), when he raised his head from the position of being bowed down, would say:

"O Allah, our Lord, praise be to You, filling the heavens, and filling the earth, and filling that which is between them, and filling anything further that You want, worthy You are of praise and of glory, (which are words) that are the most truthful a servant can say of You, and all of us are servants to You. O Allah, there is no withholding what You have given, and there is no one to give what You have withheld. He who possesses (worldly) fortune will not benefit therefrom (on the Day of Judgement)."

(Related by Muslim)

٧٥ ـ كانَ رسولُ اللهِ ﷺ إذا رفعَ رَأْسَهُ مِنَ الرُّكُوعِ قال:

«اللَّهُمَّ ربَّنَا لَكَ الحَمْدُ، مِلْءَ السَّمٰواتِ، ومِلْءَ الأَرْضِ، ومِلْءَ ما بَيْنَهُما، ومِلْءَ ما شِئْتَ مِنْ شَيْءٍ بَعْدُ، أَهْلَ الثَّناءِ والمَجْدِ، أَحَقُّ[١] ما قالَ العَبْدُ، وكُلُّنا لَكَ عَبْدٌ، اللَّهُمَّ لا مَانِعَ لما أَعْطَيْتَ، ولا مُعْطِيَ لما مَنَعْتَ، ولا يَنْفَعُ ذا الجَدِّ مِنْكَ الجَدُّ[٢]».

مسلم

---

(١) أي أن الدعاء السابق (ربنا لك الحمد) هو أحق قول.

(٢) الجَد هو الحظ. والمعنى أن المرء المحظوظ في الدنيا بالثراء وغيره، لا ينفعه ذلك يوم الحساب، لأن العبرة يومئذ بالعمل الصالح.

76) Rifā^{c}ah ibn Rāfi^{c} said: One day we were praying behind the Prophet (may the blessings and peace of Allah be upon him), and when he raised his head from bowing down he said: "Allah hears him who has praised Him." A man behind him said: O our Lord, and to You is praise that is abundant, good and blessed. When he had finished the Prophet said: "Who was the person who spoke?" The man said: It was I. He said: "I saw some thirty angels hastening to see which of them could write it down first."

(Related by al-Bukhārī)

77) The Messenger of Allah (may the blessings and peace of Allah be upon him) said: "The servant is nearest to his Lord when he is prostrating himself, so multiply (your) invocations (then)."

(Related by Muslim)

٧٦ ـ وقال رِفاعَةُ بْنُ رافعٍ: كُنَّا يَوْماً نُصلِّي وراءَ النبيِّ ﷺ، فلَمَّا رَفَعَ رأْسَهُ مِنَ الرَّكْعَةِ قالَ:

«سَمِعَ اللهُ لِمَنْ حَمِدَهُ» فقالَ رَجُلٌ وراءَهُ: ربَّنَا وَلَكَ الحَمْدُ، حَمْداً كَثيراً طَيِّباً مُباركاً فيه، فلمَّا انْصَرَفَ قالَ: «مَنِ المُتكلِّمُ؟ قالَ: أنا، قالَ: رأَيْتُ بِضْعَةً وثَلاثِينَ مَلَكاً يَبْتَدِرُونَها، أَيُّهُم يَكْتُبُها أَوَّلُ».

البخاري

٧٧ ـ قال رسولُ اللهِ ﷺ: «أَقْرَبُ ما يَكونُ العَبْدُ مِنْ رَبِّهِ وهُوَ ساجِدٌ، فَأَكْثِرُوا الدُّعاءَ».

مسلم

78) The Messenger of Allah (may the blessings and peace of Allah be upon him) would say in his position of prostration: "O Allah, forgive me all my sins, the minor ones and the major ones, the first ones and the last ones, the open ones and the secret ones."

(Related by Muslim)

79) ᶜĀ'ishah (may Allah be pleased with her) said: I could not find the Prophet (may the blessings and peace of Allah be upon him) one night (in his usual place of sleeping), so I searched round for him and my hand fell on the soles of his feet while he was in prostration, and they were raised. He was saying:

"O Allah, I take refuge in Your approval from Your displeasure, and in Your remission from Your punishment, and I take refuge with You from You.

٧٨ ـ كان رسولُ الله ﷺ يقولُ في سُجودِه: «اللهُمَّ ٱغْفِرْ لي ذَنْبي كُلَّهُ، دِقَّهُ وجِلَّهُ[١]، وأَوَّلَهُ وآخِرَهُ، وَعلانِيَتَهُ وسِرَّهُ».

مسلم

٧٩ ـ وقالَتْ عائِشَةُ رَضِيَ اللهُ عنها: فَقَدْتُ النبيَّ ﷺ ذاتَ لَيْلَةٍ [مِنَ الفِراشِ] فالتَمَسْتُهُ فوَقَعَتْ يَدي على بَطْنِ قَدَمَيْهِ وَهُوَ في المَسْجِدِ[٢]، وهُما مَنْصوبَتانِ، وهو يَقُول:

«اللَّهُمَّ إني أَعُوذُ بِرِضاكَ مِنْ سَخَطِكَ، وبِمُعافاتِكَ مِن عُقوبَتِكَ، وأَعُوذُ بِكَ مِنْكَ، لا

---

(١) دِقَّه وجِلَّه: صغيره وكبيره.

(٢) أي وهو ساجد.

I cannot truly measure out praise enough for You, You are as You have praised Yourself."

(Related by Muslim)

80) The Messenger of Allah (may the blessings and peace of Allah be upon him) would say between the two prostrations: "O Allah, forgive me, and have mercy upon me, and guide me, and restore me to well-being, and protect me, and provide for me."

(Related by Abū Dāwūd)

81) The Messenger of Allah (may the blessings and peace of Allah be upon him) would say between the two prostrations: "O my Lord, forgive me. O my Lord, forgive me."

(Related by Abū Dāwūd)

أُحْصِي ثَنَاءً عَلَيْكَ[١]، أَنْتَ كَمَا أَثْنَيْتَ على نَفْسِكَ».
مسلم

٨٠ ـ كان رسولُ اللهِ ﷺ يقولُ بينَ السَّجْدَتَيْنِ: «اللَّهُمَّ اغْفِرْ لي، وارْحَمْني، وٱهْدِني، وٱجْبُرْني[٢]، وعَافِني؛ وٱرْزُقْني».

أبو داود

٨١ ـ كان رسولُ اللهِ ﷺ يقولُ بين السَّجْدتيْنِ: «رَبِّ ٱغْفِرْ لي، رَبِّ ٱغْفِرْ لي».

أبو داود

---

(١) أي لا أبلغ من الثناء ما أنت مستحق له.

(٢) اجبُرْني: اكفني وأصلح شأني.

13. On invocations during the prayers and after the recitation of Tashahhud[1]

82) The Messenger of Allah (may the blessings and peace of Allah be upon him) said: "When one of you has finished the final recitation of the Tashahhud, let him say that he takes refuge in Allah from four things: from the punishment of hell, from the punishment of the grave, from the test of life and of death, and from the evil of the False Christ."

(Related by Muslim)

1. Tashahhud: i.e., reciting the statement of faith with which each prayer is concluded.

١٣ ـ في الدعاءِ في الصلاةِ وبعدَ التشهدِ

٨٢ ـ قالَ رسولُ الله ﷺ: «إِذا فَرَغَ أَحَدُكُمْ مِنَ التَّشَهُّدِ الآخِرِ، فَلْيَتَعَوَّذْ باللهِ مِنْ أَرْبَعٍ: مِن عَذابِ جَهَنَّمَ، وَمِنْ عَذابِ القَبْرِ، ومِنْ فِتْنَةِ المَحْيَا والمَماتِ، وَمِنْ شَرِّ المَسيحِ الدَّجَّالِ».

مسلم

83) And on the authority of ᶜĀ'ishah (may Allah be pleased with her) that the Messenger of Allah (may the blessings and peace of Allah be upon him) would make the following invocation:

"O Allah, I take refuge in You from the punishment of the grave, and I take refuge in You from the test of the False Christ, and I take refuge in You from the temptation of life and of death. O Allah, I take refuge in You from sinning and from debt." Somebody said to him: How often you ask refuge from debt! And he said: "If a man is in debt, he talks and lies (in his talk), he promises and he fails to keep his promise."

(Related by al-Bukhārī and Muslim)

٨٣ ـ وعَنْ عائشةَ رضيَ اللهُ عنها أنَّ رسولَ اللهِ ﷺ كانَ يَدْعُو في الصَّلاةِ:

«اللَّهُمَّ إني أعُوذُ بِكَ مِنْ عَذابِ القَبْرِ، وأعُوذُ بكَ مِن فِتْنَةِ المَسيحِ الدَّجَّالِ، وأعُوذُ بكَ مِنْ فِتْنَةِ المَحْيَا والمَماتِ، اللَّهُمَّ إني أعُوذُ بكَ مِنَ المَأْثَم والمَغْرَمِ(١)». فقالَ لهُ قائِلٌ: ما أكْثَرَ ما تَسْتَعيذُ مِنَ المغْرَمِ؟ فقالَ: «إنَّ الرَّجلَ إذا غَرِمَ(٢) حَدَّثَ فكَذَب، وَوَعَدَ فأخْلَفَ».

البخاري ومسلم

---

(١) يعني أعوذ بك من الآثام والمعاصي. وفيها أيضاً الاستعاذة من الغُرم وهو الدَّين.

(٢) غَرِم: عليه دين وغرامة.

84) And on the authority of ᶜAbdullah the son of ᶜAmr (may Allah be pleased with them both) that Abū Bakr aṣ-Ṣiddīq (may Allah be pleased with him) said to the Messenger of Allah (may the blessings and peace of Allah be upon him): Teach me an invocation for me to say in my prayers. He said "Say: O Allah, I have greatly wronged myself, (and) there is no one but You who forgives sins, so give me forgiveness from You, and have mercy upon me, You are the Forgiving, the Merciful."

(Related by al-Bukhārī and Muslim)

85) The Messenger of Allah (may the blessings and peace of Allah be upon him) would say among the final invocations he made between the saying of the Tashahhud[1] and the Taslīm[2]:

---

1. The statement of faith as used in prayers.
2. Terminating the prayer by saying the words "As-salāmu ᶜalaykum wa raḥmatu 'llahi wa barakātuh" (Peace be upon you and the mercy of Allah and His blessings).

٨٤ ـ وَعَنْ عبدِ اللهِ بْنِ عَمْرو رضيَ اللهُ عنهما، أَن أَبا بكرٍ الصِّدِّيقَ رضيَ اللهُ عَنْهُ قالَ لِرَسولِ اللهِ ﷺ عَلِّمْني دُعاءً أَدْعُو بِهِ في صَلاتي، قال: «قُلِ: اللَّهُمَّ إِني ظَلَمْتُ نَفْسي ظُلْماً كَثِيراً، ولا يَغْفِرُ الذُّنوبَ إِلاَّ أَنْتَ. فَاغْفِرْ لي مَغْفِرَةً مِنْ عِنْدِكَ، وَٱرْحَمْني إِنَّكَ أَنْتَ ٱلْغَفُورُ الرَّحِيمُ». البخاري ومسلم

٨٥ ـ كانَ رسولُ اللهِ ﷺ يقولُ مِنْ آخِرِ ما يَقولُ بينَ التَّشَهُّدِ والتَّسْليم:

"O Allah, forgive me my early and my later sins, those I have kept secret and those I have done openly, and those in which I have exceeded all bounds and those You know of better than I. You are the Expediter and the Delayer,[1] there is no god but You."

(Related by Muslim)

86) ᶜAmmār ibn Yāsir (may Allah be pleased with him) performed a prayer and made it brief. One of the people said to him: You have reduced—or you have made brief—the prayers. He said: As to that, I said invocations in it that I had heard from the Messenger of Allah (may the blessings and peace of Allah be upon him). When he rose to leave, a man from the people (present) followed him and asked him about the invocation, and he said (that it was):

"O Allah, within Your knowledge of the unseen and Your ability to create, give me life so long as

1. These are among the Most Beautiful Names of Allah.

«اللَّهُمَّ ٱغْفِرْ لي مَا قَدَّمْتُ وما أَخَّرْتُ، وَمَا أَسْرَرْتُ وَمَا أَعْلَنْتُ، وَمَا أَسْرَفْتُ وَمَا أَنْتَ أَعْلَمُ بِهِ مِنِّي، أَنْتَ المُقَدِّمُ وَأَنْتَ المُؤَخِّر، لا إِلٰه إِلاَّ أَنْتَ».

مسلم

٨٦ ـ صَلَّى عمَّارُ بْنُ ياسِرٍ رضيَ اللهُ عَنْهُ صَلاةً، فأَوْجزَ، فقالَ له بَعْضُ القَوْم: لَقَدْ خففْتَ ـ أو أَوْجَزْتَ ـ الصَّلاةَ، فَقالَ: أَمَّا عَلَى[1] ذٰلِكَ، لَقَدْ دَعَوْتُ فِيها بِدَعَواتٍ سَمِعْتُهُنَّ مِنْ رَسولِ اللهِ ﷺ، فلَمَّا قَامَ تَبِعَهُ رَجُلٌ مِنَ القَوْمِ، فَسَأَلَهُ عنِ الدُّعاءِ فقال:

«اللَّهُمَّ بِعِلْمِكَ الغَيْبَ وقُدْرَتِكَ على

(١) أي أنه رغم تخفيف الصلاة، فقد قرأ فيها هذا الدعاء الجامع.

You know that life is best for me and give me death if You know that death is best for me. O Allah, I ask of You that I should fear You in the unseen and in the seen, and I ask of You that I speak the truth, whether in contentment or anger, and I ask of You the middle way in poverty and riches, and I ask of You grace that will not run out, and I ask of You uninterrupted peace of mind, and I ask of You contentment after destiny (has been implemented), and I ask of You ease of life after death, and I ask of You the delight of Your countenance, and the longing for meeting You in a not adverse and hurtful condition, nor in a state of discord that causes one to go astray. O Allah, attire us in the finery of faith and make of us rightly-guided guides."

(Related by an-Nasā'ī)

الخَلْقِ، أَحْيِنِي ما عَلِمْتَ الحَياةَ خَيْراً لي، وَتَوَفَّنِي إذا عَلِمْتَ الوَفاةَ خَيْراً لي، اللَّهُمَّ إِني أَسْأَلُكَ خَشْيَتَكَ في الغَيْبِ وَالشَّهَادَة، وَأَسْأَلُكَ كَلِمَةَ الحَقِّ في الرِّضا وَالغَضَبِ، وَأَسْأَلُكَ القَصْدَ[1] في الفَقْرِ والغِنىٰ، وَأَسْأَلُكَ نَعِيماً لا يَنْفَدُ، وَأَسْأَلُكَ قُرَّةَ عَيْنٍ لا تَنْقَطِعُ[2]، وَأَسْأَلُكَ الرِّضا بَعْدَ القَضَاءِ، وأَسْأَلُكَ بَرْدَ العَيْشِ بَعْدَ الْموْتِ[3]، وأَسْأَلُكَ لَذَّةَ النَّظَرِ إِلى وَجْهِكَ، والشَّوْقَ إِلى لِقائِكَ في غَيرِ ضَرَّاءَ مُضِرَّةٍ[4]، ولا فِتْنَةٍ مُضِلَّةٍ[5]، اللَّهُمَّ زَيِّنَّا بِزِينَةِ الإِيمَانِ، وَٱجْعَلْنَا هُدَاةً مُهْتَدِينَ».

النّسائي

---

(١) القصد: التوسط.

(٢) قُرة العين: ما يُرضي ويسُرّ، أي رَغَد الحياة وطيبها.

(٣) أي العيش الهنيء في الجنة.

(٤) الضراء: الشِّدة وكل ما يضر.

(٥) الفتنة: ما يبتلى به الإنسان في نفسه ومجتمعه من الأحداث والأفكار التي قد تؤدي به إلى الضلال والخطأ.

87) When the Messenger of Allah (may the blessings and peace of Allah be upon him) ended his prayers he would ask forgiveness of Allah three times and would say: "O Allah, You are Peace and from You is peace. May You be praised, O You who possess majesty and bounty."

(Related by Muslim)

88) When the Messenger of Allah (may the blessings and peace of Allah be upon him) finished his prayers he would say: "There is no god but Allah alone, He having no associate. His is the dominion and His the praise and He is omnipotent over everything. O Allah, there is no one to withhold what You have given, and no one to give what You have withheld. He who possesses (worldly) fortune will not benefit therefrom (on the Day of Judgement)."

(Related by al-Bukhārī and Muslim)

٨٧ ـ كَانَ رسولُ الله ﷺ إذا ٱنصَرَفَ مِنْ صَلاتِهِ اسْتَغْفَرَ اللهَ ثَلاثاً، وقالَ: «اللَّهُمَّ أَنْتَ السَّلامُ، ومِنْكَ السَّلامُ، تَبارَكْتَ ياذَا الجَلالِ وَالإِكْرَام».

مسلم

٨٨ ـ كَانَ رسولُ اللهِ ﷺ إذا فَرَغَ مِنَ الصَّلاةِ قَالَ: «لا إِلٰهَ إلاَّ اللهُ وَحْدَهُ لا شَريكَ لَهُ، لَهُ المُلْكُ، وَلَهُ الحَمْدُ، وَهُوَ عَلَى كُلِّ شَيءٍ قَدِيرٌ، اللَّهُمَّ لا مَانِعَ لما أَعْطَيْتَ، وَلا مُعْطِيَ لما مَنَعْتَ، وَلا يَنْفَعُ ذَا الجَدِّ مِنْكَ الجَدُّ[١]».

البخاري ومسلم

---

(١) انظر حديث ٧٥.

89) And on the authority of [c]Abdullah the son of az-Zubayr (may Allah be pleased with them both) that the Prophet used to say at the end of each prayer when concluding it: "There is no god but Allah alone, He having no associate. His is the dominion, and His the praise, and He is omnipotent over everything. There is no strength or power except in Allah. There is no god but Allah and we worship only Him. He has beneficence and He has superabundance, and to Him is goodly praise. There is no god but Allah. We are sincere to Him in religion, even if the godless dislike it." And the son of az-Zubayr (may Allah be pleased with them both) said: The Messenger of Allah used to say aloud these words at the end of every prayer.

(Related by Muslim)

٨٩ ـ وَعَنْ عَبْدِ اللهِ بْنِ الزُّبَيْرِ رَضِيَ اللهُ عَنهُما، أَنَّهُ كانَ يقولُ دُبُرَ كلِّ صَلاةٍ حينَ يُسَلِّمُ: «لا إِلٰهَ إِلا اللهُ وَحْدَهُ لا شَرِيكَ لَهُ، لَهُ المُلْكُ، وَلَهُ الحَمْدُ، وَهُوَ على كُلِّ شَيْءٍ قَديرٌ، لا حَوْلَ وَلا قُوَّةَ إِلا باللهِ، لا إِلٰهَ إِلا اللهُ، وَلا نَعْبُدُ إِلا إِيَّاهُ، لَهُ النِّعْمَةُ، وَلَهُ الفَضْلُ، وَلَهُ الثَّناءُ الحَسَنُ، لا إِلٰهَ إِلاَّ اللهُ مُخْلِصِينَ لَهُ الدِّينَ وَلوْ كرِهَ الكافِرُونَ» وقال ابنُ الزُّبَيْرِ رضِيَ اللهُ عنه: «كَانَ رَسولُ اللهِ ﷺ يُهَلِّلُ[1] بِهِنَّ دُبُرَ كُلِّ صَلاةٍ».

مسلم

(١) التهليل: قول (لا إله إلا الله). والمقصود هنا أنه ﷺ كان يدعو بهذا الدعاء بصوت مرتفع مسموع.

90) And on the authority of Abū Hurayrah (may Allah be pleased with him) that those of the Emigrants[1] who were poor came to the Messenger of Allah (may the blessings and peace of Allah be upon him) and said: The affluent have made off with the highest degrees (of meritorious acts) and lasting felicity. They pray as we pray, and they fast as we fast, and they have a superfluity of riches because of which they are able to go on Pilgrimage and on the ᶜUmrah,[2] and they wage holy war, and they give in charity. He said: "Shall I not teach you something by which to catch up with those who have surpassed you and by which you will surpass those who come after you and whereby there will be no one better than you other than he who has done as you have done?" They said: Yes indeed, O Messenger of Allah. He said: "You say subḥāna 'llāh (How far is

---

1. Those who emigrated from Mecca to Medina in the early years of Islam.
2. A shortened form of Pilgrimage which can be performed at any time of the year.

٩٠ ـ وَعَنْ أَبي هُرَيْرَةَ رضيَ اللهُ عَنْهُ، أَنَّ فُقَراءَ المهاجِرينَ أَتَوْا رَسولَ اللهِ ﷺ فَقالوا: ذَهَبَ أَهْلُ الدُّثُورِ(١) بِالدَّرَجاتِ العُلا، والنَّعِيمِ المُقيمِ، يُصَلُّونَ كما نُصَلِّي، ويَصُومونَ كَما نَصُومُ، وَلَهُمْ فَضْلٌ(٢) مِنْ أَمْوالٍ، يَحُجُّونَ بِها وَيَعْتَمِرونَ، وَيُجاهِدُونَ، وَيَتَصَدَّقُونَ. فقال: «أَلا أُعَلِّمُكُمْ شَيْئاً تُدْرِكُونَ بِهِ مَنْ سَبَقَكُمْ، وَتَسْبِقُونَ بِه مَنْ بَعْدَكُمْ وَلا يَكُونُ أَحَدٌ أَفْضَلَ مِنْكُمْ إلا مَن صَنَعَ مِثْلَ ما صَنَعْتُمْ». قالوا: بَلَىٰ يا رَسولَ اللهِ، قالَ:

(١) أهل الغنى والثروة.

(٢) زيادة.

Allah from every imperfection!) and you say al-ḥamdu lillāh (Praise be to Allah) and you say Allāhu akbar (Allah is greatest) after every prayer thirty-three times."

(Related by al-Bukhārī and Muslim)

Abu Ṣāliḥ said: He says: subḥāna 'llāh (How far is Allah from every imperfection!), al-ḥamdu lillāh (Praise be to Allah) and Allāhu akbar (Allah is greatest), until there are thirty-three of each of them.

91) On the authority of the Messenger of Allah (may the blessings and peace of Allah be upon him), who said: "He who says subḥāna 'llāh (How far is Allah from every imperfection!) at the end of each prayer thirty-three times and who says al-ḥamdu lillāh (Praise be to Allah) thirty-three times and Allāhu

«تُسَبِّحُونَ، وتَحْمَدُونَ، وتُكبِّرونَ، خَلْفَ كُلِّ صَلاةٍ ثَلاثاً وثَلاثِينَ».

البخاري ومسلم

قال أَبو صالح: يَقولُ: سُبْحانَ اللهِ، والحَمْدُ للهِ، واللهُ أَكْبَرُ، حتى يَكونَ مِنهُنَّ كُلِّهِنَّ ثلاثاً وثلاثِينَ.

٩١ ـ عَنْ رَسولِ اللهِ ﷺ قالَ: «مَنْ سَبَّحَ اللهَ في دُبُرِ كُلِّ صَلاةٍ ثلاثاً وثلاثِينَ، وحَمِدَ اللهَ

akbar (Allah is greatest) thirty-three times, and who completes the hundred by saying: There is no god but Allah, He having no associate, His is the dominion and His the praise and He is omnipotent over everything—will have his sins forgiven him, even if they be as the foam of the sea."

(Related by Muslim)

92) On the authority of the Prophet (may the blessings and peace of Allah be upon him), who said: "There are two practices[1]—or two habits[2]—which no Muslim servant (of Allah) keeps to without his going to heaven. They are easy and those who practise them are few. He says subḥāna 'llāh (How far is Allah from every imperfection!) at the end of each prayer ten times, and he says al-ḥamdu lillāh (Praise be to Allah) ten times, and he says Allāhu

---

1. Lit. traits or characteristics.
2. The narrator is uncertain as to which of the two words was used.

ثَلاثاً وثَلاثِينَ، وَكَبَّرَ اللهَ ثَلاثاً وثَلاثين، وقَالَ تَمامَ المائَةِ: لا إِلٰهَ إِلاَّ اللهُ وَحْدَهُ لا شَرِيكَ لَهُ، لَهُ المُلْكُ ولَهُ الحَمْدُ وَهُوَ على كُلِّ شَيْءٍ قَدِيرٌ. غُفِرَتْ خطَايَاهُ وإِنْ كَانَتْ مِثْلَ زبَدِ[1] البَحْرِ».

مسلم

٩٢ ـ عن النَّبيِّ ﷺ قالَ: «خَصْلَتَان، أَوْ خلَّتَانِ، لا يُحافِظُ علَيْهِما عَبْدٌ مُسْلِمٌ إلا دَخَلَ الجَنَّةَ، وَهُمَا يَسِيرٌ، وَمَنْ يَعْمَلُ بِهِما قَليلٌ: يُسَبِّحُ اللهَ في دُبُرِ كُلِّ صَلاةٍ عَشْراً، ويَحْمَدُهُ عَشْراً،

(١) زبد البحر رغوته، وكثرتها مضرب المثل.

akbar (Allah is greatest) ten times, and that makes one hundred and fifty on the tongue[1] and a thousand five hundred in the Scales.[2] He should say Allāhu akbar (Allah is greatest) thirty-four times on going to bed, and al-ḥamdu lillāh (Praise be to Allah) thirty-three times, and subḥāna 'llāh (How far is Allah from every imperfection!) thirty-three times. This makes a hundred on the tongue and a thousand in the Scales." He said: I have seen the Messenger of Allah (may the blessings and peace of Allah be upon him) counting them off on his hand. They said: O Messenger of Allah, how is it that they are easy and that those who practise them are few? He said: "He

---

1. I.e., thirty at each of the five daily prayers.
2. The Scales in which good and bad deeds are measured at the Day of Judgment. Each good deed is multiplied by ten for the purpose of this computation.

وَيَكَبِّرُهُ عَشْراً، وَذٰلِكَ خَمْسُونَ ومِائَةٌ باللِّسانِ[١]، وألفٌ وَخَمْسُمِائَةٍ في المِيزانِ[٢]. وَيُكبِّرُ أَرْبَعاً وَثَلاثِينَ إِذا أَخَذَ مَضْجَعَهُ، وَيَحْمَدُ ثَلاثاً وثَلاثِينَ، ويُسَبِّحُ ثَلاثاً وثَلاثِينَ، فَذٰلِكَ مائَةٌ باللِّسانِ وأَلْفٌ في المِيزانِ». قال: فَلَقَدْ رَأَيْتُ رَسولَ اللهِ ﷺ يَعْقِدُها بيدِهِ[٣]، قالوا: يا رَسولَ اللهِ كَيْفَ هُما يَسِيرٌ، وَمَنْ يَعْمَلُ بِهِما

(١) لأنها ثلاثون في الصلاة الواحدة، فيجتمع من ذلك العدد المذكور في صلوات اليوم الخمس.

(٢) لأن الحسنة بعشر أمثالها.

(٣) أي يَعْقِد التسبيح ويعده على أنامله.

(meaning the devil) comes to one of you (in his time of sleep), and he puts him to sleep before he has said (these invocations), and he comes to him in his prayers and reminds him of some worldly need before he says them."

(Related by Abū Dāwūd, at-Tirmidhī and an-Nasā'ī)

93) On the authority of ᶜUqbah ibn ᶜĀmir, who said: The Messenger of Allah (may the blessings and peace of Allah be upon him) ordered me to recite the Muᶜawwidhahs[1] at the end of every prayer.

(Related by Aḥmad and Ibn Ḥibbān)

94) On the authority of Muᶜādh ibn Jabal (may Allah be pleased with him) that the Messenger of Allah (may the blessings and peace of Allah be upon him) took him by the hand and said: "O Muᶜādh, by Allah I love you, so do not omit to say at the end of every prayer: O Allah, help me to remember You, to thank You and to worship You well."

(Related by Abū Dāwūd and an-Nasā'ī)

---

1. The Chapter of the Daybreak (113) and the Chapter of Mankind (114).

قَليلٌ، قالَ: «يَأْتي أَحَدَكُمْ - يَعْنِي الشَّيْطانَ - في مَنامِهِ، فيُنَوِّمُهُ قَبْلَ أَنْ يَقولَ، وَيَأْتِيهِ في صَلاتِهِ فَيُذَكِّرُهُ حاجَتَهُ قَبْلَ أَنْ يَقُولَها».

أبو داود والترمذي والنّسائي

٩٣ - عن عُقْبَةَ بْنِ عامِرٍ قالَ: «أَمَرَني رَسولُ اللهِ ﷺ أَنْ أَقْرَأَ الْمُعَوِّذاتِ[١] دُبُرَ كُلِّ صَلاةٍ».

أحمد وابنُ حِبّان

٩٤ - وعن مُعاذِ بْنِ جَبَلٍ رضيَ اللهُ عَنْهُ، أَنَّ رسولَ اللهِ ﷺ أَخذَ بِيَدِهِ وقالَ: «يا مُعاذُ إِني وَاللهِ لأُحِبُّكَ، فَلا تَدَعَنَّ في دُبُرِ كُلِّ صَلاةٍ أَنْ تَقولَ: اللَّهُمَّ أَعِنِّي على ذِكْرِكَ، وشُكْرِكَ، وَحُسْنِ عِبادَتِكَ».

أبو داود والنّسائي

(١) سورة الفلق وسورة الناس (١١٣، ١١٤).

14. Al-Istikhārah—the prayer for seeking guidance in making the best choice

95) The Messenger of Allah (may the blessings and peace of Allah be upon him) taught us (to say) the Istikhārah prayer in all matters in the same way as he would teach us a chapter of the Qur'ān, saying: "If one of you intends to do something, let him make two non-obligatory rak^cas, then let him say: O Allah, I seek from You in Your knowledge to guide me in making the best choice, and I beg You through Your power to give me power to do it, and I ask You of Your great favour, for You are able and I am not, and You know and I do not, and You are the All-knowing of the unseen. O Allah, if You know that this matter—and you name it—is better for me in my religion, my living and my final destiny, whether it be soon or late, then decree it for me and facilitate it for me, and give me Your blessings in it. And if You

١٤ ـ الاستِخـارَةُ[١]

٩٥ ـ كــانَ رَســولُ اللهِ ﷺ يُعَلِّمُنــا الاسْتِخَارَةَ في الأُمُورِ كُلِّها كَما يُعَلِّمُنا السُّورَةَ مِنَ القُرآنِ، يَقولُ: «إذا هَمَّ أَحَدُكُمْ بالأَمْرِ، فَلْيَرْكَعْ رَكْعَتَيْنِ مِنْ غَيْرِ الفَرِيضَةِ، ثم لِيَقُلْ: «اللَّهُـمَّ إنـي أَسْتَخِيـرُكَ بِعِلْمِـكَ، وأَسْتَقْـدِرُكَ بِقُدْرَتِك، وَأَسْأَلُكَ مِنْ فَضْلِكَ العَظِيمِ، فإِنَّكَ تَقْدِرُ ولا أَقْدِرُ، وَتَعْلَمُ وَلا أَعْلَمُ، وأَنْتَ عَلَّامُ الغُيوبِ، اللَّهُمَّ إنْ كُنْتَ تَعْلَمُ أَنَّ هذا الأَمْرَ ـ وتُسمِّيهِ بِاسْمِهِ ـ خَيرٌ لي في دِيني وَمَعاشِي وعَاقِبَةِ أَمْرِي، وعاجِلِهِ وآجِلِهِ، فاقْدُرْهُ لي ويَسِّرْهُ لي، ثم بارِكْ لي فيهِ، وإنْ كُنْتَ تَعْلَمُ

(١) الاستخارة: طلب الخير من الله بسؤاله الهداية إلى ما فيه صلاح الإنسان ومصلحته، عندما يختار أمراً أو يتخذ قراراً.

know that this matter is worse for me in my religion, my living and my final destiny, whether it be soon or late, then turn it away from me and turn me away from it, and decree for me that which is best wherever it may be, then cause me to be content with it."

(Related by al-Bukhārī)

No one has regretted who has sought guidance from the Creator in making a choice, has consulted (his) fellow beings and has considered carefully his matter. Allah the Almighty has said: "And consult with them upon the conduct of affairs. And when you are resolved, then put your trust in Allah."[1] Qatādah said: No people have consulted among themselves seeking the favour of Allah, without their being guided to the best way for their affair.

---

1. The Chapter of the Family of ᶜImrān 3:159.

أَنَّ هٰذا الأَمْرَ شَرٌّ لي في دِيني ومَعَاشِي وعاقِبَةِ أَمْـرِي، وعـاجِلِـهِ وآجِلِـهِ، فـاصْـرِفْـهُ عَنِّـي، وٱصْرِفْنِي عنه، وٱقْدُرْ لِي الْخَيْرَ حيثُ كانَ، ثم رَضِّنِي بِهِ».

البخاري

وما نَدِمَ مَنِ اسْتَخارَ الخالِقَ وَشَاوَرَ المخْلـوقِيـنَ وَتَثَبَّتَ فـي أَمْـرِهِ، فَقَـدْ قـالَ اللهُ تَعالىٰ: ﴿وَشَاوِرْهُمْ فِي الْأَمْرِ فَإِذَا عَزَمْتَ فَتَوَكَّلْ عَلَى اللَّهِ﴾ [آل عمران ٣: ١٥٩] قال قَتادَةُ: ما تَشَاوَرَ قَوْمٌ يَبْتَغُونَ وَجْهَ اللهِ إلا هُدُوا لأَرْشَدِ أَمْرِهِمْ.

15. What is to be said at the time of distress, anxiety and sadness

96) The Messenger of Allah (may the blessings and peace of Allah be upon him) used to say when in distress: "There is no god but Allah, the Great, the Clement; there is no god but Allah, the Lord of the Great Throne; there is no god but Allah, the Lord of the heavens and the Lord of the earth and the Lord of the Noble Throne."

(Related by al-Bukhārī and Muslim)

97) On the authority of the Prophet (may the blessings and peace of Allah be upon him) that when some matter seriously disturbed him, he would say: "O Living and Eternal One, of Your mercy I call for help."

(Related by at-Tirmidhī)

١٥ ـ ما يُقالُ عند الكَرْبِ وَالْهَمِّ وَالْحُزْنِ

٩٦ ـ كانَ رسولُ اللهِ ﷺ يقولُ عِنْدَ الكَرْبِ: «لا إِلٰهَ إِلا اللهُ العَظيمُ الحَليمُ، لا إِلٰهَ إِلاَّ اللهُ رَبُّ العَرْشِ العَظِيمِ، لا إِلٰهَ إِلا اللهُ رَبُّ السَّمٰواتِ ورَبُّ الأَرْضِ ورَبُّ العَرْشِ الكَريمِ».

البخاري ومسلم

٩٧ ـ عَنِ النبيِّ ﷺ: أَنَّه كانَ إِذا حَزَبَهُ(١) أَمْرٌ قالَ: «يا حَيُّ يا قَيُّومُ بِرَحْمَتِكَ أَسْتَغِيثُ».

التِّرْمذي

---

(١) حَزَبه أمر: اشتد عليه.

98) On the authority of Abū Bakrah (may Allah be pleased with him) that the Messenger of Allah (may the blessings and peace of Allah be upon him) said: The invocations of those in distress are: "O Allah, Your mercy I request, so do not leave me to myself for a single moment,[1] but put in order my whole state of affairs. There is no god but You."

(Related by Abū Dāwūd and Ibn Ḥibbān)

99) The Messenger of Allah (may the blessings and peace of Allah be upon him) said to Asmā' bint ᶜUmays: "Shall I teach you words to say when you are in distress—or in a state of distress: O Allah, Allah my Lord, I associate nothing with Him." And in a version (it says) that it should be said seven times.

(Related by Abū Dāwūd)

1. Lit. for the twinkling of an eye.

٩٨ ـ وَعَنْ أَبي بَكْرَةَ رَضِيَ اللهُ عَنْهُ، أَنَّ رَسُولَ اللهِ ﷺ قَالَ: «دَعَواتُ المكْرُوبِ: اللَّهُمَّ رَحْمَتكَ أَرْجُو، فَلا تَكِلْني إلى نَفْسي طَرْفَةَ عَيْنٍ، وَأَصْلِحْ لي شَأْني كُلَّهُ، لا إِلٰهَ إِلا أَنْتَ».

أبو داود وابنُ حِبّان

٩٩ ـ قال رسولُ الله ﷺ لأَسْماءَ بِنْتِ عُمَيْسٍ: «أَلا أُعلِّمُكِ كَلِمَاتٍ تَقُولِينهنَّ عِنْدَ الكَرْبِ ـ أَو في الكَرْبِ ـ اَللهُ، اللهُ رَبِّي لا أُشْرِكُ بِهِ شَيْئاً». وفي رواية أَنَّها تُقالُ سَبْعَ مَرَّاتٍ.

أبو داود

100) The Messenger of Allah (may the blessings and peace of Allah be upon him) said: “The invocation of Dhū ’n-Nūn[1] which he invoked when he was in the belly of the whale (was): There is no god but You. How far are You from every imperfection! I was of the unjust. No Muslim man has ever invoked it in relation to anything without Allah answering it for him.”

(Related by at-Tirmidhī and Aḥmad)

101) On the authority of the Prophet (may the blessings and peace of Allah be upon him), who said: “Neither worry nor sorrow has afflicted a servant (of Allah) when he has said: O Allah, I am Your servant and the son of Your servant and the son of Your bondmaid; I am under Your control;[2]

---

1. Another name for the Prophet Yunus (Jonah).
2. Lit. my forelock is in Your hand.

١٠٠ ـ قال رسولُ اللهِ ﷺ: «دَعْوَةُ ذِي النُّونِ[١] إِذْ دَعا بها وهوَ في بَطْنِ الحُوتِ: لا إِلٰهَ إِلا أَنْتَ، سُبْحانَكَ إِنِّي كُنْتُ مِنَ الظَّالِمِينَ ـ لَمْ يَدْعُ بِها رَجُلٌ مُسْلِمٌ في شَيْءٍ قَطُّ إِلاَّ اسْتَجابَ اللهُ لَهُ».

التِّرْمذي وأحمد

١٠١ ـ عَنِ النَّبي ﷺ قال: «ما أَصابَ عَبْداً هَمٌّ ولا حُزْنٌ، فَقالَ: ـ اللَّهُمَّ إِني عَبْدُكَ، وٱبْنُ عَبْدِكَ، وٱبْنُ أَمَتِكَ، ناصِيَتي بِيَدِكَ،

---

(١) ذو النون هو النبي يونُس عليه السلام الذي التَقَمه الحوت، ثم لفظه بفضل الله.

Your judgement is carried out on me; Your decision about me is just, I ask You by every name that is Yours and by which You have named Yourself or that You have sent down in Your book or have taught to one of Your creation or that You have kept with Yourself in the knowledge of the unseen that You have, to make the Qur'ān the life[1] of my heart, the light of my breast, the disperser of my sorrow, the remover of my worry—without Allah removing his worry and his sorrow and replacing them with freedom from distress."

(Related by Aḥmad and Ibn Ḥibbān)

1. Lit. the spring.

مَـاضٍ[1] فـيَّ حُكْمُـكَ، عَـدْلٌ فـيَّ قَضَـاؤُكَ، أَسْأَلُكَ بِكُلِّ اسمٍ هُوَ لَكَ سَمَّيْتَ بهِ نَفْسَكَ أَو أَنْزَلْتَهُ في كِتَـابِـكَ أَو عَلَّمْتَهُ أَحداً مِنْ خَلْقِكَ، أَو اسْتَأْثَرْتَ بِهِ في عِلْمِ الغَيْبِ عِنْدَكَ، أَنْ تَجْعَـلَ القُـرْآنَ رَبِيـعَ قَلْبِـي، ونُـورَ صَـدْرِي، وجَلاءَ حُزْني، وذهابَ هَمِّي - إلا أَذْهَبَ اللهُ هَمَّهُ وحُزْنَهُ، وأَبْدَلَه مَكَانَهُ فَرَجاً».

أحمد وابنُ حِبّان

(١) نافذ.

16. What is to be said when meeting the enemy and someone of power

102) The Prophet (may the blessings and peace of Allah be upon him) would say when he was in fear of some people:

"O Allah, verily we put You to face them and we take refuge in You from their evil ways."

(Related by Abū Dāwūd and an-Nasā'ī)

103) On the authority of the Prophet (may the blessings and peace of Allah be upon him) that he used to say on meeting the enemy: "O Allah, You are my vigour and my ally. With You I wheel about and with You I leap (upon the enemy), and with You I fight."

(Related by Abū Dāwūd, at-Tirmidhī, Aḥmad and Ibn Ḥibbān)

١٦ ـ ما يُقال في لقاءِ العَدُوِّ وذي السُّلطان

١٠٢ ـ كانَ النبيُّ ﷺ إذا خاف قَوْماً قال:

«اللَّهُمَّ إنَّا نَجْعَلُكَ في نُحورِهِم[١]، ونَعُوذُ بِكَ مِن شُرُورِهِمْ». أبو داود والنَّسائي

١٠٣ ـ عن النبيِّ ﷺ، أَنه كانَ يَقولُ عندَ لِقاءِ العَدُوِّ: «اللَّهُمَّ أَنْتَ عَضُدِي[٢] وأَنْتَ نَصِيري، بِكَ أَجولُ، وَبِكَ أَصولُ[٣]، وبِكَ أُقاتِلُ».

أبو داود والترمذي وأحمد وابنُ حِبَّان

---

(١) النحور هي الصدور والمعنى سؤال الله أن يقضي على الأعداء.

(٢) أنت قوتي.

(٣) أجول وأصول في ساحة القتال: أي أدور وأغالب.

104) ᶜAbdullah the son of ᶜAbbās (may Allah be pleased with them both) said: Allah is sufficient for us! Most Excellent is He in whom we trust! This was said by Abraham when he was cast into the fire, and it was said by Muḥammad when the people said to him: Verily the people have gathered against you.[1]

(Related by al-Bukhārī)

---

1. A reference to the Chapter of the Family of ᶜImrān 3:173.

١٠٤ ـ وقال عبدُ اللهِ بنُ عبّاسٍ رَضِيَ اللهُ عنهما: ﴿حَسْبُنَا اللهُ وَنِعْمَ الوَكِيلُ﴾ [آل عمران ٣: ١٧٣]، قالها إبراهيمُ حينَ أُلْقِيَ في النَّارِ، وقالَها مُحمَّدٌ حينَ قالَ لهُ النَّاسُ: ﴿إِنَّ النَّاسَ قَدْ جَمَعُوا لَكُمْ﴾ [آل عمران ٣: ١٧٣].

البخاري

17. On the devil intruding upon man[1]

Allah the Almighty has said: "And say: My Lord, I seek refuge in You from the suggestions of the devils, and I seek refuge in You, my Lord, lest they be present."[2]

105) On the authority of the Prophet (may the blessings and peace of Allah be upon him) that he used to say: "I take refuge in Allah the Hearer, the Knower, from the accursed devil, from his ability to derange, his pride and his noxious exhalations," referring to the words of Allah the Almighty: "And if a whisper from the devil reach you, then seek refuge in Allah. He is the Hearer, the Knower."[3]

(Related by Abū Dāwūd)

1. Lit. the son of Adam.
2. The Chapter of the Believers 23:97–98.
3. The Chapter of Fuṣṣilat 41:36.

١٧ ـ في الشيطانِ يَعْرِضُ لاِبْنِ آدَمَ

قالَ الله تعالى: ﴿وَقُلْ رَبِّ أَعُوذُ بِكَ مِنْ هَمَزَاتِ الشَّيَاطِينِ، وأَعُوذُ بِكَ رَبِّ أَنْ يَحْضُرُونِ﴾ [المؤمنون ٢٣: ٩٧ ـ ٩٨].

١٠٥ ـ عَنِ النبيِّ ﷺ أَنَّه كانَ يَقولُ: «أَعُوذُ باللهِ السَّميعِ العَليمِ مِنَ الشَّيْطانِ الرَّجيم مِن، هَمْزِهِ ونَفْخِهِ وَنَفْثِهِ[١]». لِقَوْلِ اللهِ تعالى: ﴿وَإِمَّا يَنزَغَنَّكَ مِنَ الشَّيْطَانِ نَزْغٌ فَاسْتَعِذْ باللهِ إِنَّهُ هُوَ السَّمِيعُ العَلِيمُ﴾ [فُصِّلَتْ ٤١: ٣٦].

أبو داود

(١) أنظر حديث ٦٢.

106) The call to prayers drives away the devil. On the authority of Abū Hurayrah that the Prophet (may the blessings and peace of Allah be upon him) said: "The devil, if the call to prayers is given, retreats."

(Related by Muslim)

107) Abū Zumayl said: I said to the son of ᶜAbbās (may Allah be pleased with them both): What shall I do about something I find in myself (meaning something in the way of doubt)? He said to me: If you have found anything in yourself (of doubt), then say: He is the First and the Last, and the Outward and the Inward, and He is Knower of all things.[1]

(Related by Abū Dāwūd)

1. A reference to the Chapter of Iron 57:3.

١٠٦ ـ والأَذانُ يَطْرُدُ الشيْطانَ: عن أَبي هُرَيْرةَ رضيَ الله عنه عَنِ النبيِّ ﷺ قال: «إِنَّ الشَّيْطانَ إِذا نُودِيَ بالصلاةِ أَدْبَرَ». مسلم

١٠٧ ـ وقال أَبو زُمَيْل: قُلْتُ لاِبْنِ عباسٍ رَضِيَ اللهُ عَنْهما: ما شَيْءٌ أَجِدُهُ في نَفْسي ـ يعني شيئاً من شَكٍّ ـ فقالَ لي: «إِذا وَجَدْتَ في نَفْسِكَ شَيْئاً فَقُلْ: ﴿هُوَ الأَوَّلُ والآخِرُ، والظَّاهِرُ والبَاطِنُ، وهُوَ بِكُلِّ شَيْءٍ عَلِيمٌ﴾[1]». أبو داود

---

(١) إشارة إلى الآية في سورة الحديد ٥٧: ٣.

18. On submitting to divine decree but without holding back or being remiss

---

Allah the Almighty has said: "O you who believe, be not as those who disbelieved and said of their brethren who went abroad in the land or were fighters: If only they had been with us they would not have died and been killed, lest Allah may make it anguish in their hearts, and Allah gives life and causes death, and Allah is Seer of what you do."[1]

---

1. The Chapter of the Family of ᶜImrān 3:156.

١٨ - في التَّسْليم للقضاءِ مِنْ غيرِ عَجْزٍ ولا تَفْريطٍ[١]

قالَ اللهُ تعالى: ﴿يا أَيُّها الَّذِينَ آمَنُوا لا تكُونُوا كَالَّذِينَ كَفَرُوا وقَالوا لإِخْوانِهِمْ إِذا ضَرَبُوا[٢] في الأَرْضِ أَو كانوا غُزَّىً[٣] لَوْ كَانُوا عِنْدَنَا مَا مَاتُوا وَمَا قُتِلُوا لِيَجْعَلَ اللهُ ذٰلِكَ حَسْرَةً في قُلُوبِهِمْ واللهُ يُحْيي وَيُمِيتُ واللهُ بِمَا تَعْمَلُونَ بَصيرٌ﴾ [آل عمران ٣: ١٥٦].

(١) أي لا يمنعنك الرضا بقضاء الله عن الاجتهاد لتحقيق المصلحة لنفسك، فالمؤمن إذا مرض يرضى بقضاء الله بالمرض ولكنه يسعى ويجتهد في العلاج.

(٢) سافروا للتجارة أو غيرها ثم ماتوا خارج بلادهم.

(٣) غُزَّى: أي غزاة ومجاهدين فقتلوا.

108) The Messenger of Allah (may the blessings and peace of Allah be upon him) said: "The vigorous believer is better and more loved by Allah the Almighty than the weak believer; and in each of them there is good. Strive for what will benefit you, and ask help of Allah (Exalted be He!), and do not hold back. And if something befalls you, do not say: If only I had done such-and-such, but say: Allah has decreed (it) and has done what He wished, for the words 'if only' open up the work of the devil."

(Related by Muslim)

١٠٨ ـ قالَ رسولُ اللهِ ﷺ: «المؤمِنُ القَويُّ خيرٌ وأَحبُّ إلى اللهِ تَعالى مِنَ المؤمِنِ الضَّعيفِ، وفي كُلٍّ خيرٌ. احْرِص على ما يَنْفَعُكَ، وَٱسْتَعِنْ باللهِ عَزَّ وَجَلَّ، ولا تَعْجَزْ، وإنْ أَصابَكَ شَيْءٌ فَلا تَقُلْ: لَوْ أَنِّي فَعَلْتُ كانَ كَذا وكَذا، ولٰكن قُلْ قَدَّرَ اللهُ وما شاءَ فَعَلَ، فَإِنَّ (لَوْ) تَفْتَحُ عَمَلَ الشَّيْطان».

مسلم

19. About favours bestowed on man

Allah the Almighty has said in the story of the two men:[1] "If only, when you had entered your garden, you had said: That which Allah wills (will come to pass). There is no strength other than in Allah."

109) On the authority of the Prophet (may the blessings and peace of Allah be upon him) that he would say when seeing something that pleased him: "Praise be to Allah through whose favour good things are accomplished." And if he saw something that offended him he would say: "Praise be to Allah in any event."

(Related by Ibn Mājah)

---

1. A reference to the story in the Chapter of the Cave 18:39 about two men one of whom possessed two productive gardens. He was not thankful to Allah for having bestowed them on him. The other man used to counsel him to believe in Allah and express his gratitude to Him.

١٩ ـ فيما يُنْعَمُ بِهِ على الإِنسانِ

قالَ اللهُ تعالىٰ في قِصَّةِ الرَّجُلَيْنِ[١]:

﴿وَلَوْلا إِذْ دَخَلْتَ جَنَّتَكَ قُلْتَ مَا شَاءَ اللهُ لا قُوَّةَ إلا باللهِ﴾ [الكهف ١٨ : ٣٩].

١٠٩ ـ وَعَنِ النَّبِيِّ ﷺ أَنَّه كانَ إِذا رأى ما يَسُرُّهُ قالَ: «الحَمْدُ للهِ الَّذي بِنِعْمَتِهِ تَتِمَّ الصَّالِحاتُ، وإِذا رأىٰ ما يَسُوؤُهُ قالَ: الحَمْدُ للهِ على كُلِّ حالٍ».

ابنُ ماجَه

(١) إشارة إلى القصة الواردة في سورة الكهف ١٨ :٣٩ عن رجلين، كان لأحدهما بستانان مثمران ولم يكن يشكر الله على نعمته بهما، وكان الآخر ينصحه بالإيمان وشكر الله.

20. About that which befalls a believer, both small and great

Allah the Almighty has said: "Those who say when a misfortune befalls them: Verily we belong to Allah and unto Him we are returning, such are they on whom are blessings from their Lord and mercy. Such are the rightly-guided."[1]

110) The Messenger of Allah (may the blessings and peace of Allah be upon him) said: "Let one of you say: Verily we belong to Allah and unto Him we are returning, in every matter (that befalls him) even something relating to the leather thong of his sandals, (if it breaks), for (even) that is a misfortune."

(Related by Ibn as-Sunnī)

1. The Chapter of the Cow 2:156–157.

٢٠ ـ فيما يُصابُ بهِ المؤمنُ من صغيرٍ وكبيرٍ

قالَ اللهُ تعالى: ﴿الَّذِينَ إِذا أَصَابَتْهُمْ مُصِيبَةٌ قَالُوا إِنَّا للهِ وإِنَّا إِلَيْهِ رَاجِعُونَ. أُولٰئِكَ عَلَيْهِمْ صَلَوَاتٌ مِن رَبِّهِمْ وَرَحْمَةٌ وَأُولٰئِكَ هُمُ المُهْتَدُونَ﴾ [البقرة ٢: ١٥٦ ـ ١٥٧].

١١٠ ـ قالَ رسولُ اللهِ ﷺ: «لِيَسْتَرْجِعِ[١] أَحدُكُمْ في كُلِّ شَيْءٍ، حتى في شِسْعِ[٢] نَعْلِهِ فإِنَّها مِنَ المصائِبِ».

ابن السُّني

---

(١) على المرء إذا فقد شيئاً أو أصيب في أمر، أن يسترجع، بقوله ﴿إنا لله وإنا إليه راجعون﴾.

(٢) شِسْع النعل: سَيْر النعل الذي يكون بين الإصبعين، فإذا قُطع أو فُقد فهي خسارة.

111) Umm Salamah (may Allah be pleased with her) said: I heard the Messenger of Allah (may the blessings and peace of Allah be upon him) say: "There is no servant (of Allah) who is afflicted with some misfortune and who says: Verily we belong to Allah and unto Him we are returning, O Allah, reward me for bearing my misfortune (with patience) and replace it with something better—without Allah rewarding him and replacing (his loss) with something better."

She said: When Abū Salamah died I said as the Messenger of Allah (may the blessings and peace of Allah be upon him) had ordered me and Allah gave me (someone) better than him: the Messenger of Allah (may the blessings and peace of Allah be upon him).[1]

(Related by Muslim)

---

1. Because the Messenger of Allah then married her.

١١١ ـ وقالت أُمُّ سَلَمَةَ رَضِيَ اللهُ عَنْها: سَمِعْتُ رسولَ اللهِ ﷺ يَقولُ: «ما مِنْ عَبْدٍ تُصيبُهُ مُصِيبَةٌ فَيَقولُ: إنَّا للهِ وإِنَّا إِلَيْهِ راجِعونَ، اللَّهُمَّ أَجِرْني[١] في مُصِيبَتي وأَخْلِفْ[٢] لي خَيْراً مِنْها، إلا أَجَرَهُ اللهُ في مُصيبَتِهِ، وأَخْلَفَ لَهُ خَيْراً منها».

قالتْ: فَلَمَّا تُوُفِّيَ أَبو سَلَمَةَ: قُلْتُ كما أَمَرَني رسولُ اللهِ ﷺ، فَأَخْلَفَ اللهُ لي خَيْراً مِنْهُ، رَسولَ اللهِ ﷺ[٣].

مسلم

---

(١) أَجِرْني في مصيبتي: أعطني ثواب الصبر عليها.

(٢) أَخْلِف: أعطني عِوَضاً.

(٣) لأن رسول الله ﷺ تزوجها بعد موت زوجها.

112) And she said: The Messenger of Allah (may the blessings and peace of Allah be upon him) came to Abū Salamah when his eyes were fixed (in death), and the Prophet closed his eyelids. Then he said: "When the soul is taken, the sight follows it." Some people of his relatives raised a clamour, and he said: "Do not pray for yourselves other than for good things, for the angels confirm what you say (by saying Amen)." Then he said: "O Allah, forgive Abū Salamah and raise his degree among those that have been rightly-guided, and let him be replaced by his offspring that remain, and forgive us and him, O Lord of the Worlds, and make his grave spacious and give him light therein."

(Related by Muslim)

١١٢ ـ وَقالتْ: دَخَلَ رسولُ اللهِ ﷺ على أَبي سَلَمَةَ وَقَدْ شَقَّ بَصَرُهُ[١]، فأَغْمَضَهُ ثم قال: «إنَّ الرُّوحَ إذا قُبِضَ تَبِعَهُ البَصَرُ»، فَضَجَّ ناسٌ مِنْ أَهْلِهِ، فقالَ: «لا تَدْعُوا على أنفُسِكُمْ إلا بِخَيْرٍ، فإنَّ الملائِكَةَ يُؤَمِّنُونَ على ما تَقولونَ»، ثم قال: «اللَّهُمَّ ٱغْفِرْ لأَبي سَلَمَةَ، وٱرْفَعْ دَرَجَتَهُ في الْمَهْدِيِّينَ، وٱخْلُفْهُ في عَقِبِهِ في الْغابِرينَ[٢]، وٱغْفِرْ لَنا ولَهُ يا رَبَّ العالَمينَ، وافْسَحْ لَهُ في قَبْرِهِ ونَوِّرْ لَهُ فيهِ».

مسلم

(١) شق البصرُ: انفتح وثبت علامة الموت.

(٢) اجعل له خَلَفاً في ذريته الباقية.

21. On debt

113) On the authority of ᶜAlī ibn Abī Ṭālib (may Allah be pleased with him) that a slave who had made a written contract with his master to pay off money, came to him and said: I am unable to pay off the amount that is due from me, so help me. He said: Shall I not teach you some words that the Messenger of Allah (may the blessings and peace of Allah be upon him) taught me? Were you to have upon you a debt (as big) as a mountain, Allah would discharge it for you if you were to say: "O Allah, make that which is permissible of Yours suffice me rather than that which is not permissible, and make me, through Your favour, dispense with everyone but You."

(Related by at-Tirmidhī)

٢١ ـ في الدَّيْنِ

١١٣ ـ عَنْ عليٍّ بْنِ أَبي طالبٍ رَضِيَ اللهُ عنه أَنَّ مُكَاتَباً[١] جاءَهُ فقال: إِني عَجَزْتُ عَنْ كِتَابَتِي[٢] فَأَعِنِّي، قالَ: أَلا أُعلِّمُكَ كَلِماتٍ عَلَّمَنِيهِنَّ رَسولُ اللهِ ﷺ، لَوْ كانَ عَلَيْكَ مِثْلُ جَبَلٍ دَيْناً أَدَّاهُ اللهُ عَنْكَ؟ قُلْ: «اللَّهُمَّ اكْفِنِي بِحَلالِكَ عَنْ حَرامِكَ، وأَغْنِنِي بِفَضْلِكَ عَمَّنْ سِوَاكَ».

التِّرْمذي

---

(١) المكاتَب: هو العبد كتب عليه سيده مالا يدفعه فيحرره.

(٢) عجزتُ عن كتابتي: أي عن دَفع ما كُتب عليّ من المال.

22. On ruqyah[1]

114) The Messenger of Allah (may the blessings and peace of Allah be upon him) used to say a *ruqyah* over al-Ḥasan and al-Ḥusayn (may Allah be pleased with them) (with the words): "I seek protection for the two of you with the consummate words of Allah from every devil and venomous reptile and from every evil eye." And he used to say: "Verily your father[2] would use them as a *ruqyah* for Ishmael and Isaac."

(Related by al-Bukhārī)

115) On the authority of ᶜĀ'ishah (may Allah be pleased with her) that the Prophet (may the blessings and peace of Allah be upon him) used to say a *ruqyah* over some of his relatives by passing his right hand (over the sick person) and saying: "O Allah, Lord of people, take away the harm and heal (him), for You are the Healer, there is no healing other than Your healing, a healing that will not leave any illness."

(Related by al-Bukhārī and Muslim)

---

1. An invocation for protection against evil.
2. I.e., Abraham their forefather.

٢٢ - في الرُّقَىٰ

١١٤ - كانَ رسولُ الله ﷺ يُعوِّذُ الْحَسَنَ والحُسَيْنَ رَضِيَ اللهُ عنهما: «أُعِيذُكُما بِكَلِماتِ اللهِ التَّامَّةِ مِنْ كُلِّ شَيْطانٍ وهَامَّةٍ[١]، ومِنْ كُلِّ عَيْنٍ لامَّةٍ»[٢]، ويقولُ: «إِنَّ أَباكُما[٣] كانَ يُعوِّذُ بها إِسماعيلَ وإِسْحاقَ».

البخاري

١١٥ - وعن عائشةَ رضي اللهُ عنها أَنَّ النبيَّ ﷺ، كانَ يُعوِّذُ، بعضَ أَهْلِهِ يَمْسَحُ بِيَدِهِ اليُمْنىٰ ويَقولُ: «اللَّهُمَّ رَبَّ النَّاسِ، أَذْهِبِ البَاسَ، واْشْفِ أَنْتَ الشَّافي، لا شِفاءَ إِلا شِفاؤُكَ، شِفاءً لا يُغادِرُ سَقَماً».

البخاري ومسلم

---

(١) الهامّة: الحشرة السامة من هوامّ الأرض.

(٢) اللامّة: العين الشريرة التي تنذر بالسوء والأذى.

(٣) أي إبراهيم عليه السلام.

116) On the authority of [c]Uthmān ibn Abī 'l-[c]Āṣ that he complained to the Messenger of Allah (may the blessings and peace of Allah be upon him) of a pain he had had in his body since he embraced Islam, and the Messenger of Allah (may the blessings and peace of Allah be upon him) said: "Place your hand where it hurts in your body and say: In the name of Allah—three times, and say seven times: I take refuge in the might and power of Allah from the evil of what I feel and fear."

(Related by Muslim)

117) On the authority of the Prophet (may the blessings and peace of Allah be upon him), who said: "He who visits a sick man whose time of death has not yet arrived, and who says when with him seven times: I ask Allah the Great, Lord of the Great Throne, to heal you, Allah will heal him."

(Related by Abū Dāwūd and at-Tirmidhī)

١١٦ ـ وَعَنْ عثمانَ بْنِ أَبي الْعاصِ أَنَّهُ شَكا إِلى رسولِ اللهِ ﷺ وَجَعاً يَجِدُهُ في جَسَدِهِ مُنْذُ أَسْلَمَ، فقالَ رسولُ اللهِ ﷺ: «ضعْ يدَكَ عَلَى الْذي يَأْلَمُ مِنْ جَسَدِكَ وَقُلْ: بِسْمِ اللهِ ثَلاثاً، وقلْ سَبعَ مَرَّاتٍ: أَعُوذُ بعِزَّةِ اللهِ وقُدْرتِهِ مِنْ شَرِّ ما أَجِدُ وأُحاذِرُ».

مسلم

١١٧ ـ عَنِ النبيِّ ﷺ قالَ: «مَنْ عادَ مَريضاً لَمْ يَحْضُرْ أَجَلُهُ فقَالَ عندَهُ سَبْعَ مَرَّاتٍ: أَسْأَلُ اللهَ العَظِيمَ رَبَّ العَرْشِ العَظيمِ أَنْ يَشْفِيَكَ، إلا عافاهُ اللهُ».

أبو داود والترمذي

23. On entering graveyards

118) The Messenger of Allah (may the blessings and peace of Allah be upon him) used to teach them that, when going out to the graveyards, they should say: "Peace be upon you, O people of the dwellings, true believers and those who have surrendered themselves to Allah. Verily we shall, when Allah wills, be joining you. We ask of Allah to safeguard us and you."

(Related by Muslim)

٢٣ - في دُخُولِ المقابرِ

١١٨ - كـانَ رسـولُ اللهِ ﷺ يُعَلِّمُهُـمْ إِذا خَرَجُوا إلى المقابِرِ أَنْ يقولَ قائِلُهُمْ: «السَّلامُ عَلَيْكُمْ أَهْلَ الدِّيارِ مِنَ المؤمنينَ والمسلمينَ، وإِنَّا إِنْ شاءَ اللهُ بِكُمْ لاحِقُونَ، نَسْأَلُ اللهَ لَنَا وَلَكُم العافِيَةَ».

مسلم

24. On praying for rain

119) On the authority of Jābir the son of ᶜAbdullah (may Allah be pleased with them both), who said: There came to the Prophet (may the blessings and peace of Allah be upon him) some women who were wailing,[1] and the Prophet (may the blessings and peace of Allah be upon him) said: "O Allah, send down on us a rain that is wholesome, gentle, productive, beneficial and not harmful, sooner rather than later"—and the skies opened on them.

(Related by Abū Dāwūd and al-Ḥākim)

120) On the authority of ᶜĀ'ishah (may Allah be pleased with her), who said: The people complained to the Messenger of Allah (may the blessings and peace of Allah be upon him) of the drought, so he ordered a pulpit (to be brought) and it was put down in the place for holding prayers, and he assigned for the people a day on which to go out. So the

1. Because of a drought.

٢٤ ـ في الاسْتِسْقاءِ[١]

١١٩ ـ عَنْ جابِرِ بْنِ عبدِ اللهِ رَضيَ اللهُ عَنْهما قالَ: أَتَتِ النبيَّ ﷺ بَواكٍ[٢] فقال النبيُّ ﷺ: «اللَّهُمَّ اسْقِنا غَيْثاً مُغِيثاً، مَريئاً، مَرِيعاً نافعاً غيرَ ضارٍ[٣]، عاجِلاً غيرَ آجِلٍ» فأَطْبَقَتْ عليهمُ السَّماءُ[٤].

أبو داود والحاكم

١٢٠ ـ وَعَنْ عائشةَ رَضيَ اللهُ عنها، قالَتْ: شَكا الناسُ إلى رَسولِ اللهِ ﷺ قُحُوطَ[٥] المطَرِ، فأَمَرَ بِمِنْبَرٍ فَوُضِعَ لهُ في الْمُصَلَّى، وَوَعَدَ النَّاسَ يَوماً يَخْرُجُونَ فيهِ،

---

(١) الاستسقاء: الدعاء بنزول المطر.

(٢) بواك: جمع باكية. وقد بكت النساء لجَدْب الأرض وقلة الأرزاق.

(٣) الغيث: المطر، المريء: الهنيء. المريع: الذي يملأ الأرض خصباً.

(٤) أطبقت عليهم السماء: غمرهم المطر.

(٥) قحوط المطر: احتباسه.

Messenger of Allah (may the blessings and peace of Allah be upon him) went out when the sun's rim made its appearance, and he sat down on the pulpit and said: "Allah is greatest" and "Praise be to Allah," (Exalted be He!), and then he said:

"You have complained of the dryness of your lands and of the rain holding back from you beyond its usual season, and Allah (How far is He from every imperfection!) has ordered you to invoke Him and He has promised you that He will answer you." Then he said: "Praise be to Allah, Lord of the Worlds, the Merciful, the Compassionate, Owner of the Day of Judgement.[1] There is no god but Allah, who acts as He desires. O Allah, You are Allah, there is no god but You, You are the self-sufficient and we are the needy. Bring down upon us the rain and make what You have brought down for us a power and a sufficiency for a time."

1. The Chapter of the Opening 1:1–3.

فَخَـرَجَ رسـولُ اللهِ ﷺ حيـنَ بَـدَا حـاجِـبُ الشَّمْسِ، فَقَعَدَ على المِنبَرِ فكَبَّرَ وحَمِدَ اللهَ عَزَّ وَجلَّ، ثُمَّ قالَ:

«إِنَّـكُـمْ شَكَـوْتُـمْ جَـدْبَ دِيـارِكُـمْ، وٱسْتِئْخارَ المَطَرِ عن إِبَّانِ زَمانِهِ عَنْكُمْ، وقدْ أَمَرَكُمُ اللهُ سُبْحانَهُ أَنْ تَدْعُوهُ، وَوَعَدَكُمْ أن يَسْتَجِيبَ لكُمْ»، ثـم قـالَ: ﴿الحَمْـدُ للهِ رَبِّ العالَمينَ، الرَّحمٰنِ الرَّحيمِ. مَالِكِ يَـوْمِ الدِّينِ﴾[١]. لا إِلٰهَ إِلا اللهُ يَفْعَلُ ما يُريدُ، اللَّهُمَّ أَنْتَ اللهُ لا إِلٰهَ إِلا أَنْتَ، أَنْتَ الغَنِيُّ ونَحْنُ الفُقَراءُ، أَنْزِلْ عَلَيْنا الغَيْثَ، واجْعلْ ما أَنْزَلْتَ لَنا قُوَّةً وَبَلاغاً إِلى حينٍ».

(١) الفاتحة: ١ ـ ٣.

Then he raised his hands, and he continued to raise them until one could see the whiteness of his armpits. Then he turned his back on the people, and he put the inside of his cloak outside, while raising his hands. Then he advanced upon the people, having come down (from the pulpit), and he prayed two rak^{c}as, and Allah (Exalted be He!) brought into being a cloud and there was thunder and lightning. Then, by the permission of Allah the Almighty, it rained, and he had not reached his mosque before torrents of rain flowed. When he saw the speed with which they sought shelter, he laughed (may the blessings and peace of Allah be upon him) (so much) that his molars could be seen, and he said: "I bear witness that Allah is capable of doing everything and that I am the servant of Allah and His Messenger."

(Related by Abū Dāwūd)

ثمَّ رَفَعَ يَدَيْهِ فلم يَزَلْ في الرَّفْعِ حتى بَدا بَياضُ إِبْطَيْهِ، ثم حَوَّلَ إلى النَّاسِ ظَهْرَهُ، وقَلَّبَ أو حَوَّلَ رِداءَهُ وهُوَ رافعٌ يَدَيْهِ، ثم أَقْبَلَ على الناسِ، ونَزَلَ فَصَلَّى رَكْعَتَيْنِ، فَأَنْشَأَ اللهُ عَزَّ وجَلَّ سَحابَةً، فَرَعَدَتْ وَبَرَقَتْ، ثُمَّ أَمْطَرَتْ بِإِذْنِ اللهِ تعالى، فلم يَأْتِ مَسْجِدَهُ حَتى سالَتِ السُّيولُ، فلمَّا رَأَىٰ سُرْعَتَهُمْ إلى الكِنِّ[1] ضَحِكَ ﷺ حتى بَدَتْ نَواجِذُهُ فقالَ: «أَشْهَدُ أَنَّ اللهَ على كُلِّ شَيْءٍ قديرٌ، وأَنِّي عَبْدُ اللهِ ورسولُهُ».

أبو داود

(١) الكِنُّ: ما يستر الإنسان مثل البناء وغيره.

25. About winds

121) The Messenger of Allah (may the blessings and peace of Allah be upon him) said: "Winds are from the mercy of Allah and bring mercy and bring punishment. When you see them do not curse them, and ask Allah for the best of them, and take refuge in Allah from the worst of them."

(Related by Abū Dāwūd, Ibn Mājah and Aḥmad)

122) The Prophet (may the blessings and peace of Allah be upon him), when a wind blew, would say: "O Allah, I ask You for the good of it and the good that is in it, and the good by which it has been sent, and I take refuge in You from the evil of it and the evil that is in it, and the evil by which it has been sent."

(Related by Muslim)

٢٥ - في الرِّيحِ

١٢١ - قال رسولُ اللهِ ﷺ: «الرِّيحُ مِنْ رَوْحِ اللهِ[١] تأتي بالرَّحْمَةِ، وَتَأْتي بالعَذابِ، فإذا رأَيْتُموها فلا تَسُبُّوها، وٱسْأَلوا اللهَ خَيْرَها، وٱسْتَعيذوا باللهِ مِن شَرِّها».

أبو داود وابنُ ماجَه وأحمد

١٢٢ - كانَ النَّبيُّ ﷺ إذا عَصَفَتِ الرِّيحُ قالَ: «اللَّهُمَّ إني أَسْأَلُكَ خَيْرَها، وخَيْرَ ما فِيها، وخيرَ ما أُرْسِلَتْ بِهِ، وأَعوذُ بكَ مِنْ شَرِّها وشَرِّ ما فيها وشَرِّ ما أُرْسِلَتْ بِهِ».

مسلم

(١) أي من رحمة الله بعباده.

26. What is to be said when there is thunder

123) ᶜAbdullah the son of az-Zubayr (may Allah be pleased with them both) used, on hearing thunder, to stop conversing and would say: How far is He from every imperfection! He whose praise the thunder extols, and the angels (too) in awe of Him.[1]

(Related by al-Bukhārī, al-Bayhaqī and Mālik)

1. A quotation from the Chapter of the Thunder 13:13.

٢٦ ـ ما يُقالُ عِنْدَ الرَّعْدِ

١٢٣ ـ كانَ عبدُ اللهِ بْنُ الزُّبيرِ رَضِيَ اللهُ عنهما إذا سَمِعَ الرَّعْدَ تَرَكَ الحَدِيثَ وقالَ: «سُبْحانَ الذي يُسَبِّحُ الرَّعْدُ بِحَمْدِه، والمَلائِكَةُ مِنْ خِيفَتِهِ»[١].

البخاري والبيهقي ومالك

(١) من قوله تعالى: ﴿وَيُسَبِّحُ الرَّعْدُ بحمده والملائِكَةُ مِنْ خِيفَتِهِ﴾ الرعد ١٣: ١٣.

27. What is to be said when there is rainfall

124) Zayd ibn Khālid al-Juhaniyy (may Allah be pleased with him) said: The Messenger of Allah (may the blessings and peace of Allah be upon him) led the morning prayer for us at al-Ḥudaybiyah [following rainfall during the night]. When he finished, he faced the people and said: "Do you know what your Lord has said?" They said: Allah and His Messenger know best. He said: "He said, this morning one of my servants became a believer in Me and one a disbeliever. As for him who said: We have been given rain by virtue of Allah and His mercy, that one is a believer in Me, a disbeliever in the stars; and as for him who said: We have been given rain by such-and-such a star, that one is a disbeliever in Me, a believer in the stars."

(Related by al-Bukhārī and Muslim)

٢٧ ـ ما يُقالُ عِنْدَ نزولِ الغَيْثِ

١٢٤ ـ قالَ زَيْدُ بْنُ خالدٍ الْجُهَنِيُّ رَضِيَ اللهُ عَنْهُ: صَلَّى بِنا رسولُ اللهِ ﷺ صلاةَ الصُّبْحِ بالحُدَيْبِيَةِ [في إِثْرِ سَماءٍ كانَتْ مِنَ اللَّيْلِ[١]] فلمَّا انْصَرَفَ أَقْبَلَ على النَّاسِ فقالَ: «هَلْ تَدْرُونَ ماذا قَالَ رَبُّكُمْ؟» قالوا: اللهُ ورسولُهُ أَعْلَمُ، قالَ: «قالَ: أَصْبَحَ مِنْ عِبادي مُؤْمِنٌ بِي وكافِرٌ، فأَمَّا مَنْ قالَ: مُطِرْنا بِفَضْلِ اللهِ ورحْمَتِهِ، فَذٰلِكَ مُؤْمِنٌ بي كافِرٌ بالكَوْكَبِ، وأَمَّا مَنْ قَالَ: مُطِرْنا بِنَوْءِ كذا وكذا[٢]، فَذٰلِكَ كافِرٌ بِي مُؤْمِنٌ بالكَوْكَبِ».

البخاري ومسلم

---

(١) أي عقب سقوط المطر ليلاً.

(٢) النوْء: الكوكب، ربطوا نزول المطر به، ولم يربطوه بالله مسير الكواكب.

125) Anas (may Allah be pleased with him) said: A man entered the mosque on a Friday while the Messenger of Allah (may the blessings and peace of Allah be upon him) was standing delivering his sermon. He said: O Messenger of Allah, animals have perished and we are at our wits' end, so pray to Allah to give us rain. So the Messenger of Allah (may the blessings and peace of Allah be upon him) raised his hands, then said: "O Allah, give us rain. O Allah, give us rain." Anas said: By Allah, we did not see any clouds or streaks of clouds, and there was no building or house between us and Sal^{c}.[1] Then from behind it a cloud rose up, and when it was in the centre of the sky, it spread out and then it gave rain, and, by Allah, we did not see the sun for a week.

---

1. A mountain on the north-western side of Medina. A large expanse of cloudless sky was thus visible.

١٢٥ ـ قالَ أَنَسٌ رضيَ اللهَ عنهُ: دَخَلَ رجلٌ الْمَسْجِدَ يومَ الْجُمُعَةِ، ورسولُ اللهِ ﷺ قائمٌ يَخْطُبُ، فقالَ: يا رسولَ اللهِ هَلَكَتِ الأَمـوالُ[١] وَانْقَطَعَـتِ السُّبُـلُ[٢]، فـادْعُ اللهَ يُغيثُنا، فَرَفَعَ رسولُ اللهِ ﷺ يَدَيْهِ ثُمَّ قالَ: «اللَّهُمَّ أَغِثْنا، اللَّهُمَّ أَغِثْنا»، قالَ أَنَسٌ: وَاللهِ ما نَرىٰ في السَّماءِ من سَحابٍ ولا قَزَعَةٍ[٣] وما بَيْنَنا وبَيْنَ سَلْعٍ[٤] من بُنْيانٍ ولا دارٍ، فَطَلَعَتْ مِـنْ وَرَائِـهِ سَحَـابَـةٌ فلمَّـا تَـوَسَّطَـتِ السَّمـاءَ، انْتَشَـرَتْ، ثُـمَّ أَمْطَـرَتْ، فَـلا واللهِ مـا رأَيْنـا

(١) الأموال هنا هي الأنعام من إبل وماشية.
(٢) أي انقطعت أسباب التكسب والمعيشة.
(٣) القَزَعَة: واحدة القَزَع وهي قطع السحاب المتفرقة.
(٤) سَلْع: جبل في المدينة في طرفها الشمالي الغربي.

Then the following Friday a man entered by that (selfsame) door while the Messenger of Allah (may the blessings and peace of Allah be upon him) was standing and delivering his sermon, and he said: O Messenger of Allah, animals have perished and we are at our wits' end as the roads are cut off, so pray to Allah to hold it back from us. So the Prophet (may the blessings and peace of Allah be upon him) raised his hands, then said: "O Allah, round about us and not on us. O Allah, on the hills and the low-lying mountains, on the bottoms of water-courses, and the places where trees grow"—and it cleared and we went out walking in the sun.

(Related by al-Bukhārī and Muslim)

الشَّمْسَ سَبْتاً[1]. ثم دَخَلَ رَجُلٌ من ذٰلِكَ البَابِ في الجُمُعَةِ المقْبِلَةِ وَرَسولُ اللهِ ﷺ قائِمٌ يَخْطُبُ، فقالَ: يا رسولَ اللهِ هَلَكَتِ الأَمْوالُ، وانْقَطَعَتِ السُّبُلُ[2]، فادْعُ اللهَ يُمْسِكُها عنَّا، فَرَفَعَ النبيُّ ﷺ يَدَيْهِ ثم قالَ: «اللَّهمَّ حَوَالَيْنا ولا عَلَيْنا، اللهمَّ على الآكامِ[3]، والظِّرابِ، وبُطونِ الأَوْدِيَةِ، ومَنابِتِ الشَّجَرِ»، فانْقَلَعَتْ، وخَرَجْنا نَمْشِي في الشَّمْسِ.

البخاري ومسلم

---

(١) سبْتاً: أي أسبوعاً أو فترة غير قصيرة.

(٢) انقطعت أسباب التكسب بانقطاع الطرق بعد الأمطار.

(٣) الآكام: التلال، والظِّراب: الجبال المنبسطة.

28. On seeing the crescent moon

126) The Messenger of Allah (may the blessings and peace of Allah be upon him) would say when seeing the crescent moon: "Allah is greatest; O Allah, bring it to us in safety and faith, in security and submission,[1] and in the success of what You like and approve of. Allah is our Lord and your[2] Lord."

(Related by at-Tirmidhī, Ibn Ḥibbān and al-Dārimī)

1. I.e., as Muslims.
2. He is addressing the crescent moon.

٢٨ ـ في رُؤْيةِ الهلالِ

١٢٦ ـ كانَ رسولُ اللهِ ﷺ إذا رأىٰ الهلالَ قالَ: «اللهُ أَكْبَرُ، اللَّهُمَّ أَهِلَّهُ عَلَيْنا بالأَمْنِ والإيمانِ، والسَّلامَةِ والإسلامِ، والتوفيقِ لما تُحِبُّ وتَرْضىٰ، ربُّنا وربُّكَ اللهُ».

التِّرْمذي وابنُ حِبَّان والدارمي

29. On journeying

127) On the authority of the Prophet (may the blessings and peace of Allah be upon him), who said: "He who wants to journey, let him say to those he leaves behind: I ask of Allah to take you into His safekeeping, He in whose custody nothing is lost."

(Related by Ibn Mājah, an-Nasā'ī, Ibn as-Sunnī and Aḥmad)

128) Sālim said: The son of ᶜUmar (may Allah be pleased with them both) used to say to a man intending (to undertake) a journey: Draw near to me that I may bid you farewell as the Messenger of Allah (may the blessings and peace of Allah be upon him) used to bid us farewell and say: I ask of Allah to take into His safekeeping your religion, your good faith, and your last and final actions. And in another version he—meaning the Prophet (may the blessings and peace of Allah be upon him)—when saying farewell to a man, used to take him by the hand and not let it go till the man himself had let go the hand of the Prophet (may the blessings and peace of Allah be upon him), and he said it.[1]

(Related by at-Tirmidhī)

---

1. I.e., the above invocation.

٢٩ - فِي السَّفرِ

١٢٧ - عَنِ النَّبِيِّ ﷺ قالَ: «مَنْ أَرادَ أَنْ يُسافِرَ فَلْيَقُلْ لِمَنْ يُخَلِّفُ: أَسْتَوْدِعُكُم اللهَ[١] الَّذي لا تَضِيعُ وَدائِعُهُ».

ابنُ ماجَه والنَّسائي وابن السُني وأحمد

١٢٨ - وقالَ سالمٌ: كانَ ابْنُ عُمَرَ رَضِيَ اللهُ عَنْهُما يقولُ للرَّجُلِ إِذا أَرادَ سَفراً: ادْنُ مِنِّي أُوَدِّعْكَ كما كانَ رسولُ اللهِ ﷺ يُوَدِّعُنا، فيقولُ: «أَسْتَوْدِعُ اللهَ دِينَكَ وأَمانَتَكَ وخَوَاتِيمَ عَمَلِكَ» وَمِنْ وَجْهٍ آخَرَ كانَ - يَعْنِي النَّبيَّ ﷺ - إِذا وَدَّعَ رَجُلاً أَخَذَ بِيَدِهِ، فلا يَدَعُها حَتى يَكونَ الرَّجُلُ هُوَ الَّذي يَدَعُ يَدَ النَّبِيِّ ﷺ، وَذَكَرَهُ[٢].

التِّرْمذي

(١) أسأل الله أن يقبلكم ودائع لديه، وأن يحفظكم كما تُحفظ الودائع.

(٢) أي ذكر الدعاء.

129) A man came to the Prophet (may the blessings and peace of Allah be upon him) and said: O Messenger of Allah, I intend (to undertake) a journey. Supply me with the provisions. He said: "May Allah provide you with piety." He said: Give me more. And he said: "May He forgive your sins." He said: Give me more. He said: "And may He facilitate good for you wherever you are."

(Related by at-Tirmidhī)

130) On the authority of Abū Hurayrah (may Allah be pleased with him) that a man said: O Messenger of Allah, I wish to go on a journey, so counsel me. He said: "You must have fear of Allah, and you must say Allāhu akbar[1] on every elevated place." And when the man left, he said: "O Allah, shorten for him the distance and make the journeying easy for him."

(Related by at-Tirmidhī, Ibn Ḥibbān and al-Ḥākim)

---

1. Allah is greatest.

١٢٩ ـ وجاءَ رَجُلٌ إلى النبيِّ ﷺ فقالَ: يا رسولَ الله إني أُريدُ سَفَراً، زَوِّدْني، فقالَ: «زَوَّدَكَ اللهُ التَّقْوىٰ» قال: زِدْني. قالَ: «وَغفرَ ذَنْبَكَ» قالَ: زِدْني. قال: «وَيَسَّرَ لَكَ الخَيْرَ حَيْثُما كُنْتَ».

التِّرْمذي

١٣٠ ـ وَعَنْ أَبي هُرَيْرَةَ رَضِيَ اللهُ عَنْهُ، أَنَّ رَجُلاً قالَ: يا رَسُولَ اللهِ إِنِّي أُرِيدُ أَنْ أُسافِرَ، فأَوْصِنِي، قال: «عَلَيْكَ بِتَقْوىٰ اللهِ، والتَّكْبِيرِ على كُلِّ شَرَفٍ[1]»، فَلَمّا وَلَّى الرَّجُلُ، قال: «اللَّهُمَّ اطْوِ لَهُ البُعْدَ[2]، وَهَوِّنْ عَلَيْهِ السَّفَرَ».

التِّرْمذي وابنُ حِبّان والحاكم

---

(١) الشَّرَف: الموضع المرتفع.

(٢) قرِّبه من نهاية سفره وكأن المسافة إليه قد قصرت.

30. On mounting a riding animal

131) ᶜAlī ibn Rabīᶜah said: I saw ᶜAlī ibn Abī Ṭālib (may Allah be pleased with him) when he brought an animal to mount and when placing his foot in the stirrup, saying: bismillāh,[1] and when he had seated himself on its back he said: al-ḥamdu lillāh.[2] Then he said: Gloried be He who has subdued these for us, and we were not capable of doing so; and verily to our Lord we are returning.[3] Then he said: al-ḥamdu lillāh[2]—three times. Then he said: Allāhu Akbar[4]—three times. Then he said: How far are You from every imperfection! O Allah, I have acted wrongly against myself, so forgive me, for there is no one who forgives sins but You. Then he gave a laugh, and (someone) said: O Commander of the Faithful, what did you laugh for? He said: I saw the Prophet (may the blessings and peace of Allah be upon him) do as I have done, then he gave a laugh, and I said:

---

1. In the name of Allah.
2. Praise be to Allah.
3. The Chapter of the Ornaments 43:13.
4. Allah is greatest.

٣٠ ـ فِي رُكُوبِ الدَّابَةِ

١٣١ ـ قالَ عليُّ بْنُ رَبيعَةَ: «شَهِدْتُ عليَّ بْنَ أَبي طالبٍ رَضِيَ اللهُ عَنْهُ أُتِيَ بِدابَّةٍ لِيَرْكَبَهَا، فَلَمَّا وَضَعَ رِجْلَهُ في الرِّكابِ قالَ: بِسْمِ اللهِ، فَلَمَّا اسْتَوىٰ على ظَهْرِها قالَ: الحَمْدُ للهِ، ثُمَّ قَالَ: ﴿سُبْحَانَ الَّذي سَخَّرَ لنا هٰذا وَمَا كُنَّا لَـهُ مُقْرِنيـنَ، وإِنَّـا إِلـى رَبِّنـا لَمُنْقَلِبُونَ﴾[1] [الزخرف ٤٣: ١٣]، ثم قالَ: الحَمْدُ لله ـ ثَلاثَ مَرَّاتٍ ـ، ثُمَّ قالَ: اللهُ أَكْبَرُ ـ ثلاثَ مَراتٍ ـ، ثم قال: سُبْحانَكَ ـ اللَّهُمَّ إني ظَلَمْتُ نَفْسِي، فَاغْفِرْ لي، فَإِنَّهُ لا يَغْفِرُ الذُّنوبَ إلا أَنْتَ. ثم ضَحِكَ، فَقِيلَ: يا أَميرَ المؤمنينَ مِنْ أَيِّ شَيْءٍ ضَحِكْتَ؟ قالَ: إِني رَأَيْتُ النَّبِيَّ ﷺ فَعَلَ كَمَا فَعَلْتُ، ثم ضَحِكَ،

(١) الآية في ركوب الفلك، وتنطبق على كل وسيلة سفر. سخّر: ذلّل وسهّل. مقرنين: مطيقينه وقادرين على استعماله.

O Messenger of Allah, what did you laugh for? He said: "Your Lord (How far is He from every imperfection and Exalted be He!) is pleased at His servant when he says: O Lord, forgive my sins—knowing that no one forgives sins but I."

(Related by Abū Dāwūd, an-Nasā'ī, at-Tirmidhī, Ibn Ḥibbān and al-Ḥākim)

132) The Prophet (may the blessings and peace of Allah be upon him), when seating himself on his camel to go out on a journey, would say: "Allāhu akbar"[1]—three times. He would then say: "Gloried be He who has subdued these for us, and we were not capable of doing so, and verily to our Lord we are returning.[2] O Allah, we ask of You in this journey of ours righteousness and piety, and such deeds as You would approve of. O Allah, make this journey of ours easy for us, and shorten for us its distance. You are the Companion in travelling and the One who stands in for us with the family. O Allah, I take refuge in You from the discomfort of travel and the depressing things one may see, and

1. Allah is greatest.
2. The Chapter of the Ornaments 43:13.

فَقُلْتُ: يا رَسولَ اللهِ مِنْ أيِّ شَيْءٍ ضَحِكْتَ، قَالَ: «إنَّ ربكَ سُبْحانَهُ وتعالىٰ يَعْجَبُ مِن عَبْدِهِ إذا قالَ: رَبِّ ٱغْفِرْ لي ذُنوبي، يَعْلَمُ أَنَّهُ لا يَغْفِرُ الذُّنُوبَ غَيري».

أبو داود والنّسائي والترمذي
وابنُ حِبَّان والحاكم

١٣٢ ـ كانَ النَّبيُّ ﷺ إذا اسْتوىٰ على بَعيرِهِ خارجاً إلى سَفَرٍ كَبَّرَ ثلاثاً ثُمَّ قالَ: ﴿سُبْحَانَ الَّذِي سَخَّرَ لَنا هٰذا وَمَا كُنَّا لَهُ مُقْرنين وإنَّا إِلى رَبِّنا لَمُنْقَلِبون﴾ [الزخرف ٤٣: ١٣] اللَّهُمَّ إنَّا نَسْأَلُكَ في سَفَرِنا هٰذا البِرَّ والتَّقْوىٰ، ومِنَ العَمَلِ ما تَرْضىٰ، اللَّهُمَّ هَوِّنْ عَلَيْنا سَفَرَنا هٰذا، واْطْوِ عَنَّا بُعْدَهُ[١]، أَنْتَ الصَّاحِبُ في السَّفَرِ، والخَليفَةُ في الأَهْلِ[٢]، اللَّهُمَّ إني أَعُوذُ بِكَ مِن وَعْثاءِ[٣] السَّفَرِ، وكَآبَةِ المنْظَرِ،

---

(١) قَرِّب نهايته.

(٢) المُسْتخلف في رعاية الأهل.

(٣) الوعثاء: المشقة.

from (possible) adversity in fortune and family to be met with upon return."

When he returned he would say these words and would add to them: "Returning, repentant, worshipping, giving praise to our Lord."

(Related by Muslim)

133) And in another version: The Messenger of Allah (may the blessings and peace of Allah be upon him) and his Companions, when climbing up mountain paths, would say: "Allāhu akbar,"[1] and when they were going down a slope they would say: "subḥāna 'llāh."[2]

(Related by al-Bukhārī)

---

1. Allah is greatest.
2. How far is Allah from every imperfection!

وسُوءِ المُنْقَلَبِ في المالِ والأَهْلِ».

وإذا رجعَ قَالَهُنَّ، وزادَ فِيهِنَّ: «آيِبُونَ[1]، تائِبونَ، عَابِدُونَ، لرَبِّنا حامِدُونَ».

مسلم

١٣٣ ـ وفي وَجْهٍ آخَرَ: «كانَ رَسُولُ اللهِ ﷺ وأَصحابُهُ إذا عَلَوُا الثَّنَايا[2]، كَبَّرُوا، وإذا هَبَطُوا سَبَّحُوا».

البخاري

---

(١) راجعون.

(٢) الثنايا: جمع ثَنِيَّة وهي الطريق في الجبل.

31. On alighting at a place

134) The Messenger of Allah (may the blessings and peace of Allah be upon him) said: "He who alights at a place and then says: I take refuge in the consummate words of Allah from the evil that He has created, will not be harmed by anything until he departs from that place of his."

(Related by Muslim)

٣١ - فِي الْمَنْزِلِ يَنْزِلُهُ

١٣٤ - قالَ رسولُ اللهِ ﷺ: «مَنْ نَزَلَ مَنْزِلاً ثُمَّ قالَ: أَعوذُ بكَلِماتِ اللهِ التَّامَّاتِ مِنْ شَرِّ ما خَلَقَ لَمْ يَضُرَّهُ شَيْءٌ حتى يَرْتَحِلَ مِنْ مَنْزِلِهِ ذٰلِكَ».

مسلم

32. On food and drink

Allah the Almighty has said: "O you who believe, eat of the good things wherewith We have provided you, and render thanks to Allah if it is (indeed) He whom you worship."[1]

135) The Messenger of Allah (may the blessings and peace of Allah be upon him) said: "O my son, pronounce the name of Allah and eat with your right hand, and eat of that which is next to you."

(Related by al-Bukhārī and Muslim)

136) The Messenger of Allah (may the blessings and peace of Allah be upon him) said: "When one of you eats, let him mention the name of Allah Almighty at the beginning, and if he has forgotten to mention Allah Almighty at the beginning, then let him say: In the name of Allah, both for the beginning and the end."

(Related by at-Tirmidhī)

1. The Chapter of the Cow 2:172.

٣٢ - في الطعامِ وَالشَّرابِ

قالَ اللهُ تعالى: ﴿يا أَيُّها الَّذينَ آمَنُوا كُلُوا مِنْ طَيِّباتِ ما رَزَقْناكُم وٱشْكُرُوا للهِ إِنْ كُنتُمْ إِيَّاهُ تَعْبُدُونَ﴾ [البقرة ٢: ١٧٢].

١٣٥ - قالَ رسولُ اللهِ ﷺ: «يا بُنَيَّ سَمِّ اللهَ، وكُلْ بيَمِينِكَ، وكُلْ ممَّا يَلِيكَ».

البخاري ومسلم

١٣٦ - قالَ رسولُ اللهِ ﷺ: «إذا أَكَلَ أَحَدُكُمْ فَلْيَذْكُرِ اسْمَ اللهِ تعالىٰ في أَوَّلِهِ، فإِنْ نَسِيَ أَنْ يَذْكُرَ اللهَ تعالىٰ في أَوَّلِهِ، فَلْيَقُلْ: بِسْمِ اللهِ، أَوَّلَهُ وآخِرَهُ».

التِّرْمذي

137) On the authority of Abū Hurayrah (may Allah be pleased with him) (who said): The Messenger of Allah (may the blessings and peace of Allah be upon him) never found fault with any food. If he liked it he ate it, if not he left it.

(Related by al-Bukhāri and Muslim)

138) The Messenger of Allah (may the blessings and peace of Allah be upon him) said: "Verily Allah is pleased with a servant (of His) that he should eat a meal, then praise Him for it; and take a drink (of water), then praise Him for it."

(Related by Muslim)

139) The Messenger of Allah (may the blessings and peace of Allah be upon him) said: "He who has eaten food and has said: Praise be to Allah who has given me this to eat and has provided me with it without any power from me or strength, will be forgiven all the sins he has committed."

(Related by at-Tirmidhī, Abū Dāwūd and Ibn Mājah)

١٣٧ ـ وَعَنْ أَبي هُرَيْرَةَ رَضيَ اللهُ عَنْهُ: «ما عَابَ رَسولُ اللهِ ﷺ طَعاماً قَطُّ، إِنِ اشْتَهاهُ أَكَلَهُ، وإلاَّ تَرَكَهُ».

البخاري ومسلم

١٣٨ ـ قالَ رَسُولُ اللهِ ﷺ: «إِنَّ اللهَ لَيَرْضىٰ عَنِ العَبْدِ أَنْ يأْكُلَ الأَكْلَةَ فَيَحْمَدَهُ عَلَيْهَا، ويَشْرَبَ الشَّرْبَةَ فَيَحْمَدَهُ عَلَيْها».

مسلم

١٣٩ ـ قالَ رسولُ اللهِ ﷺ: «مَنْ أَكَلَ طَعاماً، فَقَالَ: الحَمْدُ للهِ الذي أَطْعَمَنِي هٰذا، وَرَزَقَنِيهِ مِنْ غَيْرِ حَوْلٍ مِنِّي ولا قُوَّةٍ، غُفِرَ لَهُ مَا تَقَدَّمَ مِنْ ذَنْبِهِ».

الترمذي وأبو داود وابنُ ماجَه

140) On the authority of a man who had been in the service of the Prophet (may the blessings and peace of Allah be upon him) that he used to hear the Prophet (may the blessings and peace of Allah be upon him), when he brought him food, say: "bismillāh,"[1] and when he had finished his food he said: "O Allah, You have given to eat and You have given to drink and You have satisfied and gratified (us) and You have guided and You have brought to life, to You is praise for what You have given."

(Related by an-Nasā'ī and Ibn as-Sunnī)

141) The Prophet (may the blessings and peace of Allah be upon him), when he had finished his meal, used to say: "To Allah be praise, abundant, good and blessed. (This gift of food) cannot be dispensed with, cannot be done without, and we pray that it is not the final (gift), O our Lord."

(Related by al-Bukhārī)

---

1. In the name of Allah.

١٤٠ ـ وَعَنْ رَجُلٍ خدَمَ النَّبيَّ ﷺ أنَّهُ كـانَ يَسْمَـعُ النَّبِـيَّ ﷺ إذا قَـرَّبَ إليـهِ طَعـامـاً يَقولُ: «بِسْمِ اللهِ» وإذا فرَغَ مِنْ طَعامِهِ قالَ: «اللهُـم أَطْعَمْـتَ، وَأَسْقَيْـتَ، وَأَغْنَيْـتَ، وَأَقْنَيْتَ[1]، وَهَدَيْتَ، وَأَحْيَيْتَ، فَلَكَ الحَمْدُ على ما أَعْطَيْتَ».

والنّسائي وابن السُّني

١٤١ ـ كانَ النَّبيُّ ﷺ إذا رفعَ مائِدَتَه قَالَ: «الحَمْدُ للهِ كَثيراً طَيِّباً مُباركاً فِيهِ، غَيْرَ مَكْفِيٍّ[2]، ولا مُوَدَّعٍ، ولا مُسْتَغْنَىً عَنْهُ رَبَّنا».

البخاري

(١) أقْنيتَ: أرضيْتَ وأغْنيت.

(٢) غير مكفيّ: قال ابن عَلان «أي غير متروك للاغتناء عنه، فحاجة العباد إلى نعم الله مستمرة».

33. About guests and the like

142) ᶜAbdullāh ibn Busr (may Allah be pleased with him) said: The Messenger of Allah (may the blessings and peace of Allah be upon him) was a guest at my father's. We presented him with food and waṭbah[1] and he ate of it. Then he was brought dates and was eating them; when throwing away the stones, he would place them between his thumb and middle finger, holding them together, and would then throw them away. Then, being brought a beverage, he drank of it and passed it to the person on his right. He said: And my father said, taking hold of the bit of his[2] mount: Say a prayer to Allah for us, and he said: "O Allah, bless for them what You have provided them with, and forgive them and have mercy on them."

(Related by Muslim)

1. A dish made of dried dates with milk and cooking butter.
2. I.e., that of the Prophet.

٣٣ - فِي الضَّيْفِ وَنَحْوِهِ

١٤٢ - ذكَرَ عَبْدُ اللهِ بْنُ بُسْرٍ رَضِيَ اللهُ عَنْهُ قالَ: نَزَلَ رَسولُ اللهِ ﷺ على أَبي، قالَ: فَقَرَّبْنا إِلَيْهِ طَعاماً وَوَطْبَةً(١) فَأَكَلَ مِنْها، ثُم أُتِيَ بتَمْرٍ فكانَ يَأْكُلُهُ ويُلْقِي النَّوىٰ بَيْنَ إِصْبَعَيْهِ، ويَجْمَعُ السَّبابَةَ والوُسْطَىٰ، ثُم أُتِيَ بِشَرابٍ فَشَرِبَهُ، ثم ناوَلَهُ الذي عَنْ يَمِينِهِ. قالَ: فَقَالَ أَبي وأَخَذَ بِلِجَامِ دَابَّتِهِ: ادْعُ اللهَ لَنَا، فَقالَ: «اللهُم بَارِكْ لَهُمْ فِيمَا رَزَقْتَهُمْ، وٱغْفِرْ لَهُمْ وَٱرْحَمْهُمْ».

مسلم

(١) وَطْبة: تمر مطبوخ مع اللبن والسمن.

143) On the authority of Anas (may Allah be pleased with him) that the Prophet (may the blessings and peace of Allah be upon him) came to Saᶜd ibn ᶜUbādah (may Allah be pleased with him), and he [1] brought bread and oil and he[2] ate (of it). Then the Prophet (may the blessings and peace of Allah be upon him) said: "May those who are fasting break their fast with you, may the godly eat of your food, and may the angels say a prayer for you."[3]

(Related by Abū Dāwūd)

---

1. I.e., Saᶜd ibn ᶜUbādah.
2. I.e., the Prophet.
3. I.e., a prayer of mercy and blessing.

١٤٣ ـ وَعَنْ أَنَسٍ رَضِيَ اللهُ عَنْهُ أَنَّ النَّبِيَّ ﷺ جاءَ إِلى سَعْدِ بْنِ عُبادَةَ رَضِيَ اللهُ عَنْهُ، فجاءَ بِخُبْزٍ وزَيْتٍ فَأَكَلَ، ثُمَّ قَالَ النَّبِيُّ ﷺ: «أَفْطَرَ عِنْدَكُمُ الصائِمونَ، وأَكَلَ طَعَامَكُمُ الأَبْرارُ، وصَلَّتْ(١) عَلَيْكُمُ الملائِكَةُ».

أبو داود

(١) صلاة الملائكة: دعاء بالرحمة والبركة.

34. On greeting (people)

144) On the authority of ᶜAbdullāh the son of ᶜAmr (may Allah be pleased with them both) that a man asked the Prophet (may the blessings and peace of Allah be upon him): Which (action in) Islam is best? He said: "That you provide food and give salām (greetings) (both) to those you know and to those you don't know."

(Related by al-Bukhārī and Muslim)

145) The Messenger of Allah (may the blessings and peace of Allah be upon him) said: "You will not enter heaven until you (truly) believe, and you will not (truly) believe until you love one another. Shall I not, therefore, direct you to something which, if you do it, will make you love one another? Spread salām (greetings) amongst yourselves."

(Related by Muslim)

146) ᶜAmmār ibn Yāsir (may Allah be pleased with him) said: If someone has brought together three things he will have brought together faith: being honest with oneself, giving salām (greetings) to everyone, and spending (on others) (even) when in straitened circumstances.

(Related by al-Bukhārī, Ibn Abī Shaybah and Ibn Ḥibbān)

٣٤ ـ فِي السَّلامِ

١٤٤ ـ عَنْ عبدِ اللهِ بْنِ عمرٍو رَضِيَ اللهُ عَنْهما أَنَّ رَجُلاً سَأَلَ النَّبِيَ ﷺ: أَيُّ الإِسلامِ خيْرٌ؟ قالَ: «تُطْعِمُ الطَّعامَ، وتَقْرَأُ السَّلامَ على مَنْ عرَفْتَ وَمَنْ لَمْ تَعْرِفْ».

البخاري ومسلم

١٤٥ ـ قالَ رَسولُ اللهِ ﷺ: «لا تَدْخُلُوا[١] الْجَنَّةَ حتَّى تُؤْمِنُوا، ولا تُؤْمِنُوا حتَّى تَحابُّوا، أَفَلا أَدُلُّكُم على شَيْءٍ إذا فَعَلْتُمُوهُ تَحابَبْتُمْ؟ أَفْشُوا السَّلامَ بَيْنَكُم».

مسلم

١٤٦ ـ وَقالَ عَمَّارُ بْنُ ياسرٍ رَضِيَ اللهُ عَنْهُ: «ثَلاثٌ مَنْ جَمَعَهُنَّ فَقَدْ جَمَعَ الإِيمانَ: الإِنْصَافُ مِنْ نَفْسِكَ، وبَذْلُ السَّلامِ للعَالَمِ[٢]، والإِنْفاقُ مِنَ الإِقْتارِ». البخاري وابن ابي شيبة وابن حبّان

---

(١) قال ابن علان: هكذا وردت بحذف النون، وهي لغة معروفة صحيحة.
(٢) أي جميع الناس.

147) ᶜImrān ibn Ḥuṣayn said: A man came to the Prophet (may the blessings and peace of Allah be upon him) and said: Peace be upon you, and he replied to him. Then (the man) sat down and the Prophet (may the blessings and peace of Allah be upon him) said: "Ten."[1] Then another man came and said: Peace be upon you and the mercy of Allah, and he replied to him. Then he said down and he[2] said: "Twenty." Then (yet) another came and he said: Peace be upon you and the mercy of Allah and His blessings. Then he replied and the man sat down and he[2] said: "Thirty."

(Related by at-Tirmidhī and al-Bayhaqī)

148) The Messenger of Allah (may the blessings and peace of Allah be upon him) said: "The worthiest of people with Allah are those who are the first to give salām (greetings) (to others)."

(Related by at-Tirmidhī)

---

1. I.e., ten good deeds.
2. I.e., the Prophet.

١٤٧ ـ وَقالَ عِمْرانُ بْنُ حُصَيْنٍ: جاءَ رَجُلٌ إلى النَّبيِّ ﷺ، فَقالَ: السَّلامُ عَلَيْكُمْ، فَرَدَّ عَلَيْهِ، ثُمَّ جَلَسَ، فقالَ النَّبيُّ ﷺ: «عَشْرٌ»[١] ثم جاءَ آخرُ، فقالَ: السَّلامُ عَلَيْكم ورَحْمَةُ اللهِ، فَرَدَّ عَلَيْهِ، فَجَلَسَ، فقالَ: «عِشْرُونَ»، ثم جاءَ آخَرُ، فَقالَ: السَّلامُ عَلَيْكُمْ وَرَحْمَةُ اللهِ وَبَرَكَاتُهُ، فَرَدَّ عَلَيْهِ، فَجَلَسَ، فَقالَ: «ثَلاثُونَ».

التّرْمذي والبيهقي

١٤٨ ـ قال رسولُ اللهِ ﷺ: «إنَّ أَوْلَىٰ النَّاسِ بِاللهِ مَنْ بَدَأَهُمْ بِالسَّلامِ».

التّرْمذي

(١) أي عشر حسنات.

149) On the authority of the Prophet (may the blessings and peace of Allah be upon him), who said: “It is sufficient for a group of people, on passing by, that one of them gives salām (greetings), and it is sufficient for those that are seated that one of them returns the salām (greetings).”

(Related by Abū Dāwūd, Aḥmad and al-Bayhaqī)

150) Anas (may Allah be pleased with him) said: The Prophet (may the blessings and peace of Allah be upon him) passed by some boys who were playing and he greeted them.

(Related by al-Bukhārī and Muslim)

151) The Messenger of Allah (may the blessings and peace of Allah be upon him) said: “If one of you has reached an assembly of people sitting, let him give salām (greetings). And if he decides to sit down let him do so. Then, when he rises (to leave), let him give salām (greetings), for the first greeting is no more deserving than the last.”

(Related by at-Tirmidhī)

١٤٩ ـ عَنِ النَّبيِّ ﷺ قال: «يُجْزِىءُ عَنِ الجَماعَةِ إِذا مَرُّوا، أَنْ يُسَلِّمَ أَحَدُهُمْ، ويُجْزِىءُ عَنِ الجُلوسِ أَنْ يَرُدَّ أَحَدُهُمْ».

أبو داود وأحمد والبيهقي

١٥٠ ـ وقالَ أَنَسٌ رَضِيَ اللهُ عَنْهُ: مَرَّ النَّبيُّ على صِبْيانٍ يَلْعَبُونَ، فَسَلَّمَ عَلَيْهِمْ».

البخاري ومسلم

١٥١ ـ قالَ رَسُولُ اللهِ ﷺ: «إِذا انْتَهى أَحَدُكُمْ إِلى المجْلِسِ، فَلْيُسَلِّمْ، فَإِنْ بَدا لَهُ أَنْ يَجْلِسَ، فَلْيَجْلِسْ، ثُمَّ إِذا قامَ، فَلْيُسَلِّمْ، فَلَيْسَتِ الأُولىٰ بِأَحَقَّ مِنَ الآخِرَةِ».

التِّرْمذي

35. On sneezing and yawning

152) On the authority of the Prophet (may the blessings and peace of Allah be upon him) that he said: “Allah loves sneezing and He hates yawning. Thus when one of you sneezes and has said al-ḥamdu lillāh (Praise be to Allah), it behoves every Muslim who has heard it to say yarḥamuka ’llāh (May Allah have mercy on you). As for yawning, it is but from the devil. So when one of you yawns, let him resist it as much as he can, for when he yawns the devil laughs at him.”

(Related by al-Bukhārī)

٣٥ - فِي العُطاسِ وَالتَّثاؤُبِ

١٥٢ - عَنِ النَّبِيِّ ﷺ قالَ: «إِنَّ اللهَ يُحِبُّ العُطَاسَ، ويَكْرَهُ التَّثَاؤُبَ، فإِذا عَطَسَ أَحَدُكُمْ، وَحَمِدَ اللهَ، كانَ حَقاً على كُلِّ مُسْلِمٍ سَمِعَهُ أَنْ يَقولَ: يَرْحَمُكَ اللهُ. وأَمَّا التَّثاؤُبُ، فإِنَّما هُوَ مِنَ الشَّيْطانِ، فإِذا تَثاءَبَ أَحَدُكُم، فَلْيَرُدَّهُ ما ٱسْتَطاعَ، فإِنَّ أَحَدَكُم إِذا تَثاءَبَ، ضَحِكَ مِنْهُ الشَّيطانُ».

البخاري

153) On the authority of the Prophet (may the blessings and peace of Allah be upon him), who said: "If one of you sneezes, let him say al-ḥamdu lillāh (Praise be to Allah), and let his brother, or his companion, say to him, yarḥamuka 'llāh (May Allah have mercy on you). And when he has said to him yarḥamuka 'llāh (May Allah have mercy on you) let (the other) say yahdīkum allāhu wa yuṣliḥu bālakum (May Allah guide you and put you in a good state of mind). And in (another) version (it reads): al-ḥamdu lillāh ᶜalā kulli ḥāl (Praise be to Allah in every event)."

(Related by al-Bukhārī and Abū Dāwūd)

154) The Messenger of Allah (may the blessings and peace of Allah be upon him) said: "If one of you sneezes and has said al-ḥamdu lillāh (Praise be to Allah), then say to him yarḥamuka 'llāh (May Allah have mercy on you). And if he has not said al-ḥamdu lillāh (Praise be to Allah), then do not say to him yarḥamuka 'llāh (May Allah have mercy on you).

(Related by Muslim)

١٥٣ ـ عَنِ النَّبيِّ ﷺ قال: «إذا عَطَسَ أَحَدُكُمْ فلْيَقُلْ: الحَمْدُ للهِ، ولْيَقُلْ لَهُ أَخُوهُ، أَوْ صاحِبُهُ: يَرْحَمُكَ اللهُ، فإذا قالَ لَهُ: يَرْحَمُكَ اللهُ، فَلْيَقُلْ: يَهْدِيكُمُ اللهُ ويُصْلِحُ بالَكُمْ».

وفي لَفْظٍ: «الحمْدُ للهِ على كُلِّ حالٍ».

البخاري وأبو داود

١٥٤ ـ قالَ رسولُ اللهِ ﷺ: «إذا عَطَسَ أَحَدُكُمْ فحَمِدَ الله فَشَمِّتُوهُ،[١] فإن لَمْ يَحْمَدِ اللهَ، فلا تُشَمِّتُوهُ».

مسلم

(١) أي قولوا له (يرحمك الله).

36. On marriage

155) ᶜAbdullah ibn Masᶜūd (may Allah be pleased with him) said: The Messenger of Allah (may the blessings and peace of Allah be upon him) taught us the Sermon of Necessity:[1]

"Praise be to Allah [we praise Him], and of Him we seek help and of Him we ask forgiveness, and we take refuge in Allah from the evils of ourselves and from our evil actions. He whom Allah guides there is no one to make go astray, and he whom He leads astray for him there is no guide. I bear witness that there is no god but Allah alone, He having no associate, and I bear witness that Muḥammad is His servant and His Messenger. O mankind, fear your Lord who created you from a single soul and from it created its mate and from the two of them has spread abroad a multitude of men and women. Fear Allah in whom you claim (your rights) of one another and (observe) your ties of kinship. Verily Allah is a watcher over you.[2] O you who believe, fear Allah as

1. The Sermon of Necessity is given here as applicable to marriage ceremonies, maybe as a prelude to other relevant words.
2. The Chapter of Women 4:1.

٣٦ - في النّكاح

١٥٥ - قالَ عبدُ اللهِ بْنُ مَسْعُودٍ رَضِيَ اللهُ عَنْهُ: عَلَّمَنا رسولُ اللهِ ﷺ خُطْبَةَ الحَاجَةِ[(١)]:

«الحَمْـــدُ للهِ [نَحْمَـــدُهُ] ونَسْتَعِينُــــهُ، وَنَسْتَغْفِرُهُ، وَنَعُوذُ بِاللهِ مِنْ شُرُورِ أَنْفُسِنا، وَمِنْ سَيِّئاتِ أَعْمالِنا، مَنْ يَهْدِهِ اللهُ فَلا مُضِلَّ لَهُ، وَمَنْ يُضْلِلْ فَلا هَادِيَ لَهُ، وَأَشْهَدُ أَنْ لا إِلَهَ إِلا اللهُ وَحْدَهُ لا شَرِيكَ لَهُ، وَأَشْهَدُ أَنَّ مُحَمَّداً عَبْدُهُ وَرَسُولُه، ﴿يا أَيُّها النَّاسُ اتَّقُوا رَبَّكُمُ الَّذي خَلَقَكُمْ مِنْ نَفْسٍ وَاحِدَةٍ وَخَلَقَ مِنْها زَوْجَها وَبَثَّ مِنْهُما رِجالاً كَثيراً وَنِساءً واتَّقُوا اللهَ الَّذي تَسَاءَلُونَ بِهِ والأَرْحَامَ، إِنَّ اللهَ كَانَ عَلَيْكُمْ رَقِيباً﴾ [النساءُ ٤ : ١] ﴿يا أَيُّها الَّذينَ

---

(١) اعتبرت خطبة الحاجة هنا خطبة النكاح. وقد تكون صدراً لخطبة النكاح ثم يضاف إليها.

He should be feared and observe your duty to Him, and do not die other than as Muslims.[1] O you who believe, fear Allah and speak words that are just and true. He will then make right your actions for you and will forgive you your sins. Whosoever obeys Allah and His Messenger, he verily has gained a great victory."[2]

(Related by Abū Dāwūd, at-Tirmidhī, an-Nasā'ī and Ibn Mājah)

156) The Prophet (may the blessings and peace of Allah be upon him), when he gave good wishes to someone who was marrying, would say: "May Allah bless you and prosper you and may He join you together in goodness."

(Related by at-Tirmidhī)

157) On the authority of the Prophet (may the blessings and peace of Allah be upon him), who said: "If one of you were to say, when he lies with his wife: In the name of Allah; O Allah, ward off from us the devil, and ward off the devil from what You bless us with, and it is decreed that they have a child, then the devil will never harm him."

(Related by al-Bukhārī and Muslim)

---

1. The Chapter of the Family of ᶜImrān 3:102.
2. The Chapter of the Clans 33:70–71.

آمَنُوا اتَّقوا اللهَ حَقَّ تُقاتِهِ ولا تَمُوتُنَّ إلا وأَنْتُمْ مُسْلِمُونَ﴾ [آل عمران ٣: ١٠٢] ﴿يا أَيُّها الَّذينَ آمَنُوا اتَّقُوا اللهَ وَقُولُوا قَوْلاً سَديداً. يُصْلِحْ لَكُمْ أَعْمالَكُمْ وَيَغْفِرْ لَكُمْ ذُنُوبَكُمْ وَمَنْ يُطِعِ اللهَ وَرَسُولَهُ فَقَدْ فازَ فَوْزاً عَظيماً﴾ [الأحزاب ٣٣: ٧٠ ـ ٧١].

أبو داود والتّرْمذي والنسائي وابن ماجَه

١٥٦ ـ كانَ النبيُّ ﷺ إذا رَفَّأَ[١] الإنسانَ، إذا تَزَوَّجَ قال: «بارَكَ اللهُ لَكَ، وبارَكَ عَلَيْكَ، وَجَمَعَ بَيْنَكُما في خَيْرٍ».

التّرْمذي

١٥٧ ـ عَنِ النَّبِيِّ ﷺ قالَ: «لَوْ أَنَّ أَحَدَكُمْ إذا أَتَىٰ أَهْلَهُ قالَ: بِسْمِ اللهِ، اللَّهُمَّ جَنِّبْنا الشَّيطانَ، وَجَنِّبِ الشَّيطانَ ما رَزَقْتَنا فَقُضِيَ بَيْنَهُما وَلَدٌ، لَمْ يَضُرَّهُ شَيْطانٌ أَبَداً».

البخاري ومسلم

(١) رفّأ متزوجاً. دعا له بالرِّفاء والبنين، والرِّفاء هو الالتئام وجمع الشمل.

37. On giving birth

158) Abū Rāfi[c] (may Allah be pleased with him) said: I saw the Messenger of Allah (may the blessings and peace of Allah be upon him) murmur the call to prayer in the ear of al-Ḥasan ibn [c]Alī when Fāṭimah had given birth to him.

(Related by at-Tirmidhī)

159) [c]Ā'ishah (may Allah be pleased with her) said: The Messenger of Allah (may the blessings and peace of Allah be upon him), when children were brought to him, would invoke blessings on them and would soften dates and move them round in their mouths.

(Related by Muslim and Abū Dāwūd)

160). On the authority of [c]Amr ibn Shu[c]ayb, from his father, from his grandfather, from the Prophet (may the blessings and peace of Allah be upon him) that he ordered the newborn baby to be given a name on his seventh day, and that he should be cleaned, and that a sacrifice should be made.

(Related by at-Tirmidhī)

٣٧ ـ فِي الوِلادَةِ

١٥٨ ـ قال أبو رافِعٍ رَضِيَ اللهُ عَنْهُ: رَأَيْتُ رَسولَ اللهِ ﷺ أَذَّنَ فِي أُذُنِ الحَسَنِ بْنِ عَلِيٍّ حينَ وَلَدَتْهُ فاطِمَةُ رَضِيَ اللهُ عَنْها بِالصَّلاةِ». التِّرْمذي

١٥٩ ـ وَقالَتْ عائِشَةُ رَضِيَ اللهُ عَنْها: «كانَ رَسولُ اللهِ ﷺ يُؤْتَىٰ بالصِّبْيانِ فَيَدْعُو لَهُمْ بالبَرَكَةِ، وَيُحَنِّكُهُمْ»[١].

مسلم أبو داود

١٦٠ ـ وَعَنْ عَمْرِو بْنِ شُعَيْبٍ عَنْ أَبيهِ عَنْ جَدِّهِ عَنِ النَّبِيِّ ﷺ: «أَنَّهُ أَمَرَ بِتَسْمِيَةِ المَوْلودِ يَوْمَ سابِعِهِ، وَوَضْعِ الأَذى عَنْهُ، والعَقِّ»[٢].

التِّرْمذي

---

(١) التحنيك: تليين التمر لتدليك حَنَك الصبي به.

(٢) وَضع الأذى عنه: تنظيفه، والعَقُّ هو ذبح العَقيقة وهي الشاة المذبوحة.

161) The Prophet (may the blessings and peace of Allah be upon him) named his son Ibrāhīm, and Ibrāhīm ibn Abī Mūsā and ᶜAbdullah ibn Abī Ṭalḥah and al-Mundhir ibn Abī Usayd (were given names) shortly after being born.

(Related by al-Bukhārī and Muslim)

162) The Messenger of Allah (may the blessings and peace of Allah be upon him) said: "Of your names the most loved of Allah are ᶜAbdullāh and ᶜAbdurraḥmān."

(Related by Muslim)

١٦١ ـ وَقَدْ سَمَّىٰ النَّبِيُّ ﷺ ابْنَهُ إِبراهيمَ، وإِبْراهيمَ ابْنَ أَبي موسى، وعبدَ اللهِ ابْنَ أَبي طَلْحَةَ، والمُنْذِرَ ابْنَ أَبي أُسَيْدٍ قَرِيباً مِنْ وِلادَتِهِمْ[١]. البخاري ومسلم

١٦٢ ـ قالَ رَسولُ اللهِ ﷺ: «إِنَّ أَحَبَّ أَسْمائِكُم إِلى اللهِ عَبْدُ اللهِ، وعبدُ الرَّحْمٰنِ».

مسلم

(١) والمعنى جواز التسمية بُعَيْد الولادة دون انتظار لليوم السابع.

163) The Prophet (may the blessings and peace of Allah be upon him) changed objectionable names to pleasant ones. Thus Zaynab (a type of pleasant-smelling tree) used to be called Barrah (Righteous). It was said: she praises herself (by being so named). Also, he disliked it being said: He went out from being at Barrah's house, and therefore he renamed her Zaynab. He said to a man: "What's your name?" He said: Ḥazn (Rough). He said: "No, you're Sahl (Amenable)." And he changed the name of ^{c}Āṣiyah (Disobedient) and named her Jamīlah (Beautiful). He said to a man: "What's your name?" He said: Aṣram (leafless). He said: "No, you are Zur^{c}ah (Flourishing)." And he named the land called ^{c}Afrah (Dusty) Khaḍirah (Green).

(Related by Abū Dāwūd and aṭ-Ṭabarānī)

١٦٣ ـ وقد غيَّرَ النَّبيُّ ﷺ الأسْماءَ المكْروهَةَ إلى أسماءٍ حَسَنَةٍ، فكَانَتْ زَيْنَبُ تُسمَّى: بَرَّةَ. فقِيلَ تُزَكِّي نَفْسَها، فَسَمَّاها: زَيْنَبَ، وكانَ يَكْرَهُ أَنْ يُقالَ: خَرَجَ مِنْ عِنْدِ بَرَّةَ، وَقالَ لِرَجُلٍ: ما اسْمُكَ؟ قالَ: حَزْنٌ، قالَ: بَلْ أَنْتَ سَهْلٌ، وَغَيَّرَ اسْمَ عاصِيَةٍ، فسمَّاها جَمِيلةً، وَقالَ لِرَجُلٍ مَا اسْمُكَ؟ قال: أَصْرَمُ. قال: بَلْ أَنْتَ زُرْعَةُ، وسمَّى أَرْضاً يُقالُ لَها: عفْرةُ: خَضِرَةَ[1].

أبو داود والطّبراني

(١) الحَزْن: الخشن من الأرض والناس. والأصرم من الشجر: المجذوذ الفروع والورق. وعَفْرة: مُتَرَّبة.

38. On the crowing of roosters, the braying of donkeys and the barking of dogs

164) On the authority of the Prophet (may the blessings and peace of Allah be upon him), who said: "If you hear the braying of donkeys, then say: I take refuge in Allah from the devil, for they have seen a devil. And if you hear the crowing of roosters, ask of Allah His favour, for they have seen an angel."

(Related by al-Bukhārī and Muslim)

165) The Messenger of Allah (may the blessings and peace of Allah be upon him) said: "If you hear the barking of dogs and the braying of donkeys at night, say: I take my refuge in Allah from them, for they see what you do not see."

(Related by Abū Dāwūd)

٣٨ ـ في صِياحِ الدِّيكِ وَالنَّهيقِ والنُّباحِ

١٦٤ ـ عَنِ النَّبيِّ ﷺ قالَ: «إذا سَمِعْتُمْ نُهاقَ الحَميرِ، فتعوَّذُوا باللهِ مِنَ الشَّيْطانِ، فإِنَّها رَأَتْ شَيْطاناً، وإذا سَمِعْتُمْ صِياحَ الدِّيَكَةِ، فَسَلُوا اللهَ مِنْ فَضْلِه، فَإِنَّها رأَتْ مَلَكاً».

البخاري ومسلم

١٦٥ ـ قالَ رسولُ اللهِ ﷺ: «إذا سَمِعْتُم نُباحَ الكِلابِ، وَنَهيقَ الحَميرِ باللَّيلِ، فَتَعَوَّذُوا باللهِ مِنْهُنَّ، فإِنَّهُنَّ يَرَيْنَ ما لا تَرَوْنَ».

أبو داود

39. When in a gathering

166) The Messenger of Allah (may the blessings and peace of Allah be upon him) said: "No one has sat in a gathering where there has been much clamorous and idle talk, and before rising from that gathering of his, says: I glorify You, O Allah, and I praise You, and I bear witness that there is no god but You; I ask forgiveness of You and I seek repentance of You—without Allah pardoning him (such errors as he committed) in that gathering of his."

(Related by at-Tirmidhī, Ibn Ḥibbān and al-Ḥākim)

167) The Messenger of Allah (may the blessings and peace of Allah be upon him) said: "No people rise from a gathering in which they have not mentioned Allah Almighty, without having risen as from something like the carcass of a donkey. It was for them a distressing gathering."

(Related by Abū Dāwūd and al-Ḥākim)

٣٩ ـ فِي المَجْلِسِ

١٦٦ ـ قالَ رَسولُ اللهِ ﷺ: «مَنْ جلَسَ في مَجلسٍ فَكَثُرَ فيهِ لَغَطُهُ[1] فقالَ قَبْلَ أَنْ يَقومَ مِنْ مَجْلِسِهِ ذٰلكَ: سُبْحانَكَ اللَّهُمَّ وبِحَمْدِكَ، أَشْهَدُ أَن لا إِلٰهَ إِلاَّ أَنْتَ، أَسْتَغْفِرُكَ وَأَتوبُ إِلَيْكَ، إلا كَفَّرَ اللهُ لَهُ ما كانَ في مَجْلِسِهِ ذٰلِكَ».

التِرمذي وابنُ حِبّان والحاكم

١٦٧ ـ قالَ رَسولُ اللهِ ﷺ: «ما مِنْ قَوْمٍ يَقومُونَ مِن مَجْلسٍ لا يَذْكُرُونَ اللهَ تعالىٰ فِيهِ إلا قَامُوا عَن مِثْلِ جيفَةِ حِمارٍ، وكانَ لهمْ حَسْرةً»[2].

أبو داود والحاكم

168) On the authority of the son of ᶜUmar (may Allah be pleased with them both) who said: Seldom would the Messenger of Allah (may the blessings and peace of Allah be upon him) rise from a gathering until he had said these invocations for his Companions: "O Allah, decree for us such fear of You by which You will prevent us from sinning against You and such obedience to You by which You will make us attain Your Paradise, and such certainty (about You) by which You will ease for us the misfortunes of the world. O Allah, let us have the benefit of our hearing, our sight and our strength for so long as You give us life, and make it the heir to us,[1] and let us have our retaliation against those who have oppressed us, and give us victory over those who have shown us enmity. Let not any misfortune (that comes to us) be in our religion and let not this world be our chief concern or the utmost attainment of our learning, and let not those who do not have pity on us be given mastery over us."

(Related by at-Tirmidhī, Ibn as-Sunnī and al-Ḥākim)

---

1. I.e., allow us to enjoy our senses intact to the end of our time.

١٦٨ ـ وَعَنِ ابْنِ عُمَرَ رَضِيَ اللهُ عَنْهما قالَ: قَلَّمَا كانَ رَسُولُ اللهِ ﷺ يَقومُ مِنْ مَجْلسٍ حتىٰ يَدْعُو بهؤُلاءِ الدَّعَوَاتِ لأَصْحابِهِ: «اللَّهُمَّ اقْسِمْ لَنا مِن خَشْيَتِكَ مَا تَحُولُ بِهِ بَيْنَنا وَبَيْنَ مَعاصِيكَ، وَمِنْ طَاعَتِكَ ما تُبَلِّغُنا بِهِ جَنَّتَكَ، وَمِنَ اليَقِينِ ما تُهَوِّنُ بِهِ عَلَيْنا مَصائِبَ الدُّنْيا، اللَّهُمَّ مَتِّعْنا بِأَسْمَاعِنا، وأَبْصارِنا وقُوَّتِنا ما أَحْيَيْتَنَا، وَاجْعَلْهُ الوَارِثَ مِنَّا[1]، واجْعَلْ ثَأْرَنا على مَنْ ظَلَمَنا، وَٱنْصُرْنا على مَنْ عادانا، ولا تَجْعَلْ مُصِيبَتَنا في دِينِنا، ولا تَجْعَلِ الدُّنْيا أكبرَ هَمِّنا، ولا مَبْلَغَ عِلْمِنا، ولا تُسَلِّطْ عَلَيْنا مَنْ لا يَرْحَمُنا».

التِّرْمذي وابن السُّني والحاكم

(١) واجعله الوارث منا: أي متعنا بهذه الحواس المذكورة حتى نهاية العمر، فتبقى بعدنا كالميراث يخلفه صاحبه.

40. On anger

Allah Almighty has said: "And if a whisper from the devil reach you, then seek refuge in Allah. He is the Healer, the Knower."[1]

169) Sulaymān ibn Ṣurad said: I was sitting with the Messenger of Allah (may the blessings and peace of Allah be upon him) when two men began insulting each other. One of them was red in the face and his jugular veins had swelled up. The Messenger of Allah (may the blessings and peace of Allah be upon him) said: "I know of some words which, if he were to say them, the state he finds himself in would go from him. Were he to say: I take my refuge in Allah from the accursed devil, the state he finds himself in would go from him."

(Related by al-Bukhārī and Muslim)

1. The Chapter of Fuṣṣilat 41:36.

٤٠ ـ فِي الغَضَبِ

قالَ اللهُ تعالىٰ: ﴿وإمَّا يَنْزَغَنَّكَ[1] مِنَ الشَّيْطانِ نَزْغٌ فَاسْتَعِذْ باللهِ إِنَّهُ هُو السَّمِيعُ العَلِيمُ﴾ [فُصِّلت ٤١: ٣٦].

١٦٩ ـ وقال سُلَيْمانُ بْنُ صُرَدٍ: كُنْتُ جالساً مَعَ رَسولِ اللهِ ﷺ ورَجُلانِ يَسْتَبَّانِ، وأَحَدُهُما قَدْ احْمَرَّ وَجْهُهُ، وٱنْتَفَخَتْ أَوْداجُهُ. فَقَالَ رَسولُ اللهِ ﷺ: «إِني لأَعْلَمُ كَلِمَةً لَوْ قالَها لَذَهبَ عَنْهُ ما يَجِدُ، لَوْ قالَ: أَعوذُ باللهِ مِنَ الشَّيْطانِ الرَّجيمِ، ذَهَبَ عَنْهُ ما يَجِدُ».

البخاري ومسلم

(١) إذا أصابك الشيطان أو صَرَفك عن تقديم الحسنات فاستعذ بالله.

41. On seeing people afflicted with misfortune

170) On the authority of the Prophet (may the blessings and peace of Allah be upon him), who said: “He who has seen someone afflicted with misfortune and who says: Thanks be to Allah who has protected me against that with which you are afflicted and who has favoured me over many of those He has created, will not be afflicted by that misfortune.

(Related by at-Tirmidhī)

٤١ ـ في رُؤْيَةِ أَهْلِ الْبلاءِ[١]

١٧٠ ـ عَنِ النبيِّ ﷺ قالَ: «مَنْ رَأَىٰ مُبْتَلىً فقَالَ: الحَمْدُ للهِ الَّذِي عَافاني ممَّا ابْتَلاكَ بِهِ، وَفَضَّلَنِي[٢] على كثيرٍ مِمَّن خَلَقَ تَفْضِيلاً ـ لَمْ يُصِبْهُ ذٰلِكَ البلاءُ».

الترْمذي

(١) البلاء: مصيبة الإنسان بمرض أو نقص أو نحو ذلك.

(٢) التفضيل هنا إكرام المرء بصفات حُرِم منها غيره.

42. On entering the market

171) The Messenger of Allah (may the blessings and peace of Allah be upon him) said: "He who enters the market and says: There is no god but Allah alone, He having no associate, to Him is the dominion and to Him the praise, He brings life and He brings death, for He is alive and does not die; in His hand is goodness, and He is Omnipotent, Allah will write for him a thousand thousand good deeds and will erase from him a thousand thousand bad deeds, and He will raise him up a thousand thousand degrees."

(Related by at-Tirmidhī, al-Ḥākim and Ibn as-Sunnī)

٤٢ ـ في دُخُولِ السُّوقِ

١٧١ ـ قالَ رَسولُ اللهِ ﷺ: «مَنْ دَخَلَ السُّوقَ فقَالَ: لا إِلٰه إلا اللهُ وَحْدَهُ لا شَريكَ لَهُ، لَهُ المُلْكُ، ولهُ الحَمْدُ، يُحْيي ويُمِيتُ، وهوَ حَيٌّ لا يَموتُ، بِيَدِهِ الخيرُ، وَهُوَ على كُلِّ شَيْءٍ قَدِيرٌ، كتَبَ اللهُ لَهُ أَلْفَ أَلْفَ حَسَنَةٍ، وَمَحا عَنْهُ أَلْفَ أَلْفَ سَيِّئَةٍ، وَرَفَعَ لَهُ أَلْفَ أَلْفَ دَرَجَةٍ».

التِّرْمذي والحاكم وابن السُّني

43. If an animal one is riding stumbles

172) On the authority of the man who said: I was riding behind[1] the Prophet (may the blessings and peace of Allah be upon him) when his mount stumbled. I said: May the devil stumble! He said: "Do not say: May the devil stumble! for if you say that he becomes as grand as a house, saying (to himself): It was because of my power. Rather say: In the name of Allah, for if you say this he is so demeaned that he becomes like a fly."

(Related by Abū Dāwūd, an-Nasā'ī, Ibn as-Sunnī and Aḥmad)

1. I.e., on the same mount.

٤٣ ـ فِي الدَّابَةِ إذا تَعِسَتْ[١]

١٧٢ ـ عَنْ رَجُلٍ قالَ: كُنْتُ رَدِيفَ النَّبِيِّ ﷺ فعثَرَتْ دابَّتُهُ، فَقُلْتُ: تَعِسَ الشَّيطانُ[٢]، فَقالَ: «لا تَقُلْ: تَعِسَ الشَّيْطانُ، فَإِنَّكَ إذا قُلْتَ ذٰلِكَ تَعَاظَمَ حَتَّىٰ يكونَ مِثلَ الْبَيْتِ، وَيَقُولُ: بِقُوَّتي، وَلٰكِنْ قُلْ: بِاسْمِ اللهِ، فإِنَّكَ إذا قُلْتَ ذٰلِكَ تَصاغَرَ حَتَّىٰ يَكونَ مِثْلَ الذُّبابِ».

أبو داود والنّسائي وابن السُّني وأحمد

---

(١) تعست الدابة: عثرت.

(٢) دعاء على الشيطان أن يتعس.

44. On him who has been given a present and for whom an invocation has been said

173) On the authority of ᶜĀ'ishah (may Allah be pleased with her), who said: A sheep was given as a present to the Messenger of Allah (may the blessings and peace of Allah be upon him). He said: "Divide it up (and distribute it)." On the maidservant returning, ᶜĀ'ishah said: What did they say? The maidservant said: They said: May Allah bless you, at which ᶜĀ'ishah said: And may Allah bless them. We reply to them with the same words they have spoken, and our reward remains for us.

(Related by Ibn as-Sunnī)

٤٤ ـ فِيمَنْ أُهْدِيَ هَدِيَّةً وَدُعِيَ لَهُ

١٧٣ ـ عَنْ عائِشَةَ رَضِيَ اللهُ عَنْها قالَتْ: أُهْدِيَتْ لِرسولِ اللهِ ﷺ شاةٌ، قالَ: «اقْسِمِيها» فَكانَتْ عائِشَةُ إذا رَجَعَتْ الخادِمُ تقولُ: ما قالُوا؟ تَقُولُ الخادِمُ: قالوا: بارَكَ اللهُ فِيكُمْ، فتَقولُ عائِشةُ: وَفِيهِمْ بارَكَ اللهُ، نَرُدُّ عَلَيْهِمْ مِثْلَ ما قَالوا، ويَبْقىٰ أَجْرُنا لَنا.

ابن السُّني

45. On someone from whom something harmful is removed

174) On the authority of [c]Umar (may Allah be pleased with him) that he removed something (harmful) from a man's beard or from his head. The man said: May Allah avert evil from you, to which [c]Umar (may Allah be pleased with him) said: Allah has averted evil from us ever since we embraced Islam. But if something (harmful) is taken from you, then say: May your hands receive goodness.

(Related by Ibn as-Sunnī)

٤٥ ـ فِيمَنْ أُميط عَنهُ الأَذىٰ

١٧٤ ـ وَعَنْ عُمَرَ رَضِيَ اللهُ عَنْهُ أَنَّهُ أَخَذَ مِنْ لِحْيَةِ رَجُلٍ أَو رَأْسِهِ شَيْئاً، فقالَ الرَّجُلُ: صَرَفَ اللهُ عَنْكَ السُّوءَ، فَقالَ عُمَرُ رَضِيَ اللهُ عَنهُ: صَرَفَ اللهُ عَنَّا السُّوءَ مُنْذُ أَسْلَمْنا، ولٰكنْ إذا أُخِذَ عَنْكَ شَيْءٌ فَقُلْ: أَخَذَتْ يَدَاكَ خَيْراً.

ابن السُّني

46. On seeing the first fruits

175) Abū Hurayrah (may Allah be pleased with him) said: When the people saw the first of the fruit, they would bring it to the Messenger of Allah (may the blessings and peace of Allah be upon him). Then the Messenger of Allah (may the blessings and peace of Allah be upon him) would say: "O Allah, bless us in our produce and bless us in our city, and bless us in our Ṣāᶜ,[1] and bless us in our Mudd,"[1] then he would give it to the youngest person present.

(Related by Muslim)

1. Measurements for grain. The Prophet is saying an invocation for a good harvest.

٤٦ ـ في رُؤْيَةِ باكورةِ الثَّمَرِ

١٧٥ ـ قال أبو هُرَيْرَةَ رَضِيَ اللهُ عَنْهُ: كانَ النَّاسُ إذا رأَوْا أوَّلَ الثمَرِ جاؤُوا بِهِ إلى رَسُولِ اللهِ ﷺ فإذا أَخَذَهُ رَسُولُ اللهِ ﷺ قالَ: «اللَّهُمَّ بَارِكْ لَنا في ثَمَرِنا، وبارِكْ لَنَا في مَدِينَتِنا، وبارِكْ لَنَا في صَاعِنا، وبَارِكْ لنا في مُدِّنـا[١]، ثُمَّ يُعْطِيـهِ أَصْغَرَ مَـنْ يَحْضُـرُ مِنَ الوِلْدانِ».

مسلم

---

(١) الصّاع والمُدّ مكيالان، والمقصود الدعاء بوفرة الثمر والرزق.

47. On something that pleases one and against which one fears the evil eye

Allah the Almighty has said: "If only, when you entered the garden, you had said: That which Allah wills (will come to pass). There is no strength save in Allah."[1]

176) The Prophet (may the blessings and peace of Allah be upon him) said: "The evil eye is real, and if there were to be something that overrides fate, the evil eye would do so."

(Related by Muslim and Aḥmad)

177) On the authority of the Prophet (may the blessings and peace of Allah be upon him), who said: "If one of you has seen something about himself or his possessions which is pleasing to him, let him ask Allah to bless it, for the evil eye is real."

(Related by Ibn as-Sunnī, Aḥmad and al-Ḥākim)

1. The Chapter of the Cave 18:39.

٤٧ - فِي الشَّيْءِ يُعْجِبُهُ وَيَخافُ عَلَيْهِ الْعَيْنَ

قالَ اللهُ تعالى: ﴿وَلَوْلا إِذْ دَخَلْتَ جَنَّتَكَ قُلْتَ مَا شَاءَ اللهُ لا قُوَّةَ إِلاَّ بِاللهِ﴾[1]، [الكهف ١٨ : ٣٩].

١٧٦ - وَقالَ النبيُّ ﷺ: «العَيْنُ حَقٌّ، ولَو كانَ شَيْءٌ سابِقَ القَدَرَ لَسَبَقَتْهُ العَيْنُ».

مسلم وأحمد

١٧٧ - عَنِ النبيِّ ﷺ قالَ: إذا رأى أَحَدُكُمْ ما يُعْجِبُهُ في نَفْسِهِ، أَو مالِهِ، فَلْيُبَرِّكْ[2] عَلَيْه، فَإِنَّ العَيْنَ حَقٌّ».

ابن السُّني وأحمد والحاكم

(١) حَضٌّ على ذكر المشيئة الإلهية التي قدَّرتْ الازدهار لذلك البستان.
(٢) بأن يقول: بارك الله فيه.

178) Abū Saᶜīd (may Allah be pleased with him) said: The Messenger of Allah (may the blessings and peace of Allah be upon him) used to seek refuge in Allah from the djinn and from the evil eye of man until the two Muᶜawwidhahs[1] were revealed. Once they were revealed he used them to the exclusion of anything else.

(Related by at-Tirmidhī, an-Nasā'ī and Ibn Mājah)

---

1. Chapters 113 and 114 of the Qur'ān.

١٧٨ ـ وَقالَ أَبو سعيدٍ رَضِيَ اللهُ عَنْهُ:

«كانَ رسولُ اللهِ ﷺ يتَعَوَّذُ مِنَ الْجَانِّ، وعَيْنِ الإِنْسانِ، حتى نَزَلَت المُعَوِّذَتانِ، فلَمَّا نَزَلَتا تَرَكَ ما سِواهُما».

الترمذي والنَّسائي وابنُ ماجَه

48. On good and bad omens

179) On the authority of ᶜĀ'ishah (may Allah be pleased with her), who said: The Messenger of Allah (may the blessings and peace of Allah be upon him) used to be pleased by good omens. (Related by Ibn Ḥibbān and Aḥmad.) And in another Hadith the Prophet (may the blessings and peace of Allah be upon him) was asked: And what is a good omen? He said: "A good[1] word that a man hears."

(Related by al-Bukhārī and Muslim)

180) He (may the blessings and peace of Allah be upon him) said: "I saw in my dream as though I were in the house of ᶜUqbah ibn Rāfiᶜ and we were brought some of Ibn Ṭāb's fresh dates. I thus interpreted it as a lofty position for us in this world and a good outcome for us in the Hereafter, and that our religion had prospered."[2]

(Related by Muslim)

1. I.e., auspicious.
2. The interpretation lies in the meaning of the root letters of the words Rāfiᶜ and Ṭāb.

٤٨ ـ فِي الْفَأْلِ وَالطِّيَرَةِ

١٧٩ ـ عن عائشة رضي الله عنها قالت: «وكَـانَ رَسـولُ الله ﷺ يُعْجِبُـهُ الْفَـأْلُ» وفـي حديثٍ آخرَ سُئِلَ النبي ﷺ: وما الْفَأْلُ؟ قال: «الكَلِمَةُ الحَسَنَةُ يَسْمَعُها الرجلُ[(١)]».

ابنُ حِبّان وأحمد والحديث الآخر عند البخاري ومسلم

١٨٠ ـ وَقـالَ ﷺ: «رَأَيْـتُ فـي مَنَـامِـي كأَنِّي في دارِ عُقْبَةَ بْنِ رافعٍ، وأُتِينا مِنْ رُطَبِ ابْنِ طَابٍ، فَأَوَّلْتُ الرِّفْعَةَ لَنا في الدُّنيا، والعـاقِبَـةَ لَنـا فـي الآخِـرَةِ، وأَنَّ دِينَنـا قَـدْ طَابَ[(٢)]».

مسلم

(١) الكلمة الحسنة هنا هي التي توحي بالخير.

(٢) وفيه الفأل بالرؤيا الصالحة.

181) As for bad omens, Mu^{c}āwiyah ibn 'l-Ḥakam (may Allah be pleased with him) said: I said: O Messenger of Allah, there are some of us who draw evil omens (from certain things). He said: "That is something you find in your hearts, so let it not turn you away."[1]

(Related by Muslim)

Completed
by the Grace of Allah

1. I.e., from what you propose doing.

١٨١ ـ وأَمَّا الطِّيَرَةُ[١] فقالَ مُعَاويةُ بْنُ الحَكَمِ رَضِيَ اللهُ عَنْهُ: قُلْتُ يا رَسُولَ اللهِ، مِنَّا رِجالٌ يَتَطَيَّرُونَ. قالَ: «ذٰلِكَ شَيْءٌ تَجِدُونَهُ في صُدُورِكُمْ فلا يَصُدَّنَّكُمْ[٢]».

تمّ

بحَمدِ اللهِ

مسلم

(١) الطِّيَرَة: التطيُّر والتشاؤم.

(٢) أي فلا يمنعنكم ذلك من متابعة ما عزمتم عمله.